NATIONAL SERVICE

NATIONAL SERVICE
Pro & Con

EDITED AND WITH AN INTRODUCTION BY
WILLIAMSON M. EVERS

HOOVER INSTITUTION PRESS

STANFORD UNIVERSITY
STANFORD, CALIFORNIA

he Hoover Institution on War, Revolution and Peace, founded at
_tanford University in 1919 by President Herbert Hoover,
is an interdisciplinary research center for advanced study on
domestic and international affairs in the twentieth century.
The views expressed in its publications are entirely those of the
authors and do not necessarily reflect the views of the staff,
officers, or Board of Overseers of the Hoover Institution.

Hoover Press Publication 393

Copyright © 1990 by the Board of Trustees of the
  Leland Stanford Junior University

First printing, 1990

96 95 94 93 92 91 90   9 8 7 6 5 4 3 2 1

Simultaneous first paperback printing, 1990

96 95 94 93 92 91 90   9 8 7 6 5 4 3 2 1

Manufactured in the United States of America

Printed on acid-free paper

Library of Congress Cataloging-in-Publication Data

National service : pro & con / edited and with an
introduction by Williamson M. Evers.
        p.   cm.
  Rev. and edited papers and comments of the Hoover Institution
Conference on National Service held Sept. 8–9, 1989.
  ISBN 0-8179-8931-5 (cloth : acid free).
  ISBN 0-8179-8932-3 (paper : acid free)
  1. National service—United States—Congresses. I. Evers,
Williamson M., 1948—   . II. Hoover Institution Conference on
National Service (1989)
HD4870.U6N36 1990   90-41567
355.2'236'0973—dc20   CIP

CONTENTS

CONTRIBUTORS

MARTIN ANDERSON is a Senior Fellow at the Hoover Institution. He is the author of *Conscription: A Select and Annotated Bibliography* and the editor of two books on the draft: *Registration and the Draft* and *The Military Draft*. A former policy adviser to both Presidents Richard Nixon and Ronald Reagan, he played a major role in the abolition of the draft and the move toward an all-volunteer force in the early 1970s.

DOUG BANDOW is a Senior Fellow at the Cato Institute and a nationally syndicated columnist. He previously served as a special assistant to President Ronald Reagan, during which time Mr. Bandow worked with the Military Manpower Task Force. He is a former editor of *Inquiry Magazine* and the author of *Human Resources and Defense Manpower*, a National Defense University textbook. He has written on military manpower for such publications as the *New Republic*, the *Journal of Contemporary Studies*, the *New York Times*, and the *Wall Street Journal*.

BENJAMIN R. BARBER is the Walt Whitman Professor of Political Science at Rutgers University and the Director of the Whitman Center for the Culture and Politics of Democracy. He is the author of nine books, including *Strong Democracy*, *The Conquest of Politics*, and the forthcoming *Teaching Liberty*, as well a novel and, with Patrick Watson, the PBS television series "The Struggle for Democracy." As Chairman of the

Committee on Education for Civic Leadership and Director of the Whitman Center, he led a project that is developing a citizenship education program at Rutgers—a program that includes community service rooted in the educational process. As the program evolves, Rutgers may require all undergraduates to take citizenship education for credit in order to graduate.

Sue E. Berryman directs the Institute on Education and the Economy at Teachers College, Columbia University. The institute, a research organization, focuses on changes in the U.S. economy and how they affect job skills and U.S. educational and training institutions. From 1975 to 1985, she was a behavioral scientist with the RAND Corporation, where she researched military manpower problems. In addition to technical reports, she authored the book *Who Serves? The Persistent Myth of the Underclass Army*. Using historical documents and analyses of longitudinal data bases, *Who Serves?* assesses the social composition of the nineteenth- and twentieth-century enlisted forces.

Bruce Chapman, a Senior Fellow at the Hudson Institute, wrote *The Wrong Man in Uniform* in 1986, making the case for an all-volunteer military. A former Seattle city councilman, Washington State secretary of state, director of the U.S. Census Bureau, and presidential aide, he served recently as U.S. ambassador to the U.N. organizations in Vienna.

Donald J. Eberly is Executive Director of the National Service Secretariat in Washington, D.C. His "National Service for Peace" proposal of 1958 was one of the origins of the Peace Corps and, as a consultant to the National Advisory Commission on Selective Service in 1966, he prepared the plan for national service that was considered by the commission. He is the author of *National Service: A Promise to Keep* and, with Michael Sherraden, the editor of *National Service: Social, Economic and Military Impacts* and *The Moral Equivalent of War? A Study of Non-Military Service in Nine Nations*.

Amitai Etzioni is University Professor at the George Washington University in Washington, D.C., and director of the Center for Policy Research in New York City and Washington, D.C. He taught sociology for twenty years at Columbia University. He has been a visiting scholar at the Brookings Institution and a senior adviser at the White House. He has served on the editorial board of *Science* and on the council of the American Sociological Association. He is the author of *The Moral Dimension, The Active Society, An Immodest Agenda, Political Unification,* and other works.

TIM W. FERGUSON is the *Wall Street Journal*'s "Business World" columnist and a member of its editorial board. He was editorial features editor of the *Wall Street Journal,* 1983–1990, and editorial page editor of the *Orange County Register,* 1982–1983.

MILTON FRIEDMAN, 1976 Nobel Prize winner in economics, is a Senior Research Fellow at the Hoover Institution. He is also the Paul Snowden Russell Distinguished Service Professor Emeritus of Economics at the University of Chicago. He has written many books on economics, including *A Theory of the Consumption Function* and (with A. J. Schwartz) *A Monetary History of the United States.* Among his books in the public policy field are *Capitalism and Freedom* and *Free to Choose,* both written with Rose D. Friedman. A member of the President's Commission on an All-Volunteer Armed Force (Gates commission), he is a past president of the American Economic Association and a member of the National Academy of Sciences.

DAVID R. HENDERSON is Professor of Economics at the Naval Postgraduate School in Monterey, California. His articles on national service have appeared in *Barron's* and *Fortune,* and his unpublished paper "The Economics of National Service," done for the Chief of Naval Operations, was used by the navy to help decide on and defend its position on national service. Dr. Henderson also served as a senior economist with President Ronald Reagan's Council of Economic Advisers and wrote and collected 280 signatures on the "Economists' Statement in Opposition to the Draft."

PAUL N. McCLOSKEY, JR., is a founding partner of the law firm of McCloskey and Kays in Menlo Park, California. A Republican member of the U.S. House of Representatives from 1967 to 1983 representing California's twelfth congressional district, in 1979, he was the main sponsor in the House of the National Youth Service Act (H.R. 2206). A congressional critic of the U.S. conduct of the Vietnam War, he ran against Richard Nixon in the New Hampshire primary in 1972. He is a decorated veteran of the Korean War and retired from the Marine Corps Reserve in 1974 with the rank of colonel. Former Congressman McCloskey has been a guest professor and lecturer at Stanford University and the University of Santa Clara.

CONGRESSMAN DAVE McCURDY (D-Okla.)—first elected in 1980 and now in his fifth term—is from Norman and represents the state's fourth congressional district. Congressman McCurdy is a member of the House

Armed Services Committee and cochairman of the Coalition for the Democratic Majority's Task Force on Foreign Policy and Defense. In July 1987, he established the House Army Caucus, which promotes interaction on army-related issues among army officials, interested members of the House, and military policy experts. National vice-chairman of the Democratic Leadership Council, Congressman McCurdy played an active role in developing the council's proposal for national service. He has been the main sponsor in the House of the Citizenship and National Service Act (H.R. 660).

CHARLES C. MOSKOS is Professor of Sociology at Northwestern University. Chairman of the Inter-University Seminar on Armed Forces and Society, he is Past President of the Research Committee on Armed Forces and Conflict Resolution of the International Sociological Association. His books include *The American Enlisted Man, The Military—More Than Just a Job?* (with Frank Wood) and *A Call to Civic Service.* He serves on the board of advisers of the Democratic Leadership Council and holds the Distinguished Service Medal, the U.S. Army's highest decoration for a civilian.

THE REV. RICHARD JOHN NEUHAUS is Director of the Institute on Religion and Public Life, a research and education institute in New York City. Religion editor and columnist for *National Review*, Pastor Neuhaus is the author of *Freedom for Ministry, The Naked Public Square, Religion and Democracy in America, The Catholic Moment, To Empower People* (coauthored with Peter Berger), and other works. He is also editor of the *Lutheran Forum Letter* and a board member of the United States Institute of Peace.

WALTER Y. OI is the Elmer B. Milliman Professor of Economics at the University of Rochester in New York. He was director of the economic analysis section of the Military Manpower Policy Study for the Department of Defense in 1964; consultant to the Office of the Assistant Secretary of Defense during 1964–1965; staff economist for the President's Commission on an All-Volunteer Armed Force (Gates commission) in 1969; and cochairman of the Advisory Task Force on the Draft, National Service and Alternatives for the White House Conference on Youth in 1970.

PETER SZANTON is President of Szanton Associates, a Washington, D.C.–based consulting firm specializing in strategic planning for nonprofit organizations. He directed the RAND Corporation's work in New York City in the late 1960s and early 1970s and has twice served in the federal

Office of Management and the Budget. He is the author of several books on issues of public policy, including, with Richard Danzig, *National Service: What Would It Mean?* Mr. Szanton is a member of the board of Youth Service America and served as the first chairman of that board.

DON WYCLIFF is a member of the editorial board of the *New York Times.* He writes on a range of social policy issues, including education, youth employment, and national service.

ACKNOWLEDGMENTS

During the year and a half of planning, writing, and editing that resulted in this book, many people have helped. My principal thanks go to those whose contributions are collected in this volume. I wish to thank Martin Anderson for his all-important encouragement, advice, and counsel. Robert Hessen helped plan the Hoover Institution Conference on National Service and advised me at many points. Annelise Anderson and Milton Friedman made valuable suggestions. Angelo Codevilla helped me get in touch with people on Capitol Hill. Hoover Institution directors W. Glenn Campbell and John Raisian supported this project and provided guidance—without their leadership the work of Hoover Institution's research scholars and its research publications would be impossible.

Brenda McLean and Teresa Terry spent many hours ensuring that the conference would run smoothly. Gloria Walker, Michele Horaney, Denny Brisley, and the rest of the Hoover public affairs staff worked on publicity for the conference. Deborah Ventura found support staff when I needed it. Craig Snarr's Hoover facilities staff readied the conference room and operated the microphones and recording equipment during the conference. Kim Grose of the Haas Center for Public Service and several members of the Stanford Federalist Society volunteered at the conference, noting down the names and order of speakers from the audience.

I wish to thank my research assistant Bernadette Chi for her work on this project. Donna MacGruer, Aurora Fischer-Buck, and Nancy Edmondson transcribed the oral remarks at the conference. Pat Baker, executive director of the Hoover Institution Press, helped me plan my editorial work and (together with Marshall Blanchard, production coordinator) encouraged me along the way. Ann Wood edited the copy with diligence and skill. Lenore McCracken worked on marketing and promotion.

Finally, I wish to thank my wife, Mary Gingell, and my children, Daniel and Pamela.

Introduction:
Social Problems and
Political Ideals
in the Debate over
National Service

Williamson M. Evers

Conservatives like Sen. Sam Nunn (D-Ga.) and Sen. Charles Robb (D-Va.) want to establish national service and so do New Deal liberals like Sen. Edward Kennedy (D-Mass.). Technocratic, problem-solving neolibcherals like *Washington Monthly* editor Charles Peters favor it. Senate majority leader George Mitchell (D-Maine) has given national service a prominent place in the Democrats' legislative agenda. Senator Nunn says national service is "an idea whose time has come."

Is it?

National service has long been an issue that inspires passionate argument and provokes polarized debate. Ideologies as well as individuals clash over the issue. It raises fundamental questions about the proper role of government, the nature of citizenship and whether problems are best tackled privately or by governmental action.

I want to thank Annelise Anderson, Martin Anderson, Doug Bandow, Donald Bellante, Bernadette Chi, Roy Childs, Milton Friedman, Roger Garrison, Mary Gingell, David Gordon, Dana Harris, David Henderson, Robert Hessen, Jeffrey Rogers Hummel, Robert Knight, Brenda McLean, Catherine Milton, Ralph Raico, Sheldon Richman, Llewellyn Rockwell, Paul Seaver, and Lawrence Uzzell for reading earlier drafts of the manuscript in whole or part and offering helpful comments. I also want to thank my research assistant Bernadette Chi for her work in searching for and checking references and citations.

As Peter Szanton says in this volume,

> The people at one end [of the spectrum] feel strongly that the impera-
> tives of citizenship or morality or social integration are sufficiently
> powerful to justify some form of mandatory or semimandatory mixing
> of youth at some stage in their lives. The people at the other end of the
> spectrum feel, in an equally principled way, that such actions imposed
> by government are illegitimate and have no moral, legal, or constitu-
> tional foundation.[1]

The Hoover Institition Conference on National Service, held September 8–9, 1989, was the first conference concentrating on national
service to bring face to face a balanced panel of leading proponents and
critics of the proposal. This volume presents, in revised and edited form,
the papers given and comments made at the conference.

The proponents were

- Political theorist Benjamin Barber
- National service advocate Donald Eberly
- Sociologist Amitai Etzioni
- Former Congressman Paul McCloskey (R-Calif.)
- Congressman Dave McCurdy (D-Okla.)
- Sociologist Charles Moskos
- Policy analyst Peter Szanton
- Journalist Don Wycliff

The critics were

- Economist Martin Anderson
- Policy analyst and journalist Doug Bandow
- Policy analyst Bruce Chapman
- Journalist Tim Ferguson
- Economist Milton Friedman
- Economist David Henderson
- Theologian Richard John Neuhaus
- Economist Walter Oi

One person on the conference panel, policy analyst Sue Berryman, was
neutral on the issue.

Among the panelists were authors and editors of five books on
national service, congressional sponsors of two major legislative initiatives on national service, and authors and editors of five books on the

closely related issues of military manpower and the draft. About half the panelists had participated in the national debate over military manpower, the draft, and national service during the Vietnam War.

How can one characterize the two sides in the debate?

Opposing national service are

- Classical liberals (or libertarians) and those conservatives who emphasize individual rights, constitutional protections, and free market economics
- Those welfare-state liberals who emphasize individual rights and constitutional protections

Favoring national service are

- Those conservatives who emphasize civic virtue, citizenship, and serving the political community as the common duty and purpose of all in the society
- Those welfare-state liberals who emphasize the same things

In brief, on the issue of national service, one can speak of opposing libertarian and communitarian ideologies.

In 1989, U.S. senators introduced nine bills and members of the House of Representatives introduced eleven bills to establish one form or another of national service. Senator Nunn and Congressman McCurdy sponsored the most striking and innovative bill. It would set up a program of benefits-conditional service, in which most young people would have to complete a term of military or civilian service to be eligible for federal college aid. The multibillion-dollar Nunn-McCurdy plan would establish a large, comprehensive national service program. This bill, as the *New York Times* put it, has been "the catalyst" of the current debate.[2]

An omnibus bill sponsored by Senator Kennedy would fund small-scale experiments using several of the national service plans now on the drawing boards. President George Bush's "thousand points of light" initiative proposes to grant tax funds to successful or promising public service efforts. The White House calls the youth-oriented part of this initiative Youth Engaged in Service to America.

The Nunn-McCurdy bill would pay national service participants with educational and other vouchers and would cut off eligibility for federal college aid for most students who did not enlist. Without changing the federal student aid program, the Kennedy omnibus bill would pay volunteers to work in public service programs. It would also aid the programs themselves. The Bush administration's bill would only aid programs. It would not pay volunteers.

Since the Hoover Institution conference, congressional proponents of national service have worked to enact national service legislation with budgetary outlays somewhere between the $300 million in Senator Kennedy's original omnibus bill and the $25 million in the Bush administration's bill. Such legislation includes experiments with payments to volunteers.[3]

WHAT IS NATIONAL SERVICE?

American proponents of national service want to enlist many if not all young people in military or civilian service programs run by or approved by the federal government. How did this idea come to be called national service? The history of proposals along these lines illustrates how people in Britain and the United States have come to use the term *national service* as they currently do.

Britain and World Wars I and II

In late 1916 two different British cabinets proposed a policy of full national service combining military and civilian labor conscription. Although Britain did not implement such a policy in World War I, the government called its military conscription laws National Service Acts and its wartime executive department for manpower, the Ministry of National Service.[4]

In the winter before the Munich conference—when, in B. H. Liddell Hart's words, "an influential section of the people were more impressed by the social developments of the Nazi system than alarmed by its dangers"—proponents launched a campaign for universal national service in Britain. In a March 1938 letter to the London *Times,* Lord Lothian said that under national service, the government would allocate "every individual" to a particular form of service "whether in peace or emergency."[5]

During World War II, Parliament in the 1940 Emergency Powers Act authorized the minister of labor and national service to "direct any person" in Britain to perform whatever work the minister specified. Starting in mid-1941, Minister of Labor and National Service Ernest Bevin began to assign civilians to first scores of thousands and then hundreds of thousands of compulsory jobs.[6] He told the public that the time had come for "national service on a more intense scale."[7] Bevin's biographer Alan Bullock points out that the British government mobilized men and women "to a higher point" than the German or Italian governments did, "despite their boasted totalitarian organization."[8]

The United States and World War II

Before U.S. entry into World War II, there were two prominent proposals for national service: that of American veterans of the World War I–era Plattsburg training camps movement and that of President Franklin D. Roosevelt.[9] The Plattsburg veterans, led by Wall Street lawyer Grenville Clark, pushed for a peacetime military draft. They advocated a system that would ultimately combine military conscription and civilian labor conscription.[10]

While Clark's lobbying group pushed for immediate peacetime military conscription, President Roosevelt opposed such a military measure until public opinion was ready to support it. In late June 1940, Roosevelt's press secretary announced plans to conscript young people for civilian tasks, but said that the plans would not include military conscription.[11]

In sum, Clark advocated an immediate military draft followed by a civilian draft (a "national service act"); the White House advocated an immediate civilian draft followed by a military draft. President Roosevelt's plans never fully matured, however, and Congress superseded them by narrowly passing immediate peacetime military conscription in September 1940.

After the Japanese attack at Pearl Harbor, Clark and his friends Secretary of War Henry Stimson and Under Secretary of War Robert Patterson continued to push for civilian labor conscription. Clark encouraged and promoted a congressional national war service bill that was introduced early in 1943, and President Roosevelt called for civilian labor conscription in his 1944 State of the Union address. But labor union leaders denounced the 1943 proposal as a "forced labor bill" and a "serfdom bill." Though Stimson, Patterson, and the War Department backed the 1943 bill and another, less-comprehensive bill in 1945, neither passed.[12]

The United States and the Vietnam War

During the Vietnam War some critics of selective military service suggested a system (called *national service*) of combined military and civilian conscription as an alternative that they said would remove perceived inequities in the existing military draft. On May 18, 1966,

Secretary of Defense Robert S. McNamara, speaking to the American
Society of Newspaper Editors, said,

> It seems to me that we could move toward remedying [the] inequity [of
> selective military conscription] by asking every young person in the
> United States to give two years of service to his country—whether in
> one of the military services, in the Peace Corps, or in some other
> voluntary developmental work at home or abroad.[13]

But Congress never adopted McNamara's suggestion. Instead it enacted
a draft lottery to defuse some of the criticisms of the draft's inequities.[14]

Current Usage

Thus in Britain the term *national service* usually means the military
service of conscripts, whereas *universal* or *full* national service means a
manpower system that combines military and civilian conscription.

In the United States (until President Richard Nixon halted use of
the military draft in 1973), *national service* usually meant a system
combining military and civilian conscription. But in recent years, proponents of a wide variety of government-sponsored or government-
assisted service programs have advanced them under the rubric of
national service. Many of these recent programs do not have a military
service component, and participants would enlist in them voluntarily,
though proponents often hope to transform a small voluntary program
into a universal compulsory one.

American usage of the term is now in a muddle. I caution readers
of this book to look at the particulars of the policies and programs
proposed or opposed. Do not expect those debating national service to
share a precise meaning for the term.

The Debate

Though both sides have something to say on every facet of the
debate, each side emphasizes some arguments more than others. In
outlining the debate, I discuss first the arguments that proponents stress
(military manpower, unmet social needs, the future of young blacks
from poor families, equity, social integration, welfare benefits without
corresponding duties, building character, citizenship, and national purpose). I then discuss the arguments critics stress (the costs, the nature of
service, the nature of politics, moral instruction by the government, and

the nature of a free society). In describing the debate, I rely heavily on the Hoover Institution conference proceedings in this volume, but, when appropriate, I supplement those proceedings with outside material.

Military Manpower

Current national service proponents Roger Landrum, Donald Eberly, and Michael Sherraden ask, "Why is it that the only time a president seriously considers national service appears to be when war is in the making [and the government] needs [young people] to fight a war?"[15]

This important question pinpoints the essential reason some of those at the top of the U.S. political system have sponsored national service proposals: They find national service an attractive way to meet military manpower requirements and mobilize the population, especially in wartime and during a prewar buildup.[16]

Preparedness is the principal reason that former Congressman McCloskey, a Republican progressive in the tradition of Theodore Roosevelt, has sought to bring back the military draft or establish a national service system that includes the military. In his remarks in this volume, he says American troops need rigorous training—in the summer in the desert or the jungle, in the winter in the Arctic—to be prepared to go into battle. He then outlines the multioption plan for national service that he introduced in 1979, a plan he says would improve readiness and the quality of enlistees.[17]

Today's Democratic Leadership Council (DLC), an organization of conservative Democrats, is also part of this tradition of emphasizing military preparedness. In 1988 the DLC pointed to the "coming demographic squeeze" and proposed a tax-funded national service program that would channel manpower into the military "as the youth population shrinks in the years ahead."[18]

But critics of national service respond that the decline in U.S.-Soviet tensions means lower military manpower needs. They add that the all-volunteer force is currently filling its ranks with people who are smarter and better educated than the general population of young people.

Doug Bandow contends that there is no necessary connection between a military draft of national service and preparedness. The U.S. military was drafting young men at the time the Korean War began, but the U.S. military was not prepared to fight in Korea.[19]

Though proponents of national service point to the high budgetary costs of the all-volunteer force, critics of national service say the full economic costs of national service or a military draft would be higher. This is discussed further in the section on costs below.

Unmet Social Needs

Proponents of national service maintain that putting men and women in service will enable the government to address a multitude of unmet social needs. In this volume and elsewhere, Eberly, Charles Moskos, and Congressmen McCurdy list what they would suggest or what others have suggested those in civilian service would do:

- Care for those with AIDS and Alzheimer's disease
- Prepare reading materials for the blind
- Assist the U.S. Border Patrol
- Care for children
- Work on conservation and cleanup projects
- Help drug abusers
- Care for the elderly
- Care for the homeless
- Work in libraries
- Work in mental institutions
- Drive and maintain paratransit vehicles that carry the infirm and handicapped
- Work as prison guards
- Work as teacher's aides[20]

Moskos emphasizes that this work needs to be done and that it would be too expensive to hire regular government employees to do these jobs.[21] Morris Janowitz contends that the manpower "generated" by national service is "essential to achieve the goals of the welfare state."[22]

Moskos contends that convincing the public that these needs can only be addressed by instituting national service, would give it the "securest" possible foundation.[23]

Critics of national service point out that if costs are not considered, needs are limited only by one's imagination.[24] I discuss the critics' argument about costs in a separate section below.

The Future of Young Blacks from Poor Families

Although unemployment is low for the entire U.S. population at present, it is high for black teenagers. Some believe that the government could use national service to try to prevent young blacks from spending the rest of their lives in the underclass.[25]

For example, Vernon Jordan, past president of the National Urban League, fears that black youth are "endangered" as a generation and that too many of them are on an "express train to oblivion." In his view, "piecemeal programs" cannot successfully address this problem. He believes that a national service, "open to all," but concentrating on recruiting poor youth, would perform the needed rescue mission.[26]

Likewise, policy analyst Peter Szanton says in this volume that there exists a subpopulation whose members often come from broken families, are likely to pick up bad habits and values, and have poor prospects in life. He believes that young people from this subpopulation can be turned around by participating in government-funded public service work.[27]

One such local program is the California Conservation Corps, set up by Jerry Brown when he was that state's governor. He describes the corps as "an attempt to promote values." He says his idea was to take young people, particularly from the inner cities, out of their usual surroundings and place them in a new, "tightly controlled" environment where discipline would inspire them to be "better citizens."[28]

National service proposals like Jordan's and Szanton's encounter criticisms from two directions. From one direction, economist Milton Friedman says the Boy Scouts, Girl Scouts, Campfire, Boys' Clubs, mountaineering clubs, and church groups can organize outdoor cleanup crews and camps dedicated to conservation projects and raise money for them.[29] Friedman sees no necessity for the government to act as sponsor or to take money for them from the taxpayer.

Promarket critics of national service like Friedman and Martin Anderson would also question whether national service would create more jobs or improve job skills better than steps such as tax cuts, eliminating the minimum wage, loosening the rules governing the youth minimum wage, or expanding apprenticeship programs and job training.

The Rev. Richard John Neuhaus fears for the future of the millions of young Americans who are growing up in the underclass in fatherless households. But he would not compel or induce those young people to enlist in national service. Compulsory regimentation, he believes, takes away the free choice about their lives to which these young people are entitled and would in effect suspend their constitutional liberties.[30]

From another direction, some proponents of a more broadly based national service say that a targeted program places a disproportionate burden on the poor. Charles Moskos says that the public sees programs designed specifically to help poor young people and those who are members of racial minorities not as public service programs, but as "welfare in disguise."[31] Moskos adds that national service is doomed politically if the public sees it as a program that hires more bureaucrats and makes more people dependent on government handouts.[32] Eberly and Sherraden oppose targeted, selective national service, maintaining that it "falls short" of the "promise of national service," but they offer no further elucidation.[33]

Benjamin Barber says in this volume that some national service proposals (for example, the Nunn-McCurdy bill) require the poor to work to earn their citizenship, while requiring no work by the rich.[34] (He holds that citizenship should not be a term for rights Americans are born with, but rather a status that one has earned through national service.)[35] In the early 1980s, Sen. Sam Nunn himself opposed any system that allowed some young people, particularly those from wealthy families, to escape from federal military and civilian service programs.[36]

Equity

Benjamin Barber, though a proponent of national service, sees the Nunn-McCurdy plan as flawed because of its effect on the pattern of who has what and who does what in society. Barber maintains that the state should distribute the rights and benefits of citizenship on an egalitarian basis; he likewise maintains that citizens should share the duties and burdens of citizenship equally.[37] Moskos believes that there is degrading work (his example is caring for old people who are sick) that must be done and that justice requires that the burden of doing this work be spread equally.[38]

There are, of course, other principles (moral merit, needs) besides egalitarianism by which one could judge the pattern of roles, jobs, and possessions in society. But some political philosophers—for example, Robert Nozick in his *Anarchy, State, and Utopia*—reject all accounts of justice that require that distribution follow a set pattern and instead see justice as whatever outcome results from a just process of acquiring possessions and taking on roles and jobs. Political theorist James Dick maintains that the "fundamental reason" Nozick rejects imposing such patterns is that "the value of liberty requires it."[39]

Not surprisingly, no critic of national service in this volume tackles the issue of distributive justice by accepting Barber's and Moskos's assumptions and defending an alternative set pattern of jobs and roles. Instead, Martin Andersen and Doug Bandow say that people should be paid directly for doing difficult or unpleasant work or that people should volunteer to do it under private auspices. Anderson and Bandow find it morally repugnant to establish as government policy an enforceable duty to do degrading work.[40]

Social Integration

Some communitarians believe that national service would integrate Americans from different racial, religious, and class backgrounds into one nation with a sense of common citizenship. Amitai Etzioni speaks of national service's potential as a "great sociological mixer."[41] Moskos says that under a "comprehensive" national service program, all races and classes would take part in "a common civic enterprise."[42]

Criticism of such goals comes from several quarters. Some people defend cultural pluralism and diversity and oppose tax-funded efforts to increase homogeneity. Others, such as Peter Szanton, who consider social integration attractive do not believe that its attractions outweigh the fact that in a Nunn-McCurdy–type service program participants sacrifice too little and are paid much too much.[43]

Some proponents of national service see the current racial makeup of the military as undesirable. The conservative Democratic Leadership Council says that "Americans should be concerned that our armed forces are not representative of society as a whole."[44] It plans to use national service to change that makeup. Morris Janowitz favored using national service as an instrument to prevent the creation of "a predominantly or even all-Negro enlisted force in the Army, an 'internal foreign legion,'" which, Janowitz said, would be "disastrous" for America.[45]

In discussing the makeup of the current military, which operates under an all-volunteer system, there are factual disagreements and political controversies. In this volume, Sue Berryman primarily addresses questions of fact. She takes aim at two myths: (1) that the U.S. military is currently filled with recruits from the bottom rank of society and (2) that the makeup of the military was or would be much different under a draft.[46]

Doug Bandow points out that military recruitment—whether based on a military draft, national service, or an all-volunteer system—will not notably affect the proportion of blacks in the army and in the combat arms (infantry, artillery, and armor), as long as blacks are allowed to volunteer and to reenlist. (Blacks volunteer and reenlist in proportionally larger numbers than whites.)[47] Given the current pattern of choices by blacks, the only way to achieve the racial proportions that some desire would be to impose a mandatory ceiling on black participation in the army or to pay blacks lower wages than whites.[48]

The critics of large-scale black participation in the military conjure up the specter of an "internal foreign legion" or a largely black army. But they do not explain what they fear from black soldiers and why. Until the critics of large-scale black participation explain further, proponents of the all-volunteer force are blocked from addressing this complaint in more detail.

Welfare Benefits without Corresponding Duties

The Nunn-McCurdy bill would make federal benefits contingent on federally approved service. According to Moskos, to the extent possible, those who receive tax-funded benefits should earn those benefits, especially when the recipients are using their benefits to increase their lifetime earnings.[49] Moskos cites an opinion survey showing that the public overwhelmingly agrees that persons who receive college aid should be "required to repay that support through some type of public service."[50]

Congressman McCurdy says that college aid should be an "earned benefit," not an entitlement,[51] and that the federal government is "too large" and "out of control" because of the "entitlement society" that has come into existence in America. "The entitlement society is killing us," he believes. It may be politically impossible for Congress to take away entitlements, but he would like the government to get "something in return" from the recipients.[52] (By "something in return," Congressman McCurdy means not repayment of student loans in cash, but participation in national service.)

Opposition to this approach comes most strongly from college administrators and supporters of the idea of volunteer service. In the section below on the nature of service, I discuss the views of the supporters of volunteer service.

College administrators prefer a needs-based federal program of aid to college students rather than a service-contingent program. They and their political allies say that the Nunn-McCurdy plan would fund fewer students, cost more, and grant some students less aid than before.[53] In contrast to the college administrators, David Henderson in this volume attacks federal student aid because it taxes relatively poor people to subsidize people who will be relatively rich after they graduate from college.[54]

Building Character

Some proponents of national service view it as a morally acceptable, indeed morally instructive, substitute for activities, attitudes, or institutions thought to be vice-ridden. They say that national service supplies a character-building alternative to tempting vices and thus can minister to perceived flaws in youth both from the underclass and from wealthier backgrounds.

During the Progressive Era, reformers often found it attractive to establish the "moral equivalents" of vices. In Walter Lippmann's Progressive Era classic, *A Preface to Politics,* he argues that prohibitory laws would not reform human beings. Instead social engineers ("political inventors," "constructive" reformers) should channel people—making use of people's natural desires, impulses, and instincts—into courses of action the reformers hold would be better for them. Attractive vices can only be supplanted by attractive virtues. Instead of vainly trying to place a taboo on natural instincts, many Progressive Era reformers sought to rechannel and redirect them. Lippmann cites a socialist mayor of Milwaukee who called for the city government "to go into competition with the devil" by providing clean popular entertainments.[55]

Likewise some Progressive Era reformers considered the ethos of the military and youth gangs depraved and sought substitutes for them. Progressive Era juvenile court judge Ben Lindsey did not seek to break up youth gangs. He thought gangs were natural organizations, basically marred by their disloyalty to the social order and the government. He founded a Kid Citizens' League to rechannel the loyalty of gang members back to the government.[56] Lippmann adds that the Boy Scouts are an instrument for making boys' gangs a force "valuable to civilization."[57]

Lippmann devotes two pages in his *Preface to Politics* to extensive quotations from William James's 1906 speech "The Moral Equivalent of War," in which James proposed national service. James believed young men—particularly young men from the "luxurious classes"—needed a harsh, challenging environment in which to develop their characters. He wanted that environment to be a conscripted civilian youth service rather than the military. James would have the government summon these young men to a war against nature (digging in coal mines, catching fish at sea in the winter, carving tunnels out of rock). Paid unskilled laborers should not "toil and suffer pain" and do work that is "repulsive"; instead the government should compel young men to do such work in service to the collectivity that, he says, "owns" them.[58]

The need for positive substitutes for vices may indeed be a valid psychological insight. Yet critics of national service point out that making use of this insight does not require compulsory enrollment, government sponsorship, or tax funding. Milton Friedman notes that private voluntary donations and membership fees support the Boy Scouts and Boys' Clubs.[59] But Amitai Etzioni retorts that the Boy Scouts and such private groups are not doing enough and that a program under government auspices would improve matters.[60]

Tim Ferguson thinks—as do many proponents of national service—that undertaking disciplined service and working for pay can improve people's moral character. But he wants such a program only if it is noncoercive and "fiscally responsible."[61]

The Rev. Richard John Neuhaus contends that, according to the vision of America's founders, the society's cultural institutions (primarily religious and educational) should be what shapes people's characters and that the cultural realm should be kept "distinct" from the government. Neuhaus acknowledges, indeed denounces, the flight of the mainline churches in recent years from responsibility for character formation. He also laments the weakness in the inner city of the family, the neighborhood, and voluntary associations. But he believes that only such institutions can provide opportunities for service consistent with the founders' vision and that only such institutions, when revitalized, can help those in the underclass regain their self-respect.[62]

Citizenship

Many proponents of national service describe it as a form of civic education or citizenship training. But citizenship has different meanings in different political philosophies. Most liberals hold that citizens are those who enjoy the common liberties of the society. Communitarians, however, often look back to the city-states of ancient Greece and the way in which their citizens are said to have shared in the political life of the state and served the state.[63]

Hence some proponents of national service find such service appealing because it offers the possibility of transforming young U.S. citizens into something like the legendary ancient Greek citizens. Leaving aside the question of whether Plutarch's account of Lycurgus is historically accurate, Plutarch's description of the Spartan lawgiver's training for citizenship has inspired many imitators, including many advocates of national service:

> He trained his fellow-citizens to have neither the wish nor the ability to
> live for themselves; but like bees they were to make themselves always
> integral parts of the whole community, clustering together about their
> leader, almost beside themselves with enthusiasm and noble ambition,
> and to belong wholly to their country.[64]

Many communitarian conservatives and welfare-state liberals hope that national service would create or recover a sense of community in

American life, especially at the national level.[65] Barber contends that the state makes community life possible and that you owe a duty of civic service "to yourself as a social person, a person who is a member of . . . the greater community to which all communities belong, which is finally the state." Thus in practice, you owe the duty to the state.[66] Don Wycliff says that the idea of national service is to "cause people to appreciate their citizenship" by having them do altruistic deeds with civic purposes.[67]

Such emphasis on service to the state provokes some dissent. Martin Anderson and Milton Friedman ask, Who is served when the state is served? Barber says that it can be the people who are served, but Anderson and Friedman doubt that this is usually the case.[68]

National Purpose

It is not unusual for proponents of programs of national reconstruction or social change to see their programs as uplifting the morale of the people and identifying a set of common national goals—mobilizing and unifying the citizenry in the way that war does. In 1942, the English historian E. H. Carr said that war provides "a sense of meaning and purpose" many believe is lacking in modern life. For the English-speaking peoples, World War II provided a moral purpose that "revived the national will" and "increased the sense of cohesion and mutual obligation." The postwar world, Carr said, requires a substitute moral purpose if civilization is to survive. The world, according to Carr, requires a new creed that "will lay more stress on obligations than on rights, on services to be rendered to the community rather than benefits to be drawn from it."[69]

When William James advocated national service as the moral equivalent of war, he wanted a way to toughen young men as war does, without war's mass killing. But he also had in mind another, related use for national service: unifying the society.

He cited favorably the belief of sociologist S. Rudolf Steinmetz that war hammered and welded people into unified political communities ("cohesive states") and that human beings can only develop their capacities in such political communities. James sought to assuage the worries of those like Steinmetz who wondered, What, in a future era of peace, would replace the fear of the enemy? Would the people of cohesive states degenerate and disintegrate in the absence of military foes?

James believed that "surrender of the private interest," "obedience to command," and other martial virtues would continue to be "the rock upon which states are built." "So far," he said, war has been "the only force that can discipline a whole community." As a substitute for the discipline of war, he would have the government conscript young men to serve in factories, steel mills, and mine pits and on fishing ships at sea.[70]

Eberly says in this volume that people who go into the military share a common experience. Veterans of World War II, he says, talk about the war years as "the best years of their lives." Those who participate in national service will likewise, Eberly says, share a common experience—one which they will remember positively.[71]

Moskos, in his book *Call to Civic Service,* says that World War II gave Americans a "feeling of common purpose." By the close of the war, this unity of purpose had produced a public-spirited "national euphoria." But since the war, he says, this sense of common purpose has broken up and scattered. Race riots, political scandals, and divisions over the Vietnam War have torn the "national fabric."[72]

According to Moskos, a "breakdown of civic consensus" has vexed American society since the 1960s. The generation that became interested in political questions in the 1960s is "divided," and "two distinct political cultures" exist. This, he says, "augurs ill" for the republic. The "factions" in the current generation may never be able to unite after what they have been through. But by establishing national service, Moskos says, the current generation would unify future generations within "a common civic framework." "Civic solidarity" is a necessity, and national service would "nurture good citizenship" in the generations to come.[73]

In contrast, the Rev. Richard John Neuhaus says that national service will not do as an embodiment of national purpose. He concurs with many proponents of national service who say that in America's history our sense of national purpose almost always has been shaped "in antithesis with clear and threatening alternatives," mainly during war or hostilities verging on war.[74] But, Neuhaus says, there is no equivalent of war. No one should want equivalents of war. War is so horrible, so severe a remedy that ethical theorists in the Judeo-Christian tradition disallow it in almost all circumstances.[75]

Instead of looking to "wars" against poverty or drug abuse or other social ills to forge a sense of national purpose, America should look to its founding principles. According to these principles, the national purpose is to sustain pluralism, to sustain a diversity of purposes.[76]

Public-spiritedness in America, according to Neuhaus, lives in the diverse institutions that pluralism allows—the family, the church, the neighborhood, and voluntary associations. These are the institutions, Neuhaus says, that need to be strengthened when we seek ways of providing service.[77]

The Costs

National service, both compulsory and voluntary, has its economic critics. An economist like Walter Oi would say that compulsory national service is like the corvée of France during the ancien régime in that both compulsory national service and the corvée let government officials obtain the people's labor at less than the market rate. National service conscripts must work at low wages set by the government unless they prefer to leave the country or go to jail. They are forced to pay a hidden tax *in kind* (in this case, in their labor power), rather than paying in money.[78]

The full economic costs of staffing military and public service jobs are higher with compulsory national service than without. Without national service conscription, the government would take taxes in money from the governed. It would pay employees market wages to work in military and public service jobs. These market wages would disclose the full economic costs of the work assigned to national service conscripts. Hiring people on the market would encourage government officials to use them efficiently and productively. In contrast, if there is conscription, officials will tend, more than otherwise, to assign the wrong people to jobs because the costs of doing so are disguised. With conscription, the payroll costs (budgetary costs) of national service work would be lower, but the true costs (full economic costs) would be higher.

A compulsory plan raises serious moral problems about individual choice and coercion that the participants in the Hoover Institution conference discuss throughout the proceedings.[79] I am not going to resolve those problems here. Some of them are addressed in the section on the nature of a free society below. I will, however, put such a compulsory plan to one side as politically impossible, except perhaps in wartime.

If Congress establishes a tax-funded national service with voluntary enlistment, there is no tax in kind as there is in compulsory service. The government would pay national service participants enough to attract them to enlist. The participants would believe that time spent in the program was worth (to them) as much as time spent in the next most valuable activity (going to school or holding a regular civilian or military job).

Would a dollar that the government collects from a taxpayer to pay an unskilled young person to participate in national service be better spent some other way? This is the basic question an economic critic like Oi asks.

The national service participants receive money, vouchers, or in kind payments.[80] They receive some training, which is likely worth little because of the conditions of rapid turnover in national service. They receive moral and civic instruction. Public officials will decide what that instruction is, and it may be good or bad for the participants and the rest of us.

The payments participants receive from national service divert them, at public expense, from their most attractive available alternative—going to school, holding a job, or receiving relief for the needy. Whatever valuable work the national service participants do or training they receive must be compared with whatever they would otherwise have done outside of national service. As Doug Bandow writes,

> Paying young people to sweep floors entails the cost of foregoing whatever else we could do with that money and the cost of foregoing whatever else those young people could do with their time. An additional dollar spent on medical research might be a better investment than one used to add an extra hospital helper; an additional young person who finished school and entered the field of biogenetics might increase the social welfare more than one more kid shelving books in a library.[81]

In national service, the participants would do unskilled work in jobs that public officials designate as appropriate. Under current proposals for decentralized national service, the federal government will subsidize the costs of local service agencies obtaining the labor of national service participants. These subsidies will disguise the true costs of national service labor. Because of these distortions, local service officials will tend more than otherwise, to assign the wrong people to jobs. In labor economist Eli Ginzberg's formulation, "The more manpower there is, and particularly the more manpower there is paid for by somebody else, the less effectively it will be utilized."[82] In local national service assignments, computer programmers will peel potatoes, as they would in a conscript military or in compulsory national service. In addition, local agencies will tend to substitute the federally subsidized unskilled labor of national service participants for that of their regular employees, whose payroll costs have to be met in full by local taxpayers.[83]

Hundreds of thousands or millions of young people will not volunteer for small, below-market payments because to do so would disrupt their career plans, as Morris Janowitz says.[84] Only a compulsory plan (backed by a threat of jail) or making national service a prerequisite for receiving major federal benefits (as the Nunn-McCurdy bill does) could attract large numbers of young people.[85]

In this volume, Oi discusses the costs and benefits of the Nunn-McCurdy bill in detail. He finds that the Nunn-McCurdy plan would pay participants in its military program 63 percent more than a regular enlisted man or woman gets. The flow of national service participants in and out of the military could easily increase turnover and the costs that accompany it. The disparity in earnings between those in national service and those in the regular enlisted force could easily disrupt regular recruitment.[86]

Similarly, Oi finds that the Nunn-McCurdy plan would pay lucrative amounts to participants in its civilian program (19 percent more to young men than the wages of comparable young men; 44 percent more to young women than the wages of comparable young women). He says that taxpayers would be subsidizing rather unproductive, highly paid work by those "lucky enough" to get into the national service program. These subsidies would make participants the envy of those not admitted to the program.

At the same time, Oi says, national service participants will displace many existing jobholders. Provisions in the Nunn-McCurdy bill that rule out displacing currently employed workers will be difficult to enforce.[87]

David Henderson makes what he calls a "generous estimate" of the productivity of the labor of national service participants. He then says that costs of the civilian program of the Nunn-McCurdy plan would outweigh benefits by $3.5 to $4.5 billion.[88]

National service of the sort envisioned by the bill may well be politically impossible. A tax-funded benefits-conditional service plan relying on voluntary enlistments inevitably faces a problem in paying enlistees. The payments problem takes this form: Can one design a Nunn-McCurdy–type plan that will at the same time (1) attract youth in large numbers, (2) preserve a public-spirited sense of sacrifice, and (3) operate at a reasonable cost?

Richard Danzig and Peter Szanton find a Nunn-McCurdy–type plan an unattractive proposal.[89] When, however, they look at another hypothetical tax-funded national service program with voluntary enlistments, they assign a large value to the program's effects on its participants and say that benefits might well exceed costs. They also say that such a national service program might help the poor and unemployed more efficiently than job training programs do.[90].

The Nature of Service

Underlying many of the disputes about national service are different ideas of what constitutes service. One widely held idea is that service requires sacrifice. This idea is found in the Judeo-Christian religious tradition and in ethical theories that emphasize altruism.[91] In this volume, Bruce Chapman, for example, contends that something cannot be service unless it entails personal sacrifice.[92] Bandow likewise says that activity motivated by a desire to serve stands apart from paid work or work in which one's expenses are reimbursed.[93] Thus these critics argue that payments high enough to induce large numbers of young people to participate would also be high enough to deprive those young of any sense of sacrifice in the service of others.

The Rev. Richard John Neuhaus says that "government as well as other institutions must be brought to a better understanding of service as altruism. We should be skeptical of service premised upon incentives, for such incentives become enticements, which quickly become irresistible pressures on young people to conform to a certain line backed by governmental power."[94] In contrast, Moskos says that he finds "singularly unpersuasive" the view that only those who serve without reward are "worthy" and providing true service.[95]

The Nature of Politics

Many critics of national service dismiss proponents' estimates of the "work that needs to be done."[96] The critics point out that needs are infinite, while resources are finite. But when national service proponents assess the needs for certain jobs, their choice of these jobs (say, caring for the insane) rather than other jobs (say, computer consulting or religious missionary work) does tell us what sort of work they want to see done.

Critics of national service, such as Doug Bandow, Walter Oi, and Bruce Chapman, point out that a bureaucratically managed program like national service is bound to become corrupt and to deliver political favors rather than disinterested service.[97]

Also critics of national service, such as theologian John Swomley and Chapman, raise another question. Why should a governmental national service program certify or disallow work in a church, hospital, or community agency? In a society with liberal political institutions, a person should be able to serve others as a volunteer without authorization from or accountability to a government agency. Indeed, Swomley and Chapman argue, any requirement that volunteer groups and service projects must meet government standards of acceptability would destroy their independent character.[98]

One can consider these controversies—the extent of needs, the possibility of corruption, and certifying public service work—independently. But for some, these controversies are part of an overall dispute about politics.

Many proponents of national service would acknowledge that there is an infinity of needs. But these proponents would say, let's set priorities through the political process. They would acknowledge the potential for corruption, but would say, let's strive for good government anyway. They would acknowledge, at least in part, the critics' worries about certification. But these proponents would say, let's use our intelligence to develop the best regulations we can. The answer suggested in all these cases is that the proper solution is a political one.

In essence, these proponents—Benjamin Barber and Don Wycliff in this volume—see politics as an ennobling activity through which people can be the best they can be. Human beings are best fulfilled as citizens, and political participation is the road to good citizenship.[99]

In contrast, many critics—especially Milton Friedman in this volume—see politics as a necessary evil at best. Friedman argues that political choices inevitably mean all-or-nothing options, package deals, and compulsion, whereas voluntary choices (purchases on the market or donations of money or volunteer service) can be tailored and particularized and are not compulsory. Politics, Friedman says, almost invariably means that a concentrated special interest constituency can get its way at the expense of a diffuse general interest constituency. The incentives inherent in the political process, Friedman would say, make it likely that politicians and bureaucrats will use national service labor for self-serving purposes, will use certification requirements to suppress maverick providers of service, and will decide what constitutes service according to their own convenience.

In short, according to Friedman, national service cannot and will not achieve the idealistic goals of its proponents. Instead it will be perverted into the opposite of what its idealistic proponents say they intend. This result, Friedman says, is not an accident, but inevitable, given the perverse nature of politics.[100]

Moral Instruction by the Government

Some proponents of national service have narrowly practical goals, but others have grander aims. These grander aims inspire proponents of national service, but cause other people to have misgivings and become critics.

Remembering Robespierre's reign of virtue, most liberals have historically been skeptical toward public officials who proclaim themselves moral tutors and who plan to transform and uplift the morals of the governed. Such skepticism, most liberals believe, is reasonable. As liberal political theorist Stephen Holmes puts it, "transformative politics is not always benign."[101] But today communitarian conservatives and some modern liberals believe that governments may legitimately tax people or take charge of their lives in order to change moral attitudes.

Critics of national service such as John Swomley, Walter Oi, and Virginia Postrel, who oppose granting public officials the authority to instruct on morals, expect that national service participants would be a captive audience for those who wish to instill a state-sponsored conception of the moral good or of public virtue.[102] Proponents of national service interpret matters somewhat differently, saying that it will teach the virtues of democracy, hard work, cooperation, and helping others. In the words of Morris Janowitz, "the cooperative endeavors of national service will serve as a form of education that produces positive responses for a democratic society engaged in building a welfare state."[103]

The Nature of a Free Society

The tradition of Lockean liberal individualism is central to American political culture.[104] Individualist beliefs run counter to compulsory national service and support keeping volunteer service activity independent of government direction. Because of this, proponents of national service often attack what they consider a misplaced devotion to individual liberty.

Benjamin Barber says that some people associate freedom with the absence of government. These people then see coercion as "solely" governmental and see "all" nongovernmental activity as voluntary or free. He then describes a hypothetical young person who has quit high school. He asks, is it reasonable to think of this young person one afternoon deciding (in a meaningful sense) between listening to a grand opera or watching a soap opera? Through argument and example, Barber says that some people have fewer resources than others and that—in part because of this inequality—many people have wrong ideas about their own true self-interests.[105] Amitai Etzioni also questions whether people can voluntarily decide matters if they depend for their economic survival on others with more resources.[106]

Liberals would respond that it is doubtful that people can better discover their true self-interests through the government directing them than through making their own choices and decisions (including those about collecting information and consulting experts). Liberal doctrine does not say that people always know their own interests best. It says instead that people should have the right to pursue their interests as they think best. Liberals would say that a top government official in the capital city probably knows less about a peasant's interests than does the peasant himself. They would say that the opposite view—that the government official probably knows the peasant's interest better—is a doctrine that imperils liberty.[107]

Barber, a communitarian, says that "when you do not have citizenship," liberty is insecure. Unless people show they are citizens of the government at the national level by participating in politics and by bearing civic burdens, he does not see how liberty can be maintained in any society. He views national citizenship as a precondition for liberty and pluralism. Only the sovereignty of the state permits orderly pluralism; thus those living under its rule have, according to Barber, a duty to serve the state in ways that support that sovereignty.[108] Jean-Jacques Rousseau gave a classic, aphoristic formulation to this view in 1755: "The homeland cannot subsist without liberty, nor liberty without virtue, nor virtue without citizens; you will have everything, if you train citizens."[109]

Communitarians like Barber have a concept of liberty that is imbedded in their concept of citizenship. Congressman McCurdy, a communitarian conservative, says that in his view the U.S. system of government is premised on the view that rights and privileges bestowed by the government entail obligations to the government. He says that questioning the idea that citizens have obligations to the government endangers the political structure in the United States.[110]

Martin Anderson challenges the communitarians' subordination of liberty to their concept of citizenship. He says that individuals have rights to life, liberty, private property, and the pursuit of happiness and that these rights are theirs whether or not they participate in politics by voting or serve the state by building roads and emptying bedpans.[111]

The difference between the communitarians' concepts of liberty and voluntary choice and the libertarians' concepts comes out most starkly in this volume when libertarian Milton Friedman quotes Barber as saying, "You can teach someone what volunteering means by forcing them to do community service." Friedman contends that the word *voluntary* means one thing to him and something quite different to Barber.[112]

THE PROSPECTS FOR NATIONAL SERVICE

Whether Congress establishes a large-scale national service program in the near future depends in large part both on the attitude of promilitary members of Congress and on the attitude of young people. If Congress were to establish national service, the civilian program and the U.S. military would compete to attract young people to their ranks. President Jimmy Carter's 1980 report on selective service reform said that the president saw as "deleterious" to the military's morale, discipline, and enlistment efforts a civilian program that would compete with the military for the "same pool" of qualified persons.[113]

Thus any national service program—even in a time of high unemployment—whose proponents did not wish to be tarred as antimilitary has had to give priority to the military's perceived manpower needs. Programs like the McCloskey bill, the Nunn-McCurdy bill, the Democratic Leadership Council's proposal, and Charles Moskos's proposal, which channel young people into the military, have had greater potential for popularity in the Pentagon and with the executive branch than have strictly civilian service programs.

Although competition for manpower with the military will remain a problem for any federal civilian service program (because of baby-bust demographics), it may be less important than it was once, given reduced tensions between the United States and the Soviet Union and hence reduced U.S. military manpower needs.

Reduced international tensions give proponents a chance to emphasize civilian service programs. But reduced tensions may detach promilitary politicians from the coalition supporting national service. Charles Moskos contends that adherents of two "very distinct schools" of thought support national service. One school wants national service as a way of "making [military] conscription more politically palatable." The other school wants to see large-scale civilian public service work.[114]

If these two bases of support stay distinct, Congress will enact large-scale national service only when its members believe that the country simultaneously needs many more people in the military and much more public service work. In 1989 the number of members of Congress who believed both these needs were pressing was not enough to pass the Nunn-McCurdy bill. Since then, because of reduced U.S.-Soviet tensions, Congress has begun to believe that the military needs *fewer* people. Hence, as Doug Bandow points out, lower military manpower requirements mean that fewer members of Congress want to establish national service.[115]

Moskos proposes an ideological solution to the split that divides the supporters of national service. He believes that both sorts of supporters agree that everyone owes several years of service under government auspices. He looks to "the banner of civic duty" to hold together a coalition of national service proponents and inspire them to push for national service.[116]

Many members of Congress who have supported a large, well-funded military have also supported establishing national service. If they remain supportive in a time of reduced cold war tensions and declining military manpower needs, this would improve the chances of any bill that would create a large-scale national service program.

Despite opinion poll results that seem to show widespread support for national service among young people, in fact, according to Morris Janowitz, the majority of college students have strong reservations. According to Janowitz, the "typical young male or female" does not want to lose a year or two in "the struggle to find a place in the occupational structure."[117] At the same time, young people are participating in increasing numbers in volunteer public service work. If this flow of young people into volunteer public service becomes a popular social-political movement that unambiguously demands a national service program, such a development would alter the attitude of now-skeptical lawmakers.

Yet both such possible developments run counter to the normal American pattern. Usually the American people want demobilization in time of peace, and American young people value individual liberty and personal independence.[118] Young people may well prefer to pursue their interest in public service as independent volunteers rather than as participants in national service.

The proponents and opponents of national service are debating fundamental issues—individual rights, civic duties, and the scope of government authority. Adopting a large-scale, broadly inclusive program of national service is one of the few proposals on the public policy agenda today that would markedly change the American way of life as we know it.[119] As such, national service is a proposal that deserves full and extended debate.

NOTES

1. Szanton, in this volume, p. 189. Szanton places himself in the middle, between the two ends of the spectrum.

2. "Service with a Smile: Experts Debate the Merits of a Civilian Volunteer Force," *New York Times*, August 6, 1989, sec. 4, "Education Life," p. 35. Compare "Nunn-McCurdy Plan Ignites National Service Debate," *Congressional Quarterly Weekly Report* 47, no. 12 (March 25, 1989): 645–48.

3. "Bill to Spur Community Service Wins Approval in Senate," *Congressional Quarterly Weekly Report* 48, no. 9 (March 3, 1990): 669–70.

4. R. J. Q. Adams and Philip P. Poirier, *The Conscription Controversy in Great Britain, 1900–18* (Columbus: Ohio State University Press, 1987), pp. 89–92, 181–

82, 186, 190–92, 250. See also Arthur Lee, *The Need of Compulsory National Service: Lessons of the War* (London: National Service League, 1915).

In the United States, Theodore Roosevelt privately proposed in 1915 "universal" and "compulsory" national service during wartime. Several magazines editorially supported a civilian labor draft in 1917. See John Whiteclay Chambers II, "Conscripting for Colossus: The Adoption of the Draft in the United States in World War I" (Ph.D. diss., Columbia University, 1973), pp. 184, 344–45.

During World War I, Franklin Roosevelt advocated "national government service" in civilian work or military service in war and peace for all men and women at some time in their lives. See Frank Freidel, *Franklin D. Roosevelt*, vol. 1 (Boston: Little, Brown, 1952–73), pp. 258, 331; John T. Flynn, *Country Squire in the White House* (New York: Doubleday, Doran, 1940), p. 100.

5. B. H. Liddell Hart, *Why Don't We Learn from History?* rev. ed. (New York: Hawthorn Books, 1971), p. 49; London *Times*, March 14, 1938, p. 15e.

6. Alan Bullock, *The Life and Times of Ernest Bevin*, vol. 2, *Minister of Labour, 1940–1945* (London: William Heinemann, 1967), pp. 15, 139–42; Mark Stephens, *Ernest Bevin—Unskilled Labourer and World Statesman, 1881–1951* (1981; reprint, Stevenage, Herts.: SPA Books, 1985), pp. 95, 100.

7. Bullock, vol. 2, p. 140.

8. Ibid., pp. 139, 271.

9. In August 1915, Plattsburg, New York, was the site of the first of a series of volunteer citizens' military-training camps run by and for wealthy lawyers and businessmen. The site gave its name to the training camp movement, which Wall Street lawyer Grenville Clark led and Maj. Gen. Leonard Wood advised. Before U.S. entry into World War I, Plattsburgers advocated universal military training and increasing the size of the army. See Walter Millis, *Road to War: America 1914–1917* (Boston: Houghton, Mifflin, 1935), pp. 95, 199, 209–11; Michael Pearlman, *To Make Democracy Safe for America: Patricians and Preparedness in the Progressive Era* (Urbana: University of Illinois Press, 1984), chap. 3; J. Garry Clifford, *The Citizen Soldiers: The Plattsburg Training Camp Movement, 1913–1920* (Lexington: University Press of Kentucky, 1972).

10. J. Garry Clifford and Samuel R. Spencer, Jr., *The First Peacetime Draft* (Lawrence: University Press of Kansas, 1986), pp. 23, 73, 100–101.

11. Ibid., pp. 98–99. See also pp. 26, 55–56, 95, 163, 191–92; Advisory Commission on Universal Training, *A Program for National Security* (Washington, D.C.: Government Printing Office, 1947), pp. 391–92; Roger Landrum, Donald J. Eberly, and Michael W. Sherraden, "Calls for National Service," in Sherraden and Eberly, eds., *National Service: Social, Economic and Military Impacts* (New York: Pergamon Press, 1982), pp. 32–33; Charles C. Moskos, *A Call to Civic Service: National Service for Country and Community* (New York: Free Press, 1988), p. 36. During a June 18, 1940, news conference, Franklin Roosevelt called for disciplining all young people, male and female, through "universal government service"—a program of government training and labor assignments to civilian and

military tasks. His press secretary's remarks, referred to in the text of this essay, were an official clarification made the next day in order to drop the military part of the proposal.

Earlier in the same month, First Lady Eleanor Roosevelt had likewise called for civilian labor conscription of young people. Clifford and Spencer, p. 259, n. 80; Arthur A. Ekirch, Jr., *The Civilian and the Military* (New York: Oxford University Press, 1956), p. 267. Compare Eleanor Roosevelt, "Road to Security," in Julia E. Johnsen, ed., *Peacetime Conscription*, The Reference Shelf, vol. 18, no. 4 (New York: H. W. Wilson Company, 1945), pp. 65–68; Moskos, *Call to Civic Service*, p. 195, n. 31.

12. George Q. Flynn, *The Mess in Washington: Manpower Mobilization in World War II* (Westport, Conn.: Greenwood Press, 1979), chap. 4; George T. Mazuzan, "The National Service Controversy, 1942–1945," *Mid-America* 57, no. 4 (October 1975): 246–58; *Program for National Security,* pp. 393–97, 400–401; Moskos, *Call to Civic Service,* p. 36; Ekirch, pp. 266–67. See also editorial, "Involuntary Servitude," *New Leader* 27, no. 5 (January 29, 1944): 1; William Henry Chamberlin, "It Would Be a National Disservice Act," *New Leader* 27, no. 6 (February 5, 1944): 16.

13. Robert S. McNamara, "Voluntary Service for All Youth," in John Whiteclay Chambers, ed., *Draftees or Volunteers: A Documentary History of the Debate over Military Conscription in the United States, 1787–1973* (New York: Garland, 1975), p. 552; *New York Times,* May 19, 1966, p. 11. In his speech to the newspaper editors, McNamara spoke of remedying the "inequity" of the existing draft. Critics of the draft pointed to a wide variety of inequities. The "inequity" McNamara wanted to correct was the fact that the military only drafted a few of the young men eligible.

14. Congress established the draft lottery in part in response to those who said that the effects of the selective service system's educational deferments were inequitable.

15. Landrum, Eberly, and Sherraden, "Calls for National Service," in Sherraden and Eberly, *National Service,* p. 36.

16. For a discussion of the Korean War and national manpower planning, see Joel Spring, "The Channeling of Manpower in a Democratic Society," in *The Sorting Machine: National Educational Policy Since 1945* (New York: David McKay, 1976), pp. 52–92. In 1947, James B. Conant proposed a plan that tied federal student aid to an obligation to serve governmental priorities. Ibid., p. 79.

17. McCloskey, in this volume, pp. 179, 183–84.

18. *Citizenship and National Service: A Blueprint for Civic Enterprise* (Washington, D.C.: Democratic Leadership Council, May 1988), pp. 28, 26.

19. Bandow, in this volume, p. 186.

20. Eberly, "A Supporting Role for the Federal Government in National Service," in this volume, pp. 224, 232; Moskos, "National Service and Its Enemies," in this volume, pp. 195, 203; Moskos, *Call to Civic Service,* pp. 173–74;

McCurdy, "Citizenship and National Service," in this volume, pp. 61–62. Compare Anderson, in this volume, pp. 248–50.

21. Moskos, in this volume, pp. 195, 221–22.

22. Janowitz, "National Service and the Welfare-Warfare State," *Social Service Review* 57, no. 4 (December 1983): 530.

23. Moskos, *Call to Civic Service*, p. 173. Compare Moskos, "National Service and Its Enemies," in this volume, p. 202.

24. Bandow, "Current National Service Initiatives," in this volume, p. 9.

25. Sherraden and Eberly, "Why National Service," in Sherraden and Eberly, *National Service*, pp. 12–15.

26. Vernon E. Jordan, Jr., "Black Youth: The Endangered Generation," *Ebony* 33, no. 10 (August 1978): 86–90, esp. p. 88.

27. Peter Szanton, in this volume, p. 190.

28. William Schneider, "JFK's Children: The Class of '74," *Atlantic Monthly* 263, no. 3 (March 1989): 55.

29. Milton Friedman, in this volume, p. 153.

30. Richard John Neuhaus, in this volume, p. 130.

31. Moskos, *Call to Civic Service*, p. 69. See also Moskos, "National Service and Its Enemies," in this volume, p. 197; Moskos, in this volume, pp. 114–15.

32. Moskos, *Call for Civic Service*, p. 165.

33. Eberly and Sherraden, "A Proposal for National Service for the 1980s," in Sherraden and Eberly, *National Service*, p. 101.

34. Benjamin Barber, in this volume, p. 80.

35. See, for example, the subtitle of Barber's paper for this volume: "Civic Duty as an Entailment of Civil Right." George Kateb points out that in Barber's proposal for strong democracy, "greater popular participation is acceptable only if there is at the same time the universal requirement of periods of compulsory military or civilian service. One tendency in recent theories of citizenship like Barber's is to yoke citizenship to legally mandatory self-denial. Participation is paid for by conscription, by involuntarily living for others or for an abstraction. [Thus] the fear of passivity . . . can lead to proposals that work, on balance, in the direction of increased popular docility." Kateb, "Individualism, Communitarianism, and Docility," *Social Research* 56, no. 4 (Winter 1989): 933.

36. Landrum, Eberly, and Sherraden, "Calls for National Service," in Sherradan and Eberly, *National Service*, p. 29.

37. Barber, in this volume, p. 80.

38. Moskos, in this volume, p. 26. Compare Michael Walzer, "Hard Work," in *Spheres of Justice: A Defense of Pluralism and Equality* (New York: Basic Books, 1983), pp. 165–83.

39. Robert Nozick, *Anarchy, State and Utopia*, pt. 2 (New York: Basic Books, 1974); James C. Dick, "How to Justify a Distribution of Earnings," *Philosophy and Public Affairs* 4, no. 3 (Spring 1975): 255.

40. Anderson, in this volume, pp. 242–51; Bandow, "National Service Initiatives," in this volume, p. 8; Bandow in this volume, p. 21. Compare the view of Philip Gold who says national service is "utterly pernicious" in satisfying some people's desire to ensure equity "by spreading hardship." Gold, *Evasions: The American Way of Military Service* (New York: Paragon House, 1985), p. 151.

41. Amitai Etzioni, *An Immodest Agenda: Rebuilding America Before the Twenty-first Century* (New York: McGraw-Hill, 1983), p. 160. Compare the view of the spokesmen of the pre–World War I Plattsburg movement who said their training camps would integrate Americans of different backgrounds. See Clifford and Spencer, *First Peacetime Draft*, pp. 18–19.

42. Moskos, "National Service and Its Enemies," in this volume, p. 197.

43. Szanton, in this volume, p. 190. Compare Richard Danzig and Peter Szanton, *National Service: What Would It Mean?* (Lexington, Mass.: Lexington Books, 1986), pp. 246, 255.

44. *Citizenship and National Service*, p. 24.

45. Janowitz, "The Logic of National Service," in Sol Tax, ed., *The Draft: A Handbook of Facts and Alternatives* (Chicago: University of Chicago Press, 1967), p. 75; Janowitz, "American Democracy and Military Service," *Trans-action* 4, no. 4 (March 1967): 9.

46. Sue E. Berryman, "Civilian Service and Military Service: How Well Could They Mesh?" in this volume, pp. 157–78.

47. Bandow, in this volume, p. 186.

48. Robert D. Tollison, "Racial Balance and the Volunteer Army," in James C. Miller III, ed., *Why the Draft? The Case for a Volunteer Army* (Baltimore: Penguin Books, 1968), pp. 156–57.

49. Moskos, "National Service and Its Enemies," in this volume, p. 193.

50. Ibid., pp. 197–98.

51. McCurdy, "Citizenship and National Service," in this volume, pp. 58, 60, 61, 66.

52. McCurdy, in this volume, p. 56.

53. William D. Ford, "Bill in Congress on Public Service for Young People Shows Confusion about Student Aid and Patriotism," *Chronicle of Higher Education*, March 15, 1989, p. A40; Barbara Vobejda, "National Service Plan: Fair to Poor, Minorities?" *Washington Post*, February 6, 1989, p. A9.

54. Henderson, in this volume, pp. 212–13.

55. Walter Lippmann, *A Preface to Politics* (1914; reprint, Ann Arbor: University of Michigan Press, 1962), p. 36.

56. Lincoln Steffens, *Uplifters* (1909; reprint, Seattle: University of Washington Press, 1968), pp. 124–25, 130. Compare Josiah Royce, *The Philosophy of Loyalty* (1908; reprint, New York: Hafner, 1971), p. 265.

57. Lippmann, *Preface to Politics*, p. 43.

58. Ibid., pp. 40–42; William James, "The Moral Equivalent of War,"

International Conciliation 27 (February 1910): 3–20. Lord Baden-Powell, Ian Buruma points out, sought through the Boy Scout movement to "revive the warrior spirit in peacetime." Baden-Powell hoped to use the warrior spirit to bring about world brotherhood. Buruma, "Boys Will Be Boys," review of *The Boy-Man: The Life of Lord Baden-Powell*, by Tim Jeal, *New York Review of Books* 37, no. 3 (March 15, 1990): 19. Compare Royce, *Philosophy of Loyalty*, p. 40 (on the warrior spirit), p. 237 (on the rarity of civic service in America), and pp. 296–98 (on peacetime service as an alternative to war as a "moralizer of humanity").

In contrast, for a nineteenth-century liberal's attack on fostering social institutions that mimic the military, see Herbert Spencer, "Re-barbarization," in *Facts and Comments* (New York: D. Appleton, 1902), pp. 172–88.

59. Milton Friedman, in this volume, p. 153.

60. Amitai Etzioni, in this volume, p. 154.

61. Ferguson, in this volume, pp. 72–73.

62. Neuhaus, "National Service—Serving What?" in this volume, pp. 121, 126.

63. See Michael Walzer, "The Problem of Citizenship," in *Obligations: Essays on Disobedience, War, and Citizenship* (Cambridge, Mass.: Harvard University Press, 1970), pp. 203–28. For a revisionary account of political participation in ancient Athens, see Blair Campbell, "Paradigms Lost: Classical Athenian Politics in Modern Myth," *History of Political Thought* 10, no. 2 (Summer 1989): 189–213.

64. Plutarch, "Life of Lycurgus," in *Plutarch's Lives*, vol. 1, trans. Bernadotte Perrin, Loeb Classical Library (London: William Heinemann, 1914–26), p. 283, sec. 25. On the admiration of Edward Bellamy, a pioneer proponent of national service, for Plutarch's *Lives*, see Arthur E. Morgan, *Edward Bellamy* (New York: Columbia University Press, 1944), pp. 213–14.

On Spartan institutions of national service, see J. B. Bury, *A History of Greece to the Death of Alexander the Great*, 2d ed. (London: Macmillan, 1913), pp. 130–36; J. T. Hooker, *The Ancient Spartans* (London: J. M. Dent & Sons, 1980), pp. 132–44; Douglas M. MacDowell, *Spartan Law* (Edinburgh: Scottish Academic Press, 1986), pp. 52–70; Anton Powell, *Athens and Sparta: Constructing Greek Political and Social History from 478 B.C.* (London: Routledge, 1988), pp. 214–62.

65. Danzig and Szanton, *National Service* p. 57; Randall Rothenberg, "National Service," in *The Neoliberals* (New York: Simon and Schuster, 1984), pp. 208–20; Moskos, *Call to Civic Service*, pp. 4–6.

66. Barber, in this volume, p. 56.

67. Wycliff, in this volume, pp. 16, 260.

68. Anderson, in this volume, p. 51; Friedman, in this volume, p. 51.

69. Edward Hallett Carr, *Conditions of Peace* (London: Macmillan, 1942), pp. 113–25. Compare Edward Bellamy, "How I Came to Write 'Looking Backward,' " Boston *Nationalist* 1, no. 1 (May 1889): 2–3; Josiah Royce, *The Hope of the Great Community* (New York: Macmillan, 1916), pp. 44, 50–51 (I am indebted to David Gordon for this reference); Sidney Hook, *Political Power and Personal Freedom*, 2d ed. (New York: Collier Books, 1962), p. 432; Michael Walzer, *Radical*

Principles: Reflections of an Unreconstructed Democrat (New York: Basic Books, 1980), pp. 296–99.

70. James, "Moral Equivalent of War," pp. 10–20; Sebald Rudolf Steinmetz, *Die Philosophie des Krieges* (Leipzig: Johann Ambrosius Barth, 1907). See also Morris Janowitz, *The Reconstruction of Patriotism: Education for Civic Consciousness* (Chicago: University of Chicago Press, 1983), p. 171; Moskos, *Call to Civic Service*, p. 9.

71. Eberly, in this volume, p. 218. Compare Etzioni on the need for a common experience in a society. See Etzioni, in this volume, p. 146.

72. Moskos, *Call to Civic Service*, p. 39.

73. Ibid., pp. 180–81.

74. Richard John Neuhaus, "National Service—Serving What?" in this volume, p. 119.

75. Ibid.

76. Ibid., pp. 119, 125–26.

77. Ibid., pp. 120, 123, 126.

78. Oi, "National Service: Who Bears the Costs and Who Reaps the Gains," in this volume, p. 81. See also Richard V. L. Cooper, "A National Service Draft?" Rand Paper Series, no. P-5880 (Santa Monica, Calif.: Rand Corporation, 1977).

79. On some of the moral questions raised by involuntary service, see Stephen R. L. Clark, "Slaves and Citizens," *Philosophy* 60, no. 231 (January 1985): pp. 27–46. This article is not a discussion of compulsory national service, but a general discussion of involuntary service, citizenship, and the state.

80. Proponents making federal student aid contingent on performing service often point to America's experience with the GI Bill after World War II. Under a benefits-conditional service plan (for example, the Nunn-McCurdy bill), those who serve will receive educational vouchers. Proponents of such plans say these vouchers will widen access to higher education as, they say, the original GI Bill did. See Moskos, "National Service and Its Enemies," in this volume, pp. 195, 197; Forrest Studebaker, in this volume, p. 52. In fact, the original GI Bill had no effect on the trend of college enrollments. See Keith W. Olson, *The G. I. Bill, The Veterans, and the Colleges* (Lexington: University of Kentucky Press, 1974), pp. 46–47. I am indebted to Walter Oi for this reference.

81. Doug Bandow, "National Service: The Enduring Panacea," Policy Analysis no. 130 (Washington, D.C.: Cato Institute, March 22, 1990), p. 16.

82. Eli Ginzberg, "Manpower Dimensions of National Service," in Donald J. Eberly, ed., *National Service: Report of a Conference* (New York: Russell Sage Foundation, 1968), p. 55.

83. The preceding paragraphs are largely drawn from Oi, "National Service," in this volume, pp. 82–85.

84. Morris Janowitz, foreword, in Sherraden and Eberly, *National Service*, p. ix; Janowitz, "National Service and the Welfare-Warfare State," pp. 540–41; Janowitz, *Reconstruction of Patriotism*, pp. 188–89, 201–2. Compare Timothy

Noah, "We Need You: National Service, an Idea Whose Time Has Come," *Washington Monthly* 18, no. 10 (November 1986): 39; Moskos, *Call to Civic Service*, p. 168.

85. Anderson, in this volume, p. 241; Henderson, in this volume, p. 210. Compare the view of national service proponent Timothy Noah, who says that compulsory service is the "only method" of implementing national service that would ensure "full participation." Noah, "We Need You," p. 36.

86. See testimony of Pentagon manpower chief Grant S. Green, quoted in George C. Wilson, "Proposals to Link School Aid to Service Criticized," *Washington Post*, March 9, 1989, p. A5.

87. Oi, "National Service," in this volume, pp. 96, 91–92, 94–95.

88. Henderson, in this volume, pp. 211–12.

89. Danzig and Szanton, *National Service*, pp. 230–33.

90. Ibid., chap. 7. Compare Szanton, in this volume, p. 190.

91. Chapman, "Politics and National Service: A Virus Attacks the Volunteer Sector," in this volume, pp. 133–34.

92. Ibid., pp. 134, 139; Chapman, in this volume, pp. 152, 255.

93. Bandow, in this volume, pp. 23, 219. Compare comments by Congressman Daniel R. Coats (R-Ind.), White House staffer Gretchen M. Pagel, and President Bush in Robert D. Hersey Jr., "Washington Talk: The Ideal of Service by Youth Is Revived," *New York Times*, September 15, 1989.

94. Neuhaus, "National Service—Serving What?" in this volume, p. 125.

95. Moskos, "National Service and Its Enemies," in this volume, p. 199.

96. The phrase "work that needs to be done" comes from Sherraden and Eberly, "Why National Service," in Sherraden and Eberly, *National Service*, p. 15.

97. Bandow, "Current National Service Initiatives," in this volume, pp. 4–5, 10–11; Oi, in this volume, pp. 110, 260; Chapman, in this volume, pp. 137, 255.

98. John M. Swomley Jr., "The National Service Proposal," in Chambers, *Draftees or Volunteers*, pp. 558–59; Chapman, "Politics and National Service," in this volume, pp. 134–35; Chapman, in this volume, p. 25. A fuller treatment of this issue would require discussing government-sponsored and tax-funded enhancement of opportunities versus government-sponsored and tax-funded crowding out of options and activities.

99. Benjamin Barber, "Service, Citizenship, and Democracy," in this volume, pp. 27–43; Don Wycliff, in this volume, pp. 16, 260. See also Barber, *The Conquest of Politics: Liberal Philosophy in Democratic Times* (Princeton, N.J.: Princeton University Press, 1988). For a classic statement of this outlook, see Bernard Crick, *In Defence of Politics*, 2d ed. (Chicago: University of Chicago Press, 1972).

100. Milton Friedman, in this volume, pp. 154–55. See also Norman P. Barry, "A Defence of Liberalism Against Politics," *Indian Journal of Political Science* 41, no. 2 (June 1980): 171–97. A few liberal theorists (for example, John Stuart Mill) are favorable to politics. See John Stuart Mill, "Grote's History of Greece

[II]," *Collected Works*, ed. John M. Robson (Toronto: University of Toronto Press, 1963–), vol. 11, pp. 307–37; *Considerations on Representative Government, Collected Works*, vol. 19, chap. 3, pp. 399–412. Compare Stephen Holmes, "The Permanent Structure of Antiliberal Thought," in Nancy L. Rosenblum, ed., *Liberalism and the Moral Life* (Cambridge, Mass.: Harvard University Press, 1989), pp. 240–41.

In contrast to Friedman's view, Barber attacks the constant choices and bilateral exchanges of the market as a "kind of Brownian motion" of atomistic individuals not possessing the pattern that politics would impose. Barber, "Liberal Democracy and the Costs of Consent," in Rosenblum, pp. 61, 65.

101. Rosenblum, *Liberalism*, p. 247.

102. Chambers, *Draftees or Volunteers*, p. 561; Oi, in this volume, pp. 84, 110; Postrel, in this volume, p. 217. Compare the statement of Sen. Paul Tsongas, who supports national service because his service in the Peace Corps was "the formative experience of his life" and transformed his ideological values. Quoted in Moskos, *Call to Civic Service*, p. 170.

103. Janowitz, "National Service and the Welfare-Warfare State," p. 538.

104. Moskos, "National Service and Its Enemies," in this volume, p. 193; Moskos, *Call to Civic Service*, p. 169. See also Louis Hartz, *The Liberal Tradition in America: An Interpretation of American Political Thought since the Revolution* (Cambridge, Mass.: Harvard University Press, 1962).

105. Barber, "Service, Citizenship and Democracy," in this volume, p. 28. One should treat the persons whom Barber describes as those who associate freedom with "the absence of government" as constructs of Barber's, created to emphasize a point about ideology or psychology. All actual classical liberal theorists acknowledge nongovernmental coercion (by bandits, murderers, rapists). No classical liberal theorists see coercion as "solely" governmental.

106. Etzioni, in this volume, pp. 153–54.

107. See Jeremy Bentham, *Manual of Political Economy*, in *Jeremy Bentham's Economic Writings*, vol. 1, ed. W. Stark (New York: Burt Franklin, 1952), pp. 229–31; Rosenblum, p. 239.

108. Barber, in this volume, pp. 55, 131.

109. Jean-Jacques Rousseau, "Discourse on Political Economy," in *Rousseau's Political Writings*, ed. Alan Ritter and Julia Conaway Bondanella, trans. Julia Conaway Bondanella (New York: W. W. Norton, 1988), p. 72. Rousseau goes on to say: "If [men] are trained early enough never to consider their own persons except in terms of their relations with the body of the state, they may finally succeed in identifying themselves in some way with this greater whole, in feeling themselves members of the homeland, in loving it with that exquisite sentiment which every isolated man feels only for himself, in perpetually lifting up their souls toward this great objective, and thus transforming into a sublime virtue that dangerous disposition [self-love] from which all our vices arise." p. 73.

For Rousseau's advocacy of national service, see Rousseau, "On Social Contract," bk. 3, chap. 15, in *Rousseau's Political Writings*, ed. Ritter and Bondanella,

p. 143; Rousseau, "The Government of Poland," in Rousseau, *Political Writings*, ed. and trans. Frederick Watkins (Edinburgh, Scotland: Nelson, 1953), pp. 231–32, pp. 239–41; "Constitutional Project for Corsica," pt. 1, pp. 318–19.

110. McCurdy, in this volume, p. 78. Compare McCurdy, "Citizenship and National Service," in this volume, pp. 58–59.

111. Anderson, in this volume, pp. 77–78. Compare the distinction between the communitarians' concept of liberty and the libertarians' concept with Constant's classic distinction between the liberty of the ancients and the liberty of the moderns. See Benjamin Constant, "The Liberty of the Ancients Compared with That of the Moderns," in *Political Writings*, ed. and trans. Biancamaria Fontana (Cambridge, Eng.: Cambridge University Press, 1988), pp. 307–28.

112. Friedman, in this volume, p. 44.

113. *Presidential Recommendations for Selective Service Reform: A Report to Congress Prepared Pursuant to P.L. 96–107* (Washington, D.C.: Government Printing Office, February 11, 1980), p. 42 (referring to voluntary broad-based national service). See also Danzig and Szanton, *National Service*, pp. 147, 274.

114. Moskos, *Call to Civic Service*, p. 117.

115. Doug Bandow, "National Service Was 1989 Casualty," *Chicago Tribune*, December 30, 1989, p. 15.

116. Moskos, *Call to Civic Service*, p. 117.

117. See references at n. 84.

118. On national demobilization in the aftermath of war, see Moskos, *Call to Civic Service*, p. 22.

119. Compare Danzig and Szanton, *National Service*, p. ix.

1

NATIONAL SERVICE INITIATIVES

Doug Bandow

National service may be but a gleam in the eyes of a handful of philosophers and politicians in the United States, but it is a widely used tool in many other nations. The People's Republic of China, the latest country to impose a service requirement on the young, announced in August 1989 a twofold plan: students must spend up to a year in military camps before entering the university, and once they graduate they must work one to two years in factories or villages before furthering their studies. Two goals of these new requirements are instilling discipline and inculcating what the government believes to be proper citizenship values and attitudes.[1]

Although circumstances in the United States are quite different than the circumstances in China—no Tiananmen Square massacre by an aging totalitarian oligarchy, for instance—a number of American philosophers and policymakers have articulated goals similar to those advanced by China's leaders. For instance, earlier in this century William James argued that "the martial virtues, although originally gained by the race through war, are absolute and permanent human goods." His means of instilling those values in peacetime was national service:

> To coal and iron mines, to freight trains, to fishing fleets in December, to dishwashing, clothes-washing, and window-washing, to road-building and tunnel-making, to foundries and stoke-holes, and to the frames of

> skyscrapers, would our gilded youths be drafted off, according to their choice, to get the childishness knocked out of them, and to come back into society with healthier sympathies and soberer ideas.

After serving, he argued, participants "would tread the earth more proudly, the women would value them more highly, they would be better fathers and teachers of the following generation." Such was what James called "the 'moral equivalent' of war."[2]

This desire to make others serve has taken various forms in the United States. The New Deal spawned massive public works programs such as the Civilian Conservation Corps. In 1940, Congress instituted the first peacetime draft, which persisted, with one brief interruption, until 1973. Proposals for universal military training abounded during the late 1940s and early 1950s. In the late 1970s Congressman Pete McCloskey (R-Calif.) devoted much time and energy to pushing a national service program. In 1979 the Potomac Institute published *Youth and the Needs of the Nation,* which offered a service plan in hopes of ending "the present depression of the national spirit."[3]

More recently legislators of both parties have been pushing for national service. The major 1988 presidential candidates promoted civic service plans during the campaign. Massachusetts governor Michael Dukakis supported the concept of national service—but only after the election did he announce his support for the specific proposal by the Democratic Leadership Council (DLC), made up largely of hawkish liberal legislators in the tradition of the late Sen. Henry (Scoop) Jackson.[4] Candidate George Bush proposed his Youth Engaged in Service (YES) initiative. National service might have become a serious issue had not the candidacy of Gary Hart, a private advocate of forced service who publicly pushed a voluntary program, collapsed so ignominiously.

One of the first bills introduced in the new Congress, S. 3 (the Citizenship and National Service Act of 1989), was the DLC scheme, and there are now three approaches, reflected in a dozen different pieces of legislation circulating in the nation's capital. The first and least ambitious one is represented most prominently by Bush's YES plan, which would create a foundation to pass out annually $25 million in federal grants to local service efforts. Strategy number two is the National Guard model advanced by Senator Barbara Mikulski (D-Md.) that would give old and young alike three thousand dollars toward schooling or a home for spending two weekends a month and two weeks in the summer in public service. The third and most serious national service initiative comes from several DLC members, including Senators Charles Robb (D-Va.) and Sam Nunn (D-Ga.) and Congressman David McCurdy (D-Okla.), whose Citizen Corps would make federal educational benefits conditional on one or two years of participation in civilian projects or the military. All three strategies raise serious questions, but because the president and a host of influential Democratic legislators are pushing for some variant of national service—Majority Leader George Mitchell has made passage of such legislation a priority—Congress will most likely enact something.

STRATEGY ONE: THE OPEN CHECKBOOK

The first approach is to hand out money to private organizations. President Bush's YES program, for instance, which would create the Points of Light Foundation funded jointly by the federal government and private groups, would provide up to $50 million a year to promote volunteer efforts to combat illiteracy, hunger, and homelessness. White House aide Gregg Petersmeyer contends that "this isn't a federal program. This is a movement."[5]

Rather more expensive is Senator Edward Kennedy's (D-Mass.) Serve America proposal, which would give, through the Department of Education, $100 million annually to schools, colleges, and local public agencies to create both full- and part-time service opportunities for young people. The bill would also require federal agencies to use current programs to provide better service opportunities.

Grander still is the American Conservation and Youth Service Corps Act. Offered by Senator Christopher Dodd (D-Conn.) and Congressman Leon Panetta (D-Calif.), along with several cosponsors, this act would establish a conservation corps and a youth corps operating under the Departments of Interior and Agriculture and ACTION, respectively, and would provide states with matching grants for volunteers in conservation and social service work. Service would be limited to two years; participants would be primarily full-time and would earn between 100 percent and 160 percent of the minimum wage. The cost is estimated at $152.4 million annually for 13,500 volunteers. (A similar proposal, not formally embodied in any piece of legislation, is National Service Secretariat executive director Donald Eberly's National Youth Service program for 60,000 youths that would be administered by local agencies, but partially financed by a federal national service foundation.)

Contrasting minimalist approaches are provided by Senators Bob Graham (D-Fla.) and Pete Domenici (R-N.Mex.). Graham is pushing the Business and Citizen Volunteers in Schools Act that would provide $5 million through the National Center for Leadership in School Volunteer and Partnership programs (part of the Department of Education) as seed money to help schools start volunteer programs. Domenici has introduced the "Kids Helping Kids" bill to promote demonstration projects involving high school juniors and seniors assisting younger students. The Department of Education would cover expenses such as transportation and curriculum development. The bill gives no cost estimate, but according to Domenici aide Andy Bush, "not very much would be needed for it, maybe a couple of million dollars."[6]

Finally, there is the omnibus Democratic bill offered by the congressional leadership to combine all three strategies, though it relies most heavily on federal grant making. The program, announced by Mitchell, Kennedy, and Nunn, would provide $330 million annually to (1) states to promote school-based service plans, (2) a national service board to fund state public service activities, (3) a national service demonstration project to provide education and housing vouchers for full- and part-time service, and (4) existing federal social service programs to expand their activities. If passed this Christmas tree will be the new starting point from which advocates of all three strategies will begin pushing for their pet schemes.

No one objects to President Bush or any political leader urging people to help one another or, even better, setting an example by being one of the president's "thousand points of light." But a purely exhortatory campaign, however well conducted, could never live up to the high political billing given the initiative by politicians of both parties. Says Chief of Staff John Sununu, "National service could emerge as a defining aspect of this presidency. There is no policy area to which the president is more committed."[7] Therefore, President Bush and a large number of legislators want to use taxpayer funds to encourage personal philanthropy through strategy number one.

What does the administration predict for its open checkbook? "I expect there will be literally millions of young people who will become involved in community service and who would not had this initiative not started," says Petersmeyer.[8] But for all their good intentions, these various plans all carry the trappings of public relations gimmicks and the potential for becoming pork barrels, as have many other federal grant initiatives, especially federally funded job programs such as the Comprehensive Employment and Training Act (CETA).

In particular, proponents of the grant-making approach have yet to detail how federal funds for volunteer groups will not merely duplicate existing programs such as the Student Community Service Project and the Office of Project Demonstration and Development. Petersmeyer says the money is supposed to be "seed capital" to "create and stimulate activity."[9] Yet an infinite variety of private, philanthropic activity is already under way. Without a major federal program some 92 million Americans, more than one-third of the population, currently participate in the activities of some volunteer group. Private efforts continue to increase. "If the '80s were the Age of Avarice, then the '90s are shaping up as the Age of Altruism," concluded a special *Newsweek* report.[10] How will dumping federal money into private local groups that are already operating successfully improve their work?

Several congresspeople have focused their efforts on increasing the number of programs for students, yet many volunteers are already young people—more than one-third of college students, for instance, now work in social service projects, up from 20 percent in 1985. Says Frank Newman, president of the Education Commission of the States, which organized the Campus Compact through which 150 different educational institutions promote community service, "The 'Me Generation' is over. College students are becoming more aware that they have a responsibility to the community. They are already responding to the urgent needs they see around them and becoming deeply involved in public service."[11] Another important umbrella group is the Campus Outreach Opportunity League, created by students in 1984, which coordinates activities through 450 colleges and two hundred local and national organizations. What makes these efforts so impressive is that they are voluntary, arising spontaneously to meet social needs.[12]

Advocates of Uncle Sam as sugar daddy do not seem to realize that federal subsidies might squelch individual volunteer spirit and corrupt service groups, changing their focus from helping people to collecting government funds. (Many philanthropic groups, such as Habitat for Humanity, refuse to accept public funds to avoid the control that inevitably accompanies government money.)

Another important issue is the proper level of government responsibility. All these programs encourage local efforts; why shouldn't the localities fund as well as run such programs? The federal government, whose deficit is in the range of $161 billion as of 1990, certainly does not have extra money. True, Uncle Sam controls the printing press, but should he run it even faster to finance new national service programs?

Moreover, programs are most likely to be well run if financing and accountability remain together. As long as activities are "free," localities have less incentive to make sure that useful work is performed. CETA, the archetypal pork barrel, allowed municipalities to create boondoggles that local taxpayers would probably not have accepted.[13] National service monies could be similarly abused unless drafters of the legislation now before Congress have discovered how to take the politics out of political programs, something they have yet to share with the rest of us.

STRATEGY TWO: THE NATIONAL GUARD MODEL

The second approach to national service uses the National Guard as a model. Senator Mikulski's Corporation for National Service provides a three thousand dollar voucher, redeemable for education or housing. About 50,000 participants would work two weekends a month and two weeks a year for between three and six years at a cost of $250 million annually. Senator John McCain (R-Ariz.) has offered an initiative whose details differ—the voucher would be two thousand dollars, the monthly obligation would be 24 hours, the period of service would be shorter, the number of participants, greater, and the agency's name would be different (the National Service Foundation)—but whose cost and operating principle would be the same. (The most important difference is that McCain's bill requires the president to develop a mandatory program within three years of the measure's passage.)

Both these programs raise many of the same questions as do the Uncle Sam–as–banker schemes. Mikulski herself acknowledges that today, even without a major federal initiative, there are no end of opportunities for people who want to serve: "We already know how to use volunteers in public service and community projects ranging from the Boy Scouts to hospitals."[14] Why, then, do people need to be paid to help? Do we want to risk turning charitable work into a de facto job, recruiting participants for the money—her three thousand dollar reward is the equivalent of about twelve thousand dollars for a standard work year—instead of their being motivated by compassion to respond to human needs?

Yet if one of national service's most important goals is the inner transformation of individuals and if people sign up essentially to moonlight and their employers treat their free labor as most institutions treat free labor, what values will be communicated? "Patriotism and citizenship cannot be legislated," argued conservative Congressman Sonny Montgomery (D-Miss.) when he testified against the national service proposals. "They must be inspired and the example set by those in positions of leadership."[15]

Moreover, what would prevent the government from funding valueless make-work? Under the Reagan administration's short-lived Young Volunteers in Action initiative, some participants ended up working as gardeners' helpers and envelope stuffers. Groups benefiting from free assistance through Mikulski's program would have little incentive to ensure that volunteers' activities were worthwhile; in fact, officials would likely assign participants to tasks left undone because no one felt they were worth doing. Finally, imagine the potential administrative mess. Who would ensure that volunteers showed up and did their job? Could the local service group fire volunteers who performed poorly? Would participants be guaranteed a hearing before they could be laid off and lose their three thousand dollars? And so on.

STRATEGY THREE: REAL NATIONAL SERVICE

The third approach is what most people think of as national service. The most prominent plan is the DLC proposal, which would create a Corporation for National Service to administer a Citizen Corps of an estimated 800,000 young people as well as a few Senior Service members over the age of 65. The latter would receive whatever pay rate was set by the corporation; youth participants would collect subsistence benefits plus an educational/housing voucher. The Citizen Corps would offer opportunities for both social and military service.

A much smaller effort is envisioned by the Voluntary National Service and Education Demonstration Act introduced by Senator Claiborne Pell (D-R.I.). He would provide $50 million annually through the Department of Education to fund roughly four thousand volunteers in new and established community service programs. Participants would earn $600 a month plus up to $7,200 in educational benefits for each year of service. A somewhat different tack is taken by Senator Dale Bumpers (D-Ark.), who would partially cancel outstanding loans to college graduates who worked in the Peace Corps, Volunteers in Service to America (VISTA), or "comparable" private sector endeavors. (Current law allows for deferment of government loans by Peace Corps and VISTA participants.)

Finally, Senator Patrick Moynihan (D-N.Y.) wants to spend $75 million annually to employ 28,000 young people in the American Conservation Corps (ACC), patterned after the New Deal Civilian Conservation Corps. Under the Departments of Interior and Agriculture, which administer federal property (the latter has authority over forestland), the ACC would act primarily as a provider of grants to state and local agencies that would manage the conservation activities. In contrast to the Bush and other grant-making plans, however, the ACC would approve the activities undertaken and cover the full cost; the operational bureaucracy would be state or local rather than federal. The ACC would offer full-time employment for two years; pay scales would be tied to those of enlisted servicepeople.

Although proponents of this third approach emphasize the importance of changing what they consider to be America's selfish ethic, their program is aimed mostly at the young. The elderly are allowed to enroll in the DLC program, but only as an afterthought. The Citizen Corps also principally hires young people, probably because the most convenient time to serve is between high school and college (or after retirement). The impact of service on the server, however, would probably be greater on a 35-year-old investment banker making a six-figure income. Bush's plan encourages and Mikulski's allows those people as well as young people and the elderly to serve. The DLC plan, in contrast, ignores the very Americans who are potentially the most selfish.

The program also shares some of the problems of Senator Mikulski's initiative. The Citizen Corps would also pay for service in a land awash with volunteers, turning supposedly compassionate service into a job rewarded by one hundred dollars a week, health insurance, a ten or twelve thousand dollar (untaxed) annual voucher for tuition or home purchase, and "such other assistance as the corporation considers necessary and appropriate." This might not be a great reward for someone bound for Harvard, but for a lower-middle class kid just out of high school it would beat pumping gas.

The Citizen Corps would seem to transform today's admittedly obnoxious entitlement ethic—college students are entitled to a taxpayer-subsidized education—into another entitlement ethic—they are entitled to a taxpayer-subsidized education if they perform certain government-approved tasks. Moreover, this obligation would apply only to low-income youth, those most reliant on federal subsidies for a college education. As Hoover Institution senior fellow Martin Anderson points out, the DLC proposal is an attempt to "force low-income kids to build roads and empty bedpans."[16] If young people wrongly believe that life is full of benefits and that they have no responsibilities, we should eliminate unjust perquisites for everyone, not impose a peculiar new duty on poor kids.

In terms of accomplishing socially useful work, a serious defect in the DLC program is that it fills only jobs not worth paying for. The legislation dictates that the Citizen Corps neither displace any current worker nor impair "existing contracts for services or collective bargaining agreements" nor result in "any infringement of the opportunities of any currently employed individual for promotion." Local national service councils would have to ensure that no displacement occurred; each state would have to establish a grievance procedure. (Other bills, such as Moynihan's American Conservation Corps Act, have similar protectionist provisions.) The result would almost certainly be constant conflict between volunteer groups and labor unions, with participants being relegated to tasks with the least value.

Under these circumstances, what work would Citizen Corps members perform? (Although sponsors anticipate 800,000 participants, roughly 3.5 million people turn eighteen every year, all of whom would be eligible to serve two years.) National service proponents argue that an enormous number of "unmet social needs" can be supplied only through some form of government-supported service. The number 3.5 million has been bandied about, with extensive lists generated as to exactly how many people should go where (for example, 1.2 million to education, 200,000 to libraries). But as long as human wants are unlimited, the number of unfilled social needs, as well as unmet business needs, is infinite. Unfortunately, labor is not a free resource, which means that most such needs are not worth meeting.

In fact, the government has never found many useful social service tasks for people. The number of VISTA workers peaked at five thousand annually in 1980. The United States put only 30,000 conscientious objectors (COs) into alternative service positions from 1951 to 1965. Between 1965 and 1970, 170,000 people were classified as COs, but only about half of them were assigned to service jobs. The Depression-era public works programs employed millions of people, but largely to build roads and undertake similar projects, not to "do good." What does the DLC suggest? Working with the terminally ill, helping in day-care centers, building playgrounds, handling police paperwork, and installing smoke detectors in the homes of senior citizens. But do such activities justify a massive new federal program? Congressman William Ford (D-Mich.) warns that the DLC program is "an approach reminiscent of Stalinist industrialization in the 1930s: throw legions of untrained and inexperienced young amateurs at the problem."[17]

Sponsors of the current service initiatives also ignore what economists call *opportunity costs,* that is, young people sweeping floors entails the cost of forgoing whatever else they could be doing. An aging population will make it increasingly difficult for small start-up firms, which provide valuable services and products to society, to attract the low-wage help they need to succeed.

Yet the DLC program would delay for a year or two the move of hundreds of thousands, or millions, of people out of school and into the work force. Might we all not be better off if we let the premed student finish his education instead of paying him to spend a year or two picking up cigarette butts? The premed student will probably continue on and become a doctor, but some less-motivated students might not finish their schooling. The National Center for Education Statistics reports that students are most likely to earn a baccalaureate if they attend college immediately after high school. Eduardo Pena, chairman of the League of United Latin American Citizens' Foundation, worries that a national service program would interrupt "the educational cycle," creating "too many situations that tend to siphon off students from continuing their education."[18] Not everyone should go to college, of course, but it is hard to see the social benefit of discouraging interested students from completing their studies.

Would service make participants, whether the premed student or the marginal student who drops out, better people? Almost certainly yes—if they volunteered. But advocates of the Citizen Corps have yet to show how paying people to sweep floors in a public library will improve their characters, for if that is all it takes, then students could presumably gain the same benefit by taking a part-time job sweeping floors in the campus library. A monster-sized new federal program cannot provide people with a desire to serve.

Indeed, the bureaucracy required to administer a system involving hundreds of thousands, or millions, of young people would threaten the viability of the very local volunteer groups that are supposed to carry out the program. A corporation for national service would decide what kind of national service was appropriate for members of the Citizen Corps and then monitor the participants to ensure that they completed their jobs. The corporation would be empowered to make grants to states and local service councils, but the legislation requires state governments to establish "a national service plan" and to maintain existing expenditures on community service programs. Local national service councils, composed of community groups along with local government officials, businesspeople, school representatives, and labor unions, would hire staff, prepare plans, and oversee their implementation. Council members would have to be certified by the governor; local plans would have to be drafted in conformity with the state plan and approved by the state. The corporation could require groups to pay up to one thousand dollars for every volunteer they received.

An example of the harm that can come from Uncle Sam's helping hand is the Meals on Wheels program, which started out as a private effort to provide meals for elderly shut-ins. So effective was the program that the government took it over and destroyed the private charitable impulses that gave rise to the program in the first place.[19]

Placing bureaucratic deadwood in charge of local operations that are supposed to be developing innovative and inexpensive means of assisting needy people is one problem, but another equally serious difficulty would be the politicization of the entire process. Observes Woody West of *Insight* magazine: "Can't you imagine the partisan and ideological cat fights in dividing the goodies?"[20] Today, if a government agency attempts to close regional offices, congresspeople intervene, and if it tries to contract out work, labor unions protest; grant applicants try to pull legislative and executive strings to advance their causes while interest groups battle each other over federal dollars and regulations. A corporation for national service could drag small volunteer groups into these same destructive political struggles.

Where is the money going to come from? The cost of the initiatives varies, but true national service would be expensive: proponents of the Citizen Corps estimate that it would cost about $13.6 billion, $8.3 billion of which would come from phased-out educational programs. If, however, the number of participants was more than 800,000 (some 3.9 million undergraduates receive some form of federal financial aid), the expense would be far higher. Were all present beneficiaries of student loans to participate in the national service program, critics estimate that the cost would be anywhere from $30 billion to $50 billion.

Although some people would forgo student aid rather than spend a year shelving books at the local library, the DLC initiative would not eliminate student loan and grant programs. Rather, it would cut off aid for those who had not participated in the Citizen Corps, with several important exceptions (former DLC policy director Will Marshall estimated that 33 to 40 percent of the current loan recipients over the age of 24 would still qualify for assistance). People who performed their year or two of service could collect their ten thousand dollar voucher and *then* apply for Pell grants, guaranteed student loans, work-study assistance, and other government education subsidies. The supposed $8.3 billion in savings from phasing out federal educational assistance would thus be largely illusory.

One justification for the added expense might be to recruit additional qualified young people to the All-Volunteer Force (AVF); in fact, proponents of the Citizen Corps point to their provision for the enlistment of two-year "citizen-soldiers" who would collect a $24,000 voucher to make up for their reduced pay. But the AVF is already recruiting young people who are smarter and better educated than the general youth population. Indeed, in 1988, 93 percent of the Pentagon's recruits were high school graduates, compared with 75 percent of the youth population generally; 95 percent of its new enlistees scored in the top three categories of the Armed Forces Qualification Test, which tests intelligence, compared with 69 percent among civilian youth. Thus, creating a massive civilian service program will not help the military. "We're in great shape and should not tamper with the effective tools we've given the military," argues Congressman Montgomery, a longtime hawk.[21]

The Citizens Corps, however, is not just unnecessary for the armed forces, it is counterproductive because federal civilian service would likely draw people away from the military. "We don't want high-caliber people who might otherwise join the army off planting trees instead," says Thomas Byrne of the Association of the U.S. Army, a private organization.[22] Moreover, an influx of short-term citizen-soldiers would reduce the experience and skill level of the armed forces and increase turnover. This would not only hike training costs but require added re-enlistment incentives to maintain an adequate-sized career force. As a result a DLC-type program could *increase* military costs.

Assistant Secretary of Defense for Force Management and Personnel Grant Green testified before Congress that national service legislation would "reduce recruit quality, increase training costs, and adversely affect the productivity of military personnel," as well as increase "minority participation" in the armed forces, a phenomenon long criticized by many national service advocates.[23] A Pentagon-funded study by Syllogistics, an independent firm, concluded that reductions in the military personnel budget would not occur unless accession quality, overall force experience, and effectiveness levels deteriorate substantially and that accession quality would not improve significantly under any of the service proposals and would be *reduced* under a compulsory or draft-based plan.[24]

In the unlikely event that recruiting adequate numbers of qualified young people becomes a serious problem, killing or restricting the existing student aid programs would solve it. Military service would then be more attractive because it would be the only federal program offering educational benefits.

CONCLUSION

All three major national service strategies involve voluntary participation, but this is more a matter of tactics than of principle because many advocates of national service would prefer a mandatory program. Charles Moskos, for instance, the DLC's intellectual guru who just published *A Call to Civic Service: National Service for Country and Community* (New York: The Free Press, 1988), has admitted that "if I could have a magic wand, I would be for a compulsory system."[25] In 1979, Senator Nunn wrote that mandatory service "for *all* youth . . . would ultimately be of great benefit to the nation."[26] At an Atlantic Council forum in early

1989, Republican senator McCain criticized the DLC program because it was not compulsory and subsequently introduced legislation that would establish a mandatory system.

China is now reinstituting service requirements, and some national service advocates in this country once viewed China as a model. For instance, during 1977–1978 two members of a Potomac Institute study committee went to China and, according to the organization's report, "came back impressed and challenged by the extraordinary mobilization of the talent of young people possible under authoritarian, postrevolutionary conditions. They came back . . . more determined than before to try to devise a democratic equivalent."[27] But a democratic equivalent is hard to imagine. Despite the best efforts of President Bush and a number of legislators and philosophers at different points on the political spectrum, government-sponsored national service, if elective, will likely duplicate private efforts, stifle existing organizations, and waste money; if mandatory, it will likely subvert the compassionate impulses that animate true voluntarism and violate the principles of a free society. There is no shortage of plans to choose from, but judging from the legislation now before us we would do more good by encouraging individual service, rather than enacting a program of government service.

NOTES

1. See, for example, "Class of '93 at Beijing U. to Go to Army School First," *Washington Times*, August 15, 1989, p. A9; Nicholas Kristof, "China Is Planning 2 Years of Labor for Its Graduates," *New York Times*, August 13, 1989, p. 1; Daniel Southerland, "China Plans Training of Students," *Washington Post*, August 15, 1989, p. A1; and Sheryl WuDunn, "Chinese College Freshmen to Join the Army First, *New York Times*, August 15, 1989, p. A13.

2. William James, *Essays on Faith and Morals* (Cleveland, Ohio: World Publishing Company, 1962), pp. 323, 325, 326.

3. Potomac Institute, *Youth and the Needs of the Nation* (Washington, D.C.: Potomac Institute, 1979), p. 19.

4. Morton M. Kondracke, "Nunn's Story," *New Republic* 199, no. 23 (December 5, 1988), p. 16. Since then Dukakis has changed his position once again. He now rejects making student aid conditional on national service and has returned to his 1988 campaign stance on service programs. Goldie Blumenstyk, "State Leaders Are Wary of Federal Efforts to Link Student Aid to Volunteer Service," *Chronicle of Higher Education*, March 22, 1989, p. A20.

5. Quoted in Gerald Seib, "Bush, With 'Points-of-Light' Plan, Calls for Volunteers to Fight Social Problems," *Wall Street Journal*, June 23, 1989, p. A2.

6. Interview with the author, August 24, 1989.

7. Ralph Hallow, "White House Hopes to Make Volunteerism Its Hallmark," *Washington Times*, April 10, 1989, p. A1.

8. Ibid.

9. Quoted in *NonProfit Times*, April 1989, p. 10.

10. Barbara Kantrowitz, "The New Volunteers," *Newsweek*, July 10, 1989, p. 36.

11. Quoted in William Raspberry, "Not All Students Are Greedy," *Washington Post*, February 3, 1988, p. A19.

12. School-based service programs, such as the one advanced by Professor Benjamin Barber at Rutgers University, are becoming increasingly popular at both the college and the high school level. But they do not truly represent a *national* service program as do the various initiatives before Congress, though mandatory participation requirements at public institutions raise serious concerns.

13. See, for example, James Bovard, "The Failure of Federal Job Training," Cato Institute Policy Analysis, no. 77, August 28, 1986, p. 4.

14. Barbara Mikulski, "A New Kind of National Service," *Washington Post*, July 17, 1988, p. C7.

15. G. V. (Sonny) Montgomery, Testimony before the Senate Committee on Labor and Human Resources, March 14, 1989.

16. Quoted in Jeffrey Sheler, David Whitman, and Joseph Shapiro, "The Push for National Service," *U.S. News & World Report*, February 13, 1989, p. 23.

17. William Ford, "Bill in Congress on Public Service for Young People Shows Confusion About Student Aid and Patriotism," *Chronicle of Higher Education*, March 15, 1989, p. A40.

18. Douglas Martinez, "Would the National Service Proposal Help or Harm Hispanics?" *San Diego Union*, May 7, 1989, p. C8.

19. See, for example, Michael Balzano, *Federalizing Meals-on-Wheels: Private Sector Loss or Gain?* (Washington, D.C.: American Enterprise Institute, 1979).

20. Woody West, " 'National Service': Out of Step," *Insight*, May 29, 1989, p. 64.

21. Montgomery, Testimony before the Senate.

22. Quoted in Sheler, "The Push for National Service," p. 22.

23. Quoted in George Wilson, "Proposals to Link School Aid to Service Criticized," *Washington Post*, March 9, 1989, p. A5. For a detailed study that refutes the claim that the military draws disproportionately from the poor, see Sue E. Berryman, *Who Serves? The Persistent Myth of the Underclass Army* (Boulder, Colo.: Westview Press, 1988).

24. Syllogistics, "The Effects of National Service on Military Personnel Programs" (September 1988), p. iv. This view is not unanimous, but reflects the majority opinion within the services. Compare Juri Toomepuu, "Effects of a

National Service Program on Army Recruiting," United States Army Recruiting Command (February 1989), with Charles McCloskey, "Dissenting Views on the Draft Paper 'Effects of a National Service Program on Army Recruiting,' " Memorandum to Commander, U.S. Army Recruiting Command, March 24, 1989.

25. Quoted in Jacob Lamar, "Enlisting with Uncle Sam," *Time,* February 23, 1987, p. 30.

26. Quoted in Frank Bubb, "National Service: A Solution in Search of a Problem," *Human Events,* August 6, 1988, p. 22.

27. Potomac Institute, *Youth and the Needs of the Nation,* p. 18.

COMMENT

Don Wycliff

When I opened my *New York Times* a few weeks ago and read about China's new national service requirement, I knew it would become an argument against the concept in this country—actually less an argument than an exhibit, a way of suggesting a threat and a kind of guilt by association with that odious regime. But the notion that we ought to be put off from having national service because a totalitarian regime has it is like saying we ought to be put off from having an educational system because a totalitarian regime also has one. In fact, national service would have its greatest value as part of the educational system in this country and should be among our arrangements for encouraging a sense of patriotism; attachment to community, region, and country; and appreciation for certain useful values.

To begin with, I do not know how we got stuck with the term *national service. Community service* might be better because people engage in these activities at the community level. I suspect that national service stems from a direct transfer of military language and thinking to the civilian sector. Community service, although nowadays connected to people like Rob Lowe, John Zaccaro, and Oliver North, is a better term because it designates certain activities that are altruistic in motivation and whose purposes are to enhance our communal life. [Rob Lowe is a young motion picture actor who agreed in 1989 to perform community service if prosecutors would drop charges that he had sex with a minor. John

Zaccaro is a New York City businessman and the husband of 1984 Democratic Vice Presidential nominee Geraldine Ferraro. In 1985, he was sentenced to perform community service for inflating his worth. Oliver North is a former National Security Council aide and Marine colonel who in 1989 was sentenced to perform community service for crimes committed during the Iran-Contra arms scandal.]

I make that clarification to make a point about Mr. Bandow's remarks. He focused, understandably, on national service initiatives at the federal level, but there are many state and local governmental programs, as well as private ones. Neither the New York City Volunteer Corps, nor the San Francisco Conservation Corps, nor the California Conservation Corps have so far posed the threat of Big Brother that seems to be apprehended in a federal national service program.

But to go back to the point about national service as part of education, both Bush's YES to America Program, which exists only as an outline, and Kennedy's Serve America Plan, which now is Title I of the Senate bill, focus on school-based service. Mr. Bandow criticizes this, saying that President Bush and legislators would "use taxpayer funds to encourage personal philanthropy." Then he makes specific criticisms: it could evolve into a pork barrel, duplicate existing efforts, squelch the volunteer spirit, and remove the control that comes from local funding of local efforts.

The general criticism leaves me overwhelmed. Education is about encouraging certain habits and attitudes. When President Bush says any definition of a successful life must include serving others, he is tapping into a widely held American sentiment that does not threaten our way of life. Most Americans would readily subscribe to having such a subject in a school curriculum.

About Mr. Bandow's pork barrel criticism, it is a danger in any government program. You design it as well as you can, exercise oversight, and pray. That is life, that is why we have a Congress; that is why we have the GAO [General Accounting Office] and other institutions. In President Bush's program with $25 million and the Kennedy bill, with $100 million spread over an entire nation, you are not going to find many duplicate efforts.

As to squelching the volunteer spirit, that is for the volunteer organizations to concern themselves with. If they believe that by accepting federal money their purpose would in some way be vitiated, then they should not accept it. There are Hillsdale Colleges [a college in Hillsdale, Michigan that refuses to accept federal funds] in this country, but they must safeguard their mission themselves.

As for local funding and accountability, I share that concern. I was concerned to see CETA [Comprehensive Employment and Training Act] held up as an example of unaccountable spending. A better example of that would have been federal revenue sharing. It is going to continue. We are not going to roll back the tide on it. This is how this country has evolved handling the federal relationship.

As for strategy two, the National Guard model, I share Mr. Bandow's skepticism on that one. A criticism that he did not mention, which I will, is that the National Guard has two meetings a month and serves two weeks a year. It can do this because its purpose is to be *ready* to do something. In contrast, service is about doing something. It cannot be episodic or the service will not get done. Meals on Wheels delivers every day because people cannot wait.

The third strategy is Congressman McCurdy and Senator Nunn's. Mr. Bandow criticizes the youth bias in the program. I cannot take this seriously. Why do we waste youth or education on the young? Why do we do anything when people are young? Because that is when you do these things. Any middle-aged Wall Streeter who needs correction gets it from the court, which is why Rob Lowe and Ollie North are doing what they are doing.

Another criticism is that we are trading one entitlement ethic for another, one based on a willingness to do "government-approved tasks." I am baffled by the definition of the word *entitlement* here. To begin with, the right to get a loan is not an entitlement.

But what truly worries me is the attitude toward government implicit in this. There are two sides holding this attitude. On the left wing of the spectrum, I hear civil rights leaders talking about the Supreme Court having been hijacked by Reaganauts—as if it were an inert tool that could be grabbed hold of to bludgeon the rest of us into compliance with a private agenda. On the right side, I hear people talk about government as if it were an alien force imposing a different sort of private agenda on us. Neither attitude recognizes that in this country, government remains, for the most part, *of* the people.

Let us look at the argument that only poor kids will have to do service. This argument also troubles me. Poor kids can get many things from the service besides the voucher—including the value of the experience itself and the sense of attachment to the community. In New York many poor kids are not getting those things.

Another criticism points to displacement and filling jobs not worth paying for. There is a difference between a job not worth paying for and not being able to afford a job that is worth paying for. Which situation are we in? The answer is not clear. Mr. Bandow uses examples like shelving books in the library and picking up cigarette butts. In New York

City hospitals are laying off workers vital to the operation of the institution because they cannot afford to keep them. It is not at all clear that we would be filling jobs not worth paying for.

Politicization, again, is like the pork barrel, the poor, death, and taxes: it will always be with us. It is a challenge for intelligent legislators to design programs and exercise oversight of them so as to avoid that.

I am glad, however, that Congress did not simply pick up the Nunn-McCurdy bill and pass it intact this year. I hope it will get a demonstration in final legislation and a tryout; it could be useful. The Kennedy and Bush proposals—school-based, small, and relying principally on local efforts—are commendable and useful and ought to be approved.

DISCUSSION

Mr. Moskos: I am pleased to hear that your [Mr. Bandow's] new book is going to be called *National Service: The Enduring Panacea*. After listening to your talk, I would call your book *The Status Quo: The Panacea Arrived*. If you believe that one-third of the American population is donating volunteer labor, there is a bridge in Brooklyn I would like to sell you. It is nonsense to say that, on the basis of survey data, that much volunteer work is going on.

With reference to the stipend in the Nunn-McCurdy bill, you must address the question of the work the people in the San Francisco Conservation Corps are doing. Is it demeaning to those people? Does that change the work into just a job?

You have built a straw man. The whole rationale behind the Nunn-McCurdy bill is that service is at the forefront. Nobody is for meaningless or superfluous work.

What about the 70,000 German conscientious objectors working in old-age homes in Germany? This would be about 300,000 on the basis of our population. Germany is a highly unionized country, a society with an extensive social welfare program. Yet it is agreed by observers across the political spectrum that without these kids, these old-age homes would not operate.

Northwestern, my own university, also has an active volunteer program. College students do not mind working in soup lines but they do not want to go to old-age homes because the work is debilitating and demoralizing. It is something you should not have to do for the rest of your life. Who is going to do this kind of work? This is a market failure.

Mr. Bandow: One disturbing note on the German experience is that Robert Kuttner quotes you as saying that the mental hospitals are the strongest lobby in favor of the draft in Germany. [Robert Kuttner, "Economic Viewpoint: Give the Young a Better Chance to Serve Their Country," *Business Week*, March 24, 1988, p. 15.] I do not like a system that creates a constituency that likes forced service because that way it gets cheap labor. That is evil.

If you think these people are doing wonderful things in the hospitals, shouldn't the German government give the hospitals subsidies to hire the labor they need? I do not want to use a coercive mechanism. If we have particular social problems, let us talk about meeting them. I have strong reservations about an omnibus approach that funds anything and everything.

David Henderson: I want to respond to something you said, Charlie [Moskos]. You were skeptical of the survey data that Doug [Bandow] reported. Normally I am skeptical of survey data, too. I am pleased that you are skeptical because you use considerable survey data in your work, but there are two kinds of survey data. One kind surveys "what you would do if," which is the kind of survey that you and Juri Toomepuu often use in your work. That survey data is dangerous because people often do not know what they would do if they are not in that situation. Doug used the kind of survey we have when we ask census questions: "what do you do?" Although I am skeptical of that too, I have a lower degree of skepticism about that kind of survey data because people have a track record they can look back on.

Virginia Postrel, editor of Reason *magazine:*   We have seen in the child-care issue concern over the role of churches and synagogues. I do not have survey data, but philanthropic data shows that the churches and synagogues provide much of the volunteer service in the country. I would like the panel to address this in two ways. First, are any of these initiatives designed to get around the separation of church and state and allow federal money to go to the programs provided through religious institutions? Second, are the advocates of national service concerned about how the religious institutions of this country will staff themselves with the volunteers on which they depend?

Mr. Bandow: I do not remember anything in the bills specifically addressing this question. Under current constitutional law, the government could not give money to religious groups for religious activities. The city of New York contracted with the Catholic church to provide secular social services. That ended when the city passed an ordinance requiring nondiscrimination against gays. I am not aware of any challenges to a church getting funding for something purely secular such as a soup kitchen.

Mr. McCurdy: Doug [Bandow] is right. There is no prohibition against a religious organization—if it is a non-profit organization—doing charitable work. Under my legislation the state and local government would make that decision, as opposed to the federal government in Washington. As to the question of stripping the churches of their volunteers, I do not believe that would happen.

Ms. Postrel: What about churches in poor neighborhoods?

Mr. McCurdy: I do not think the target group is church volunteers. This program is not going to create a secular society. The young people—or seniors who want to work with them—will be working on illiteracy as teachers or even working on problems in the neighborhoods that are not addressed today. The idea is not to duplicate already existing services but to complement them. The people who are providing assistance today will provide leadership and guidance for those who will be coming.

Mr. Etzioni: As I see the papers, including the one presented here, if they were laid back to back, you would get a better program because there is merit in both sides of the argument. It distresses me when things get excessively polarized, and we lose the opportunity to put together something on its merits.

On the number of people volunteering, I am willing to say that it is not an accurate figure. The deeper issue is: What is the connection between somebody's working four hours a week reading to the blind and taking people out of their communities and putting them in the conservation corps full-time? Now you can be for or against national service, but you must recognize that these two programs have little to do with one another. Proponents of national service suggest taking young people out of their environment. Compare that to homemakers or executives who read to the blind. They are highly different things; we need a semantic clearance.

I just have one more comment. Your point about market failure is not well taken. Why are you using it here? If mental hospitals need more staff, then give them more money. But is it wrong to get one dollar to serve two purposes? Is there anything in free market ideology or any other set of values to prevent this? Even free market nuts accept that there are some things that the market does not provide. There is a category of unmet social needs, not Mickey Mouse needs, on which you want to spend money. If you recognize that young people need to strengthen their moral fiber, what is wrong with getting both things done for the same money?

Mr. Friedman: I want to know what you call those people who do not recognize that there is also government failure.

Mr. Etzioni: I know that the government fails many times.

Mr. Bandow: Naturally you have to look at numbers and arguments. Frank Newman is not the only person quoted in the paper who had high numbers; another coalition is involved in addition to the one he heads. There are many initiatives on the local level and considerable volunteerism, greater today than five or six years ago.

The question is volunteerism versus national service. People get a sense of community and feel a sense of compassion if they see a problem out there and do something—not because someone says go do it, not because they are paid, and not because there is reimbursement for transportation. This is volunteerism.

Presumably when you talk about unmet needs, it is because they are not being addressed. I would hope that if everyone in America were donating large amounts of time, Don [Eberly], Charlie [Moskos], and others would not see the need for this program. There would not be the support for a national service program if you found everyone in America felt a sense of community and was out meeting social needs. The question is what do you do when they aren't? These national service programs pay people to do these things, or they encourage them, or they pay expenses.

Turning to the question of doing two things with a single dollar. Keep in mind the idea of opportunity cost. You cannot just say, "Oh, great," and pay the kids to have them do things. The question is, what could that money otherwise be used for?

Mr. Etzioni: They watch television six hours a day; they will watch five. That is a statistic from the same survey—about behavior, not hypothetical actions. If you ask people what they do, they tell you they watch six hours of television. Could you put up with five?

Joanne Jacobs, columnist, San Jose Mercury News: I am puzzled by the talk about market failure. Are people saying that if nursing homes and mental hospitals raised their pay for aides by 10 percent or 50 percent, they would not be able to hire anybody? If they have volunteers working for free, doesn't that mean they do not need to raise their pay?

Mr. Bandow: I would certainly agree with you. I have problems terming this a market failure. You have to decide what social services you want to provide and how best to provide them. In my view, you provide them through the marketplace. If you need more aides, you pay more. If nursing homes cannot afford the level of service the government wants, you address that with a particularized program. Deficiencies in service are not market failures. Market failures occur when social goods, like defense, do not get produced.

Mr. Friedman: A market failure is generally something that people claim in order to promote a government failure.

Mr. Moskos: Whether it is a market failure or not, Morris Janowitz, to whom I dedicated my book, had Alzheimer's disease last year. The [nursing home] rate for that was $3,500 a month, which quickly went through his family's estate. Finally, he came back home to spend his last months in the care of his wife.

According to statistics, 70 percent of single, elderly patients reach the poverty level after thirteen weeks—somewhat longer if they are married. If that is not a failure of something, I do not know what is. Something is wrong if people have to go bankrupt when they get old and incapacitated.

Untrained, unspecialized people have done similar work effectively for a long time. Indeed the argument is that only short-term people can do this kind of work in a humane fashion, especially working with mental patients and with incapacitated and incontinent people. We do have cases in real-life societies, where the use of youth labor is more effective than is the use of the market or conventional government bureaucracy.

Walter Oi: [Alzheimer's patients are eligible for] Medicaid [once they] reach the poverty threshold, and there are various ways to reach that, such as putting your money in trust and giving your money to your heirs in advance. I would like to look at that data more carefully before deciding. The government regulations encourage becoming classified as poor. Otherwise you are ineligible for Medicaid coverage. That is a tricky problem.

Mr. Chapman: We do have opportunities for people to volunteer. Since the founding of the republic we have had a volunteer sector in our society. This is unusual in the world and one of the hallmarks of our particular civilization. It is successful, and growing, and government supports it—but only in the sense of giving a tax advantage to those who contribute money. National service, in any of its incarnations, undermines that particular system.

We have at this conference several different ideas: We have implicitly the conscription idea, whereby everybody owes an obligation, which government can command, for government-approved service. This is the original idea of national service as debated some twenty years ago. We have the Nunn-McCurdy-Moskos-DLC plan, which would provide inducements to serve in order to get loans and government grants. Then we have a plethora of various Great Society programs encompassed in the Kennedy bill. They all operate somewhat differently, and the arguments against them are somewhat different.

But they all undermine the voluntary system. Virginia Postrel, from *Reason* magazine, mentioned the churches, which is an excellent example because churches do most of the charitable work in the country and receive most of the charitable money. Our system allows the churches to decide what services to provide. Service, in their minds, is not just working in the day-care center that the church operates; it may also be missionary work. Perhaps they think that saving souls or bringing families together represents the highest order of what they can do.

The government cannot, and should not, get into approving or disapproving everything. In some churches, for example, the best use of volunteers is to send relief missions to the Sandinistas in Nicaragua. Are we going to allow the churches to do that with government money? One community thinks that is a good use of volunteer services. Another community thinks that the highest use it could make of its volunteers is to do missionary work for some particular religious denomination in Central America. Are we going to allow that?

We have plenty of opportunities in America to serve. We have a system that generates huge amounts of money to support these volunteer services. What would wreck that system is to have the government fund it and also determine what is and is not acceptable.

Mr. Barber: In talking about volunteerism, we are talking about a red herring. The volunteer sector is an old and tested sector in America. Another sector, the civic sector, is bankrupt. We have many volunteers and few citizens. I want to put this discussion back in the framework of citizenship. That is what national service is about and why people in Congress are concerned about it.

2

SERVICE, CITIZENSHIP, AND DEMOCRACY: CIVIC DUTY AS AN ENTAILMENT OF CIVIL RIGHT

Benjamin R. Barber

PART 1
DEFINING THE PROBLEM: THE DECLINE OF SERVICE AS A FUNCTION OF THE BANKRUPTCY OF CITIZENSHIP

We live in times when rights and obligations have been uncoupled, when the government has to compete with industry and the private sector to attract service people to the military, and when individuals regard themselves almost exclusively as private persons with responsibilities only to family and job, but with endless rights against a distant and alien state of which they view themselves, at best, as watchdogs and clients and, at worst, as adversaries and victims. The idea of service to country or obligations to the institutions by which rights and liberty are maintained has fairly vanished. "We the People" have severed our connections with "It" the state or "They" the bureaucrats and politicians who run It. If we posit a problem of governance, it is always framed in the language of leadership: why are there no great leaders anymore? Why can't we trust our representatives? What's gone wrong with our political institutions?

In the last decade a healthy American distrust of outsized or overbureaucratized government has become a zany antipathy toward all government; not even public schooling or progressive taxation are regarded as necessarily legitimate. As the reputation of government has declined, the reputation of markets—seen in their most abstract and innocuous eighteenth-century form—has skyrocketed. Apparently government can do nothing right, and markets can do nothing wrong. Governments are thus afflicted with every social malfunction from corruption to unintended consequences, but markets operate perfectly, right out of the textbook.

Yet those modern attitudes toward government are symptoms rather than causes of deeper changes—above all in the meaning and importance of the idea of citizenship in Western democracy. The long-term effect of representative institutions, which have been crucial in the preservation of accountability and a thin version of democracy in mass societies where more participatory forms of government seem untenable, has often been to undermine a vigorous participatory citizenship and to reinforce the distance between voters and their governors. We view the democratic state as one more hostile exemplar of those bureaucratic Leviathans that encroach on our private lives and jeopardize our private freedoms. Freedom is associated with the absence of government, and national service is regarded as a species of tyranny or involuntary servitude: "Them" coercing "Us" to serve "It" (the state). That service might be a condition of citizenship and citizenship the premise for the preservation of freedom is an argument that has little resonance in modern mass society where *voluntary* means market and *market* means a kind of formal equality (each dollar is worth each other dollar, each vote worth each other vote, and so forth) that is simply assumed, whatever the actual conditions (skewed, monopolistic, unbalanced) of real markets. Where the idea of citizenship has lost its vigor as a correlate of freedom, the idea of service appears as a function of coercion; where markets are regarded uncritically, coercion appears as solely governmental, and all behavior that is nongovernmental is, by definition, regarded as voluntary or free. Thus, the school dropout watching television all afternoon is perceived as acting voluntarily: "Let's see now, what should I do this afternoon? I can read Virgil in Latin; I can put on that new recording of *Parsifal;* or I can watch "General Hospital" . . . mmm, think I'll watch "General Hospital." The teenager washing up at McDonald's is likewise simply exercising his market freedom: "Should I be a bank president, a senator, a nuclear physicist, or a dishwasher at McDonald's? Gee, tough choice, guess I'll opt for being a dishwasher at McDonald's, I like those late-night shifts."

Yet although meaningful choice in the private sector bears no relationship to the ideal conditions assumed by advocates of the market, choice in the public sector has also been radically truncated by the erosion of citizenship. It is my argument here that service has lost much of its political potency precisely because citizenship has lost its currency. It is a notion so thin and wan nowadays that it means little more than voting, when it means anything at all. Democratic politics has become something we watch rather than something we do. As political spectators and clients of governments for which we otherwise feel no responsibility, it is no wonder that service should appear legitimate only as an alternative to government—a product of voluntarism or altruism or philanthropy. To serve retains its moral character, but as an imperative of the private person rather than a concommitant of citizenship; its obligations are entirely supererogatory and can never be the subject of political imperatives. The model is compassion: charity, where people give to others who are needy out of love or pity, but not out of duty. Charity flourishes as a counter to the private sector's vices: greed, narcissism, and privatism, which, from the point of view of competition and productivity, may be virtues, but, as conservative critics of libertarianism note, can undermine social mores. It functions as a safe antidote to Reaganism overdone: Donald Trump spending Thursday evenings in a soup kitchen feeding the homeless his runaway development projects have helped to create. To the extent that service has been reduced to charity and that civic obligation and civic service have lost their place in our nation's political vocabulary, it is because we long ago bankrupted our practice of citizenship.

These observations notwithstanding, there are ample signs of a burgeoning interest in service in the United States today, an interest for the most part, however, that has been segregated from the discussion of citizenship. Some of the bills pending in Congress tie service to the federal college loan program, and many others (along with most of the school and college service programs) embrace a spirit of private sector voluntarism that seems at odds with, rather than reinforcing of, the obligations of citizenship. We continue to think of service as an apt punishment for white-collar felons on the grand scale (Colonel Oliver North, for example). No wonder young Americans have a hard time understanding service as a function of citizenship when legislators insist it is retribution for crime or (same thing?) poverty. The successful resuscitation of the idea of service will not proceed far without refurbishing the theory and practice of democratic citizenship—which must be any successful service program's primary goal.

A vigorous conception of citizenship was not bankrupted by choice or design. Rather it has been an inevitable consequence of historical conditions that have combined with the characteristically liberal distrust of democracy to favor a less active understanding of the citizen than was current in the republican tradition from which modern democracy issued. The entire history of citizenship in the West, from ancient Athens to the great democratic revolutions of the eighteenth and nineteenth centuries, has been one in which, as the compass of citizenship has expanded, its significance has contracted. More and more people have gained access to a civic status that has entailed less and less, but grown evermore defensive and rights oriented. A small handful of property-owning males once exercised a prodigious everyday franchise; now universal suffrage permits every man and woman to cast a ballot once a year in what many think of as an exercise in meaninglessness. Or to conceive of themselves as rights bearers (a vital function of citizenship as dissent) without duties.

Before considering modern remedies to the defects of thin democracy or advancing feasible programs for strengthening service in an appropriate educational setting, let us briefly review this ironic tradition in which, as the compass of the franchise grew, the value of the citizenship it conveyed depreciated.

PART 2
A BRIEF HISTORICAL SURVEY OF THE GROWTH OF THE FRANCHISE AND THE DECLINE OF CITIZENSHIP

We derive our richest conception of citizenship from classical Athens in the fifth century when, paradoxically, a slave society that excluded women, immigrants, resident foreigners, and slaves from the ranks of its citizens nonetheless afforded that one-fifth of the population that was politically active an extraordinarily powerful role in governance. The citizen was required to participate in legislative assemblies that met every ten days or so and acted as the sovereign authority of the polis, making policy on foreign and domestic issues from war and empire to tariffs and weights and measures. The citizen also served regularly on juries with five hundred, a thousand, and sometimes more members hearing cases concerning minor civil matters as well as capital crimes and treason. He could be chosen (by sortition) for roughly half the civic magistracies by which Athens was governed on a day-to-day basis and had to pay for and serve in the military campaigns he had, as a citizen of the assembly, decided to pursue.

When Aristotle wrote in *The Politics* that man was a *zoon politikon* (political animal), he meant that man was born to civic membership in a polity. Unlike the gods and the beasts, who were capable of solitude, men were naturally sociable and found their identity in their membership in a community. Extrapolitical pursuits—both familial (regulated by women) and economic (undergirded by slave labor)—were secondary, utilitarian activities aimed at providing for procreation and sustenance, but little better than what all animals were required to do for survival and something less than constitutive of what it meant to be human.

Pericles was doing more than boasting when in Thucydides's account of the Funeral Oration he exulted: "We do not say that a man who takes no interest in politics is a man who minds his own business; we say that he has no business here at all." Even Socrates, no friend to Athenian democracy, refused to choose exile over death and reflected (in the *Crito*) on how much he owed to Athens's laws under which (he acknowledged) he was educated, provided for, and allowed to live. To a Greek, then, ostracism *was* a fate worse than death. To be outside the city, beyond the polis, was to forgo living as a human being; to be an individual was, quite literally, to be an *idiot*. When King Oedipus sought a punishment for himself as horrific as his crimes, he chose not death but exile from Thebes.

Citizenship to the Greeks was as knowledge is to philosophers: a cherished object of veneration. It entailed, to coin a term, a veritable *philopoliteia*, a love of the political so strong that it outweighed most other concerns. This powerful sense of politics has been replicated only occasionally—often in small, homogenous civic polities such as the Italian republics of the late Renaissance and the Swiss confederation of the fifteenth and sixteenth centuries—but has largely vanished in the modern world, where politics is the last refuge of scoundrels and things private are by far more venerable than things public (the old *res publica*). Nostalgic yearners for the old *philopoliteia* like Hannah Arendt or the disciples of Leo Strauss suggest that the demarcation line between antiquity and modernity is also a demarcation between virtue and corruption, justice and commerce, public goods and private greed. But the ancient ideals of civic virtue and civic participation are gone along with the belief that citizenship expresses the highest in human character, the most precious possession a man has to lose, a citizenship that—even as it facilitates common living—defines individual being.

Citizenship had already lost some of its moral luster by the time of the Romans, who learned a lesson from the example of the Athenians. The Athenians had tried futilely to extend an empire while jealously guarding the narrow boundaries of their citizenship and had ended up losing both empire and democracy. Roman citizenship grew along with imperial ambition. Beginning with their legendary conquest over the neighboring Sabines, the Romans gave to the vanquished survivors of their slaughters the gift of Roman citizenship. As their empire grew, the conquered became Romans. By the second century A.D., when Rome's territory began to match its imperial imagination, peoples in distant Gaul and Alemannia, whose language and customs were utterly alien to Rome's and who knew Romans only as efficient, irresistible warriors, nonetheless carried the name *cives* and shared mininal legal rights with those who had vanquished them. In time, all of Europe and much of the Mediterranean became Roman; the idea of Roman citizenship, however, had lost the immediacy and vitality of its Athenian cousin. Active participation had been replaced by minimal legal rights, with many more men enjoying far fewer powers. But Rome persisted where Athens had gone under, and the modern concept of citizenship as a form of thin legal personhood rather than a rich and textured human identity took root. Rights flourished, participation eroded.

After the Renaissance, and the rediscovery of Aristotle, antiquity enjoyed a renewed fashion, and early modern political theorists from Machiavelli to James Harrington again took up classical conceptions of citizenship and civic virtue and developed a tradition of republican thought that influenced polities in the burgeoning nation-states of Europe. Nationalism inspired a new understanding of the citizen-subject with obligations to the crown that included military service, and the rise of national armies—how Machiavelli admired them!—reinforced the idea of a civic polity. But the focus was shifting. The economic market, previously a locus for secondary private activity, came to be seen as the crucial arena of human productivity and, thus, of potential human virtue. As the classical weighting of the public and political over the private and economic was inverted, *liberty* ceased to mean only license and *individual* ceased to mean only anarchist or idiot. Where once commerce had been associated with the insufficiency of individuals and virtue had been understood as a wholly public commodity, by the eighteenth century commerce had come to denote a system whereby virtue might acquire a private meaning (if only by such indirect devices as the invisible hand—today's supply-side economics). Freedom became increasingly associated not only with dissent against illegitimate authority but with private agency even against a legitimate state. Thus did the state—above all the democratic state—come gradually to be perceived as liberty's primary nemesis.

The writings of Machiavelli and Montesquieu on the continent, as well as those of Harrington and his fellow republicans in England, struggled to restore vigorous citizenship and civic virtue to the political center. But the privileging of economic activity as the basis for social growth, and the concommitant stress on individual activity and private choice, both shaped and placed limits on the republican revival. The founding of new republics, above all the United States, brought to the surface the deep controversy over whether public virtue or private economic activity was to be the basis for a productive and stable society. Calvinist doctrine tried to bridge the two conceptions, as John Patrick Diggins has shown in his remarkable book *The Lost Soul of American Politics*, but even where civic virtue held its own in theory, commerce seemed to prevail in practice. For the virtuous republic modeled on antiquity relied above all on the cultivation of citizenship and demanded civic education, civic participation, and sufficient civic activism to guarantee a responsible electorate. In contrast, the new commercial republic called for a limited state whose primary function was to protect the market and for individuals whose primary motives were economic—the good citizen as productive capitalist or efficient worker—and who held the state and the democratic majority in suspicion, if not outright contempt. Religion, Tocqueville and others hoped, might continue to tether people to the civic polity and ground responsibility; but the secularism it was meant to prop up was religion's chief adversary, and public space had been stripped bare long before Richard John Neuhaus wrote his *Naked Public Square*.

Ironically, the coming of capitalism gave a push to the franchise even as it presumed a limited and privatized conception of what the franchise entailed. The final victory of capitalism over feudalism in England arrived with the nearly simultaneous abolition of the Corn Laws (and thus trade barriers) and the radical extension of the franchise in the first half of the nineteenth century. Markets, which stood for a theoretical equality that workers hoped to turn into political practice, offered a challenge to organizers, spurred the syndicalist and socialist movements, and motivated labor. Motivated labor in turn demanded the vote. In challenging feudalism in the name of capitalism, Adam Smith, David Ricardo, and Thomas Malthus assailed economic parasitism and privilege in a manner that invited an assault on political privilege and property and class limits on the franchise. If real property could not bar capital from electoral representation, why should capital bar productive (though propertyless) labor from representation? The outline of Marx was already visible to a careful reader of Ricardo and Malthus.

Democracy was thus born in the modern world with capitalism as its midwife—a capitalism that, however, was simultaneously transforming the classical values that constituted its core. More and more people shared in a power that meant less and less. Property owners without noble titles, then capitalists without real property, and in time workers with neither capital nor property won the rights of the citizen, only to discover that those rights were reactive and cautionary rather than empowering and participatory—giving them protection against the state but little control over it. Hoping to win the right to self-government, men (and in time women) found themselves relegated to the passive role of watchdogs, guardians of rights that no longer seemed to entail obligations, private persons whose liberty was defined exclusively by the absence of state power.

The advocates of strong democratic participation acknowledged that self-government by a community was feasible only under limited conditions: a homogenous population sharing a common history, a common religion, and common values; an uncomplicated economic frame characterized by modesty, relative austerity, and rough equality; and a limited territory ensuring both commonality and equality. Such conditions, theorists like Rousseau admitted, were fast disappearing in Europe and seemed incompatible with almost everything associated with modernization.

Certainly the French Revolution seemed to provide ample evidence that the attempt to introduce radical democracy in the setting of an urban, industrializing mass metropolis was likely to result in tyrannical collectivism as well as equality and in terror as well as liberty. Indeed, to the extent partisans of individualism, property, liberty, and the modern market felt threatened by the populist tradition, they argued not merely that democracy was atavistic, but that it was undesirable. Today many Americans—still students and disciples of that powerful tradition of liberalism running from William Godwin, Alexis de Tocqueville, and Benjamin Constant to Walter Lippmann, Robert Nozick, and Milton Friedman that places the fear of majoritarianism first among its many anxieties—retain a distrust of participatory democracy, equating it with mob rule or the tyranny of opinion. This fear may seem out of all proportion to the actual danger, above all in a republic as thoroughly hemmed in by constitutional constraints as ours. Louis Hartz observed with more frustration than wit that the majority in America has forever been a puppy dog tethered to a lion's leash. Neo-Hamiltonian critics still insist that the public mind must be filtered and refined through the cortex of its betters: Give the franchise to all, but don't let them do much with it. Protect them from government with a sturdy barrier of rights, but protect government from them with a representative system that guarantees they will not themselves be legislators. In short, let them vote for the governors, but do not let them govern.

The hostility to citizenship and the contempt for *res publica* have taken a toll even on the limited notion of citizenship permitted by limited government and by the dominion of market forces over political forces. Only half the eligible electorate participates in presidential elections (and the numbers fall off quickly in lesser elections), plummeting to 15 percent or less in local primaries—where, however, millions of dollars are spent by eager candidates. (Leonard Lauder, a candidate in the recent New York mayoralty primary, spent $13 million *losing* the Republican nomination!) The public airwaves are licensed to private corporations who sell them back to the public during elections at fees so exorbitant that a free electoral process can hardly be said to survive. Young Americans vote less often than old, Americans of color less than white, poor Americans less than the well-off. Whether nonvoting is, as Frances Fox Piven argues, a political act of resistance or simply a sign of the morbidity of electoral politics, democracy even in its thin version seems to be in some trouble.

Yet despite the growth of elephantine and unaccountable corporate bureaucracies, liberal and libertarian critics continue to single out the democratic state as liberty's most dangerous foe. No wonder then that the renewed call for national service uses the rhetoric of voluntarism, charity, and good works rather than the rhetoric of citizenship and responsibility. These bring us full circle to the problem with which we began: the civic vacuum in which the issue of national service is discussed today, even by its advocates.

PART 3
SERVICE UNDER THIN DEMOCRACY:
A PROPOSAL FOR MANDATORY CITIZEN EDUCATION AND
COMMUNITY SERVICE

For all the welcome interest in the idea of service today in the United States, little can be expected from it unless it inspires a renewed interest in civic education and citizenship. Simply to enlist volunteers to serve others less fortunate or those at risk (we are *all* at risk) or to conscript young people to do some form of national service in the name of improving their moral character or forcing them to repay the debt they owe their country (the language of market contracts applied to politics and the public good) will do little to reconstruct citizenship or shore up democracy. Rather it sells short the growing desire to do service, for that desire carries within it a longing for community, a need to honor what the sociologist Robert Bellah (following Tocqueville) identifies as the "habits of the heart," nurtured by membership in communal associations. This need must be met by healthy democratic forms of community in a democracy or it will breed unhealthy and antidemocratic forms: gangs, secret societies, conspiratorial political groups, hierarchical clubs, and exclusive communities. Participatory democratic communities permit an identification with others that is compatible with individual liberty.

Service to the nation is not a gift of altruists but the duty of free men and women whose freedom is wholly dependent on and can survive only through the assumption of political responsibilities. The confounding of service with altruism (charity) and volunteerism is radically ahistorical and thus particularly troublesome, for the history of the United States suggests a nation devoted to civic education for citizenship. The traditional American wellspring of service was not the nineteenth-century poorhouse or its corollaries like noblesse oblige, but the older idea of the responsible citizen as a primary objective of liberal education. In this tradition service is something we owe ourselves or that part of ourselves that is embedded in the civic community. It assumes that our rights and liberties do not come for free, that unless we assume the responsibilities of citizens we will not be able to preserve them.

For these reasons citizenship and service have historically been the first concern of the public (and private) educational system. American colleges and universities were founded in the seventeenth and eighteenth centuries on the idea of service: service to church (many began as training seminars for the ministry), service to the local community, and service to the emerging nation. Because so many wealthy parents sent their children to school in England, American schools emphasized training the young to become what the famous farmer Crevecoeur called in 1782 "this new man, the American." This was true among the schools founded before the Revolution (Harvard, William and Mary, Yale, and Princeton, to take the four oldest) and of Queens College in New Brunswick (Rutgers University in its first incarnation), chartered in 1766 to "promote learning for the benefit of the community."

By the nineteenth century, Benjamin Rush's call for the nation's colleges to become "nurseries of wise and good men" who might ensure a wise and good country had become the motto of dozens of new church-related schools and land grant colleges. The Gilded Age took its toll on this spirit, however, and by the beginning of the twentieth century Woodrow Wilson was worrying that "as a nation we are becoming civically illiterate. Unless we find better ways to educate ourselves as citizens, we run the risk of drifting unwittingly into a new kind of Dark Age—a time when small cadres of specialists will control knowledge and thus control the decision making process." Wilson urged—against the specializing spirit of the new German-influenced research universities like Johns Hopkins—that the "air of affairs" be admitted into the classrooms of America and that "the spirit of service" be permitted once again to "give college a place in the public annals of the nation."

The call for a liberal education relevant to democracy gets renewed in each generation: during World War II the fate of the war in Europe and the Pacific was seen as hinging in part on the capacity of America's schools and colleges to produce civic-minded, patriotic young Americans who understood the meaning of democracy and who (Paul Fussell notwithstanding) knew the difference between what they were fighting for and what their enemies were fighting for. In the 1960s, concern for democracy and the civic education of the young led many colleges to experimentation in the name of relevance. Few reached or waxed as hyperbolic as Rutgers' Livingston College, which issued the following inaugural bulletin toward the end of the 1960s:

> There will be freedom at Livingston College! For Livingston will have no ivory towers. It cannot; our cities are decaying, many of our fellow men are starving, social injustice and racism litter the earth. . . . We feel a strong conviction that the gap between the campus and the urban community must be narrowed.

Although many colleges' aspirations were more modest, they were led, if only by their students, to question the relationship of the ivory tower to the democratic nation, and a number tried to develop programs of some value to the country's democratic agenda.

In the 1980s the spirit that put civic questions to the complacent professionalism and research orientation of the modern university is again alive. In their 1981 study *Higher Learning in the Nation's Service,* Ernest Boyer and Fred Hechinger asked that "a new generation of Americans . . . be educated for life in an increasingly complex world . . . through civic education [that] prepares students of all ages to participate more effectively in our social institutions."

Over the past few years interest in civic education and community service has fairly exploded. At the beginning of the decade the Kettering Foundation issued "The Transition of Youth to Adulthood," a report calling for national youth service of at least a year for all young Americans. Meanwhile the Committe for the Study of National Service at the Potomac Institute issued a report, "Youth and the Needs of the Nation," asking for closer coordination between and a unified national policy for programs like the Peace Corps, Volunteers in Service to America, the Young Adults' Conservation Corps, and the Job Corps.

Charles Moskos both surveys and embraces the decade of effort in his *Call to Civic Service,* a book that has promoted the cause of service on Capitol Hill, where members of Congress have introduced nearly a dozen bills in search of a workable program of national service. These legislative efforts, along with President Bush's national Points of Light Foundation, reflect a salutary interest in service. But they do not fully connect service to citizenship and to civic education, and many draw a misleading and (to democracy) dangerous picture of service as the rich helping the poor (charity) or the poor paying a debt to their country (service for college funding).

The Rutgers Program

In the spring of 1988, the late President Edward Bloustein of Rutgers University gave a commencement address in which he called for a mandatory program of citizen education and community service as a graduate requirement for all students at The State University of New Jersey. In the academic year 1988–89, I chaired the Committee On Education for Civic Leadership charged with exploring the president's ideas and developing a program through which they could be realized.

We began with nine governing principles that are the foundation of the practical program:

1. That to teach the art of citizenship and responsibility is to practice it: so that teaching in this domain must be about acting and doing as well as about listening and learning, but must also afford an opportunity for reflecting on and discussing what is being done. In practical terms, this means that *community service can only be an instrument of education when it is connected to an academic learning experience in a classroom setting.* But the corollary is also true, that *civic education can only be effective when it encompasses experiential learning of the kind offered by community service or other similar forms of group activity.*

2. That the crucial democratic relationship between rights and responsibilities, which have too often been divorced in our society, can only be made visible in a setting of experiential learning where academic discussion is linked to practical activity. In other words, *learning about the relationship between civic responsibility and civic rights means exercising the rights and duties of membership in an actual community, whether that community is a classroom, a group project, or community service team or the university/college community at large.*

3. That antisocial, discriminatory, and other forms of selfish

and abusive or addictive behavior are often a symptom of the breakdown of civic community—both local and societal. This suggests that *to remedy many of the problems of alienation and disaffection of the young requires the reconstruction of the civic community,* something that a program of civic education based on experiential learning and community service may therefore be better able to accomplish than problem-by-problem piecemeal solutions pursued in isolation from underlying causes.

4. That respect for the full diversity and plurality of American life is possible only when students have an opportunity to interact outside of the classroom in ways that are, however, the subject of scrutiny and open discussion in the classroom. *An experiential learning process that includes both classroom learning and group work outside the classroom has the greatest likelihood of impacting on student ignorance, intolerance, and prejudice.*

5. That membership in a community entails *responsibilities and duties which are likely to be felt as binding only to the degree individuals feel empowered* in the community. As a consequence, *empowerment ought to be a significant dimension of education for civic responsibility*— particularly in the planning process to establish civic education and community service programs.

6. That civic education as experiential learning and community service must not discriminate among economic or other classes of Americans. If equal respect and equal rights are two keys to citizenship in a democracy, then *a civic education program must assure that no one is forced to participate merely because she or he is economically disadvantaged, and no one is exempted from service merely because he or she is economically privileged.*

7. That civic education should be communal as well as community based. If citizen education and experiential learning of the kind offered by community service are to be a lesson in community, *the ideal learning unit is not the individual but the small team, where people work together and learn together, experiencing what it means to become a small community together.* Civic education programs thus should be built around teams (of say five or ten or twenty) rather than around individuals.

8. The point of any community service element of civic education must be to teach citizenship, not charity. If education is aimed at creating citizens, then it will be important to let the young see that *service is not just about altruism or charity, or a matter of those who are well-off helping those who are not. It is serving the public interest,*

which is the same thing as serving enlightened self-interest. Young people serve themselves as members of the community by serving a public good that is also their own. The responsible citizen finally serves liberty.

9. Civic education needs to be regarded as an integral part of liberal education and thus should both be mandatory and should receive academic credit. Because citizenship is an acquired art, and *because those least likely to be spirited citizens or volunteers in their local or national community are most in need of civic training, an adequate program of citizen training with an opportunity for service needs to be mandatory. There are certain things a democracy simply must teach,* employing its full authority to do so: *citizenship is first among them.*

On the basis of these principles we developed a program that representatives of the student body and the Board of Governors have endorsed and duly constituted faculty bodies are currently reviewing. It calls for

A mandatory civic education course organized around (though not limited to) a classroom course with an academic syllabus, but also including a strong and innovative experiential learning focus utilizing group projects. A primary vehicle for these projects will be community service, as one of a number of experiential learning options; while the course will be mandatory, students will be free to choose community service or nonservice projects as their experiential learning group project. The required course will be buttressed by a program of incentives encouraging students to continue to participate in community service throughout their academic careers at Rutgers.

Course content will be broad and varied, but should guarantee some coverage of vital civic issues and questions, including the following:

1. The nature of the social or civic bond; social contract, legitimacy, authority, freedom, constitutionalism—the key concepts of political community.

2. The meaning of citizenship—representation versus participation, passive versus active forms of civic life; citizenship and service.

3. The university community—its structure and governance; the role of students, faculty, and administrators; questions of empowerment.

4. The place of ethnicity, religion, race, class, gender, and sexual orientation in a community: does equality mean abolishing differences? Or learning to respect and celebrate diversity and

inclusiveness? How does a community deal with differences of the kind represented by the disequalizing effects of power and wealth?

5. The nature of service: differences between charity and social responsibility; between rights and needs or desires. What is the relationship between community service and citizenship? Can service be mandatory? Does a state have the right to mandate the training of citizens or does this violate freedom?

6. The nature of leadership in a democracy: are there special features to democratic leadership? Do strong leaders create weak followers? What is the relationship between leadership and equality?

7. Cooperation and competition: models of community interaction: how do private and public interests relate in a community?

8. The character of civic communities—educational, local, regional, and national. What is the difference between society and the state? Is America a community? Is Rutgers a community? Do its several campuses (Camden, Newark, New Brunswick) constitute a community? What is the relationship between them and the communities in which they are located? What are the real issues of these communities—sexual harrassment, suicide, date rape, homophobia, racism, and distrust of authority?

A supervisory board will oversee the entire program, including its design and development, its standards and its operation. This Board will be composed of students, faculty, community representatives, and administrators who will act as the sole authority for the civic education program and who will also supervise the planning and implementation process in the transitional period. The Board will work with an *academic oversight committee,* a senior faculty committee responsible for academic design and for ongoing supervision over and review of course materials. This committee will work closely with community representatives and School of Social Work experts to assure quality control over community service and other group projects. Course sections will be taught by a combination of volunteers from faculty, graduate students, and more advanced students who have graduated from the program and wish to make seminar leadership part of their continuing service.

Variations on the basic model will be encouraged within the basic course design, with ample room for significant variations. Individual colleges, schools, and departments will be encouraged to develop their own versions of the course to suit the particular needs of their students and the civic issues particular to their disciplines or areas. The Senior Academic Committee and the Supervisory Board will assure standards by examining and approving proposed variations on the basic course. Thus, the Engineering School might wish to develop a program around the responsibilities of scientists, the Mason Gross School for the Performing Arts might wish to pioneer community service options focusing on students performing in and bringing arts education to schools and senior centers in the community, or Douglass College might want to capitalize on its long-standing commitment to encourage women to become active leaders by developing its own appropriate course variation.

Experiential learning is crucial to the program; for the key difference between the program offered here and traditional civic education approaches is the focus on learning outside the classroom, integrated into the classroom. Students will utilize group projects in community service and in other extraseminar group activities as the basis for reading and reflecting on course material. Experiential learning permits students to apply classroom learning to the real world, and to subject real world experience to classroom examination. To plan adequately for an experiential learning focus and to assure that projects are pedagogically sound and responsible to the communities they may engage, particular attention will be given to its design in the planning phase.

The team approach is a special feature of the Rutgers proposal. All experiential learning projects will be group projects where individuals learn in concert with others, where they experience community in part by practicing community during the learning process. We urge special attention be given to the role of groups or teams in the design of both the classroom format and the experiential learning component of the basic course.

Community service is only one among the several options for experiential learning, but it will clearly be the choice of a majority of students, and is in fact the centerpiece of the Rutgers program. For we believe that community service, when related to citizenship and social responsibility in a disciplined pedagogical setting, is the most powerful form of experiential learning. As such, it is central to our conception of the civic education process.

An incentive program for continuing service is built into the Rutgers project, because our objective is to instill in students a spirit of citizenship that is enduring. It is thus vital that the program, though it is centered on the freshman year course, not be limited to that initial experience, and that there be opportunities for ongoing service and participation throughout the four years of college.

Oversight and review are regarded as ongoing responsibilities of the program. In order to assure flexibility, adaptability to changing conditions, ongoing excellence, and the test of standards, every element in the program will be subjected to regular review and revision by the faculty and the student body, as represented on the Supervisory Board, the Academic Oversight Committee, and the administration. This process of review will be mandated and scheduled on a regular basis, so that it will not come to depend on the vagaries of goodwill.

CONCLUSION

The Rutgers program depicted here is only one possible model. But some form of civic education seems necessary. For democracy to be capable of withstanding the challenges of a complex, often undemocratic, interdependent world, creating new generations of citizens is not a discretionary activity. Freedom is a hothouse plant that flourishes only when it it carefully tended. It is also, as Rousseau reminded us, a food easy to eat but hard to digest, and it has remained undigested more often than it has been assimilated into a democratic body politic. Without active citizens who see in service not the altruism of charity but the necessity of taking responsibility for the authority on which liberty depends, no democracy can function properly or, in the long run, even survive. National service is not merely a good idea, it is an indispensable prerequisite of citizenship and thus a condition for democracy's preservation. The Rutgers program offers a model that integrates liberal education, experiential learning, community service, and citizen education. Using the nation's schools and colleges as laboratories of citizenship and service offers an attractive way to develop civic service for all Americans without establishing some elephantine and costly civilian surrogate for the Pentagon and provides a means by which we can restore the civic mission of our educational institutions.

COMMENT

Milton Friedman

There is a difference between the meaning that Mr. Barber assigns to words and the meaning I assign to words. His use of the word *voluntary* is different from my use of the word *voluntary*. I read you not from his conference paper, but from elsewhere in his writings: "You can teach someone what volunteering means by forcing them to do community service under the guidance of critical readings and teachers. . . ." [Benjamin R. Barber, "The Civic Mission of the University," unpublished ms., p. 16.] I agree that you can because afterward they will know what voluntary means: the opposite of what they have just experienced. As written, his words are what Bill Buckley would call an oxymoron. The word *voluntary* means one thing to him and a totally different thing to me.

The same problem arises with some of the other terms he uses. He talks about participatory democracy. He will be surprised to find that I am a strong proponent of participatory democracy. But he interprets participatory democracy as meaning majoritarianism. By my interpretation participatory democracy is the opposite of majoritarianism. Majoritarianism means some people can force other people to do things. By my notion participatory democracy means that people can jointly do things in which they separately participate because they believe in the objectives for which they are working. The best, the most effective form of participatory democracy, is the market in which all transactions are voluntary. Many years ago the SDS [Students for a Democratic Society] used to talk about participatory democracy. I said to the people in SDS and I say the same thing to you, Mr. Barber, your objectives and mine have much in common. The difference is I know how to achieve them and you do not.

Let us go directly to the so-called service program in the Nunn-McCurdy bill. People are describing that as voluntary, which it is as far as the participants are concerned. For them it is just a market transaction. The bill offers them extremely attractive terms to accept a job. Walter Oi's paper will show how attractive some of these terms are. The particular job is the one defined under the Nunn-McCurdy bill.

But is it voluntary for the people who pay for it? Money does not fall from trees. Despite the wishes of everybody, there are no free lunches. Somebody has to pay for national service, and the cost is large and will be paid for.

Is it voluntary for me as a taxpayer when my money is used for the purpose of promoting somebody else's concept of national service? It is not. If there were a proper law on truth in advertising, to talk about this as a voluntary program would make one guilty of violating that law. The taxpayers who pay for national service are forced to pay for it. It is compulsory.

Now you may tell me that they are forced to pay for many other things. Of course, and that is bad. That is why I am in favor of a limited government; I do not believe that some people should force other people to use their money for purposes they do not agree with. Now there are some cases where we cannot avoid it. We force people to pay for national defense, and I agree with that. There are a few other appropriate functions. But this far-fetched program of providing attractive opportunities to young people at the expense of people who would not freely donate for that purpose passes the limit of appropriate and moral government.

Mr. Barber speaks of "greed" as if it were a market phenomenon. Does he mean that none of those people who serve in Washington have any element of greed or narcissism or privatism? They allow themselves to be lobbied by PACs.

Mr. Barber: The difference is that it is not part of their justifying rhetoric.

Mr. Friedman: I thought we were talking about substance, not rhetoric.

My ideal of an appropriate community is not Athens but nineteenth-century America, where you had volunteerism on a large scale, volunteerism properly speaking. Much of the rhetoric in the national service argument says that the only way you can get voluntary service is by the government forcing people to volunteer. In the nineteenth century government was relatively small. Mr. Barber speaks of currently having a limited government. The government we have now is not relatively limited. It spends 45 percent of the national income, which is an understatement of the extent to which the government controls the society.

But in the nineteenth century, when federal, state, and local governments never spent more than 10 percent of the national income, what happened? That was a period in which "privately financed schools and colleges multiplied." I am quoting from something I myself wrote some years ago. "Foreign missionary activity exploded; nonprofit private hospitals, orphanages, and numerous other institutions sprang up like weeds. Almost every charitable or public service organization . . . dates from that period. . . . The charitable activity was matched by a burst of cultural activity—art museums, opera houses, symphonies." [Milton and Rose D. Friedman, *Free to Choose* (New York: Harcourt Brace Jovanovich, 1980), pp. 36–37.]

I spent fifteen minutes last night looking through the list of associations and foundations in my *World Almanac*. What did I find? B'nai B'rith began in 1843; the YMCA, in 1851; the ASPCA, in 1866; the Salvation Army, in 1880; the National Association of the Deaf, 1880; the Red Cross, in 1881; and the Indian Rights Association, in 1882. Then I skipped to later dates. I found the Boys' Club of America, 1906; the National Society to Prevent Blindness, 1908; the National Association for the Advancement of Colored People, 1909; the National Conference of Catholic Charities, 1910; and the Boy Scouts of America, 1910.

What fascinated me as I looked at the organizations that were established in the 1940s, 1950s, and 1960s was that they were almost all professional associations and trade associations whose only excuse for existence was to lobby the government. The gargantuan expansion of the government has induced people to devote their activities that are not directly productive to influencing government as opposed to serving others. Remember that the driving force of all human effort is getting somebody else's money. There are two ways you can get hold of other peoples' money—by providing something they are willing to pay for and by taking it away from them. There are no other ways. Everyone wants to spend someone else's money; nobody is immune from that. Nobody spends someone else's money as carefully as he spends his own.

A voluntary society is a society in which you have free people grouped in a community. I thoroughly agree with Mr. Barber's view that citizenship is a community concept. A decent society is a society in which communities, that is, groups of people, have common aims and promote those common objectives by common work. But the institutional structure that is best able to promote that society is not an institutional structure of centralized government in Washington doling out funds to states and localities. It is a set of institutions in which people are free to spend their own money to the largest possible extent on their own activities.

This is partly a question of words. Barber and others use the word market as if the market referred to only very narrow functions—buying and selling in the marketplace. But the market is a much broader concept. Were the charitable activities in the nineteenth century the result of market failure or market success? I regard them as market successes.

The market means voluntary activity by people who cooperate together for purposes that are common or to meet one another's desires, wishes, or wants. The establishment of nonprofit hospitals was a market activity. The establishment of the YMCA was a market activity in that sense. The development of the new modern sciences is a market activity. The establishment of the Rutgers College I graduated from was a market activity. The Rutgers University that Mr. Barber works for is not a market activity.

Let me add one more thing on which Mr. Barber and I agree. I read one of his papers in which he bemoaned the deterioration of higher education [Barber, "Civic Mission of the University"]. I agree with him 100 percent, but his explanation is wrong. Higher education has gone to hell for the same reasons that so many other activities in this country have been corrupted. Socialized industries—medicine, welfare, higher education, elementary and secondary education—are all examples of what happens when decentralized and primarily voluntary activities are taken over by the government. Success is converted to disaster.

You have profitable, private enterprise. The government takes it over, and it becomes a basket case. We had a medical system under which the country as a whole was spending about 5 percent of the national income for decades, and we were having steady medical progress. Government stepped in. Mr. Moskos cited a terrible case—the cost of the medical treatment of people with Alzheimer's disease—and he is right. Why? Because total expenditures on medicine have now reached 11 percent of the gross national product. The difference is the three-quarters made up by government funds. These not only are being wasted in an absolute sense, but are making less effective the private funds devoted to medicine. What Mr. Moskos describes would not be possible if the government had not taken over and destroyed the private activity that would solve those problems.

We had a widespread net of charitable activities. The government took over, and it became a welfare mess. Is there anybody who believes that welfare, as we now administer it, is contributing to a long-run improvement in the well-being of the underclass, or to a reduction in its numbers? Or that welfare is as effective in meeting the needs of recipients as person-to-person voluntary charity?

A major effect has been to destroy private charitable activity. To see this, it is only necessary to examine where the gifts, the private contributions, are now going. The private voluntary sector is alive. But the money is not going to the traditional charities; it is going to museums, symphonies, and, to some extent, hospital buildings. It is going to institutions of higher learning to build buildings. Universities are now in the business of selling monuments. Of course the student is getting shortchanged. Why? He should be the customer, but he isn't. The student is just a factor of production—you need students to get money from the government. As a result, universities do not pay any attention to students; they are of no importance. When I was growing up—I graduated from Rutgers College in 1932, which was not exactly a time of great prosperity in this country—the students in colleges were customers.

DISCUSSION

Mr. Chapman: I would like to ask Professor Barber what the Rutgers program is like? How far does it go? You say that citizenship entails service and that to be a citizen in good standing you have to perform service. Under these proposed rules, will university-approved service be a requirement? Will you not get a degree if you do not perform this service? The second question is, who decides what the approved service is? Does the individual or the university decide and on what terms? What about maverick perceptions of what service might be? I would expect that the university would say that helping out in a mental institution was approved service. What about the missionary activity of religious movements? What about political activity—the Young Republicans or the Young Democrats? What about tutoring? What about private tutoring?

Mr. Barber: The Rutgers program will require each student to take a one-semester course in civic education that will have as a mandatory element what we call experiential learning, out-of-the-classroom experience. Students will have the choice of opting for a service program of their choice or some other form of experiential learning. We are not mandating that they do community service. We are mandating that they take the course, and the course has a mandatory experiential learning component. Our expectation is that more than half, perhaps three-quarters, of the students will engage in community service.

Each proposal for experiential learning will be considered by an oversight group of students, people from the community, and faculty members, who will make the ultimate decision as to whether it counts. By calling this experiential learning, however, we intentionally broadened the frame and widened the spectrum of possibilities. If a group of students wanted to make a case that, by working for the local Republican committee, they could learn something about what it meant to be engaged in the community, that might pass.

Mr. Friedman: May I ask Mr. Barber whether something I did as an undergraduate would qualify? When I was an undergraduate, I and a friend, who like me was working his way through school, set up an entrepreneurial business selling students white socks, which freshmen had to wear, and ties at lower prices than the bookstore's. We also arranged to buy secondhand textbooks. (The bookstore objected strenuously and wanted to put us out of business.) We did not think we were engaged in public service, but would that count as public service, community service?

Mr. Barber: If you were anything then like you are now, anything you suggested would qualify. [laughter]

Mr. Friedman: No, do not evade the question. The implication of your comment is that you do not regard as public service serving your fellow man in a way that is mutually attractive to both of you. Take your example of working for the Republicans. I am not primarily a Republican. I am an individual; I am a citizen; I am a businessman.

Mr. Barber: There is a fundamental difference between the character of the market and the character of the civic realm. From your point of view the civic realm is coercive, elephantine, and dangerous to liberty; what you call the market and voluntary activity are conducive to liberty, human productivity, and happiness. You and I disagree, and many people in this room side one way or the other or fall somewhere in the middle. I do not think we ought to hold hostage our discussion of service to the fundamental difference between those who want to argue a pure market position or a pure government position.

Your for-profit activities would not qualify.

Mr. Anderson: I wonder, Mr. Barber, if you could answer this question. You said in your prepared remarks that "to serve retains its moral character," implying that serving the state is a moral good. Why is it moral?

Mr. Barber: What I said was that, in the discussions of service as altruism and as a feature of private voluntary behavior, service retains its moral character, but does not retain its civic character. That was a criticism in the sense that service limited to altruism is not immoral, but does not serve a civic purpose.

Mr. Anderson: Is there something intrinsically moral about serving the state?

Mr. Barber: It was not serving the state, it was serving other people. But you begin with the notion that the state is *there* and we are *here* and that we serve the state. If that is your model, my question to you is, is there anything immoral about a people serving itself? My answer is no, there is nothing immoral about a people serving itself, which is what one does when one engages in citizen service.

Mr. Anderson: My answer is no if you do so voluntarily, but yes if you are being forced to do it. If you do not agree, perhaps you could serve me. I have some interesting ideas.

Mr. Barber: You are not the people, sir.

Panelist: Who is?

Mr. Barber: We are: us, not him; us, not me; us, not Milton Friedman. The great "We" of the polity is what I am talking about.

Mr. Anderson: What do you mean, I am not the people?

Mr. Barber: Personally serving you is not serving the people, the state. Serving me is not serving the state. Serving Milton Friedman is not serving the state. Serving the Hoover Institution is not serving the state.

Mr. Friedman: Who is served when the state is served?

Forrest E. Studebaker, Professor, International Policy Studies, Monterey Institute of International Studies, Monterey, California: In the Anglo-American world, [James] Harrington developed from Machiavelli the concept of citizenship and civic virtue. This was well before Bentham and John

Stuart Mill, who defined citizenship in nineteenth century terms that allow anyone who has money to go to the university. Citizenship in the continental sense would allow the 1948 GI Bill, which put through the universities the highest number of graduates the United States has ever produced. I do not know how the market would have treated them; the market I remember some years later was shabby. As veterans, as citizens, we were able to go to universities—something that the market would not have provided.

Mr. Friedman: I went to college from 1928 to 1932. As a result of a competitive exam, I did have a slight scholarship from the state that paid most of my tuition. But beyond that, every penny of my education was paid by me working in the market. Those were not years when the market was showing itself at its best; at all times, however, the market has permitted people who did not have money to go to college and to become successful.

If you go back to the nineteenth century, there was a market in which people were poor and yet were able to go to colleges and universities. In Great Britain, James Mill, the son of a shoemaker, was able to become an educated, schooled person. John Stuart Mill, the son of James Mill, was able to do likewise. You have that same opportunity all around the world. You have it in Hong Kong today.

What you are not recognizing is the extent to which government subsidization of higher education has produced a flood of people who never should have gone to college and never should have graduated.

Mr. Barber and I agree on the extent to which the universities have been turned into trade schools and commercialized. Liberal education has been destroyed. Why? Because if you go to a state college now, it costs very little. It is a vacation. You have dropout rates of 50 percent at UCLA. You call that a government response to a market failure; I call that a government failure.

Moreover, how are we financing it? One of the most disgraceful programs in the United States is the financing of higher education. The government imposes taxes on low-income people to subsidize middle- and upper-income people to get an education. Look at the statistics on the distribution of the benefits of higher education and on the distribution of the costs. Higher education in the United States is an utter disgrace.

The GI Bill was not an example of this sort of financing, but simply an appropriate part of the compensation that people got for taking on a job at lower-than-market wages. There is nothing wrong with that. I was all in favor of the GI Bill for that reason. Do not confuse the GI Bill with the state of California's system of higher education.

Mr. Etzioni: I would like to go back to the previous discussion. The question was, why serve the state? We have serious problems in such a discussion if the two alternatives are either you serve individuals or you serve the state. Limiting matters to these alternatives removes the community and moral order as an independent realm. It is not accidental that this problem came up: In the libertarian constitution there is no mention of community. Libertarian doctrine sets up a simplistic opposition between the realm of the state and that of the individual as if these were the only two realms. The moment we eliminate the third category, we lose a lot.

This is important because a serious problem underlies and legitimates much of the criticism of national service: The government has stepped into something that should be a community problem. As a proponent, I want to acknowledge that it would be much better if the voluntary associations in the community would expand the opportunities, financing, and structures for people who want to volunteer. We would not need federal guidance, leadership, or funding.

In the heat of debate, Mr. Barber, you said, yes, we are serving the state. But I do not think it is useful to equate the state with the people.

Mr. Michael Lind, visiting fellow in foreign policy, Heritage Foundation: I would like to ask Professor Barber about history. His historical account confutes his conclusions. He spoke at great length about the desirability of republicanism. Republicanism arose in Western history in two periods—ancient Greece, and medieval and early modern Switzerland and Italy—when desirability converged with necessity, namely, economies of scale.

Athens was a state with a citizen class of about 50,000 people. It had an autarkic economy when it was a great military power in 400 B.C. A few centuries later the military economies of scale had shifted radically to incorporate the entire Mediterranean. At that point, Athens no longer made sense as an independent regime. Republicanism brought about by military and economic necessity fell apart when its underpinnings were gone.

The same thing happened in the early modern republic. Shortly after Machiavelli wrote about how important citizen-soldiers were to the strength of the state, mercenary armies—for rational economic reasons—became the order of the day in Western Europe for centuries.

My question is, is your objection to the economies of scale of the modern world—in which NATO makes sense as a military unit and in which a global economy makes sense as an economic unit—rather than the economies of scale of the nineteenth century—when economic and military units limited to a Palo Alto made sense because you had Indian raids and bandits and most of the food people consumed was grown within a day's distance of where they lived?

Mr. Barber: I do not take exception to that. That is precisely what I have been arguing. The problem of modern democracy is how, under conditions for which no republican theorist would argue it was fit, we can retain anything resembling democracy. The point is that the complacency with which we examine our own democracy leaves us in danger of losing even the thin version of democracy that we have.

In the absence of these conditions, the challenge becomes: Are there ways in which we can resuscitate a somewhat more vigorous notion of citizenship? What institutions will help us do that? Some of the service institutions that have been suggested are one way we might reinforce citizenship. Without question, it can never be revived in its Greek or early modern form.

As a social scientist, I am a pessimist. My pessimism leads me to say that those who are complacent about the market as a surrogate for democracy and who think our democracy is going to survive without support, are fooling themselves.

To exist in the market you have to have a voice. If you live in a nation where large minorities have no power to participate in the market, the market does not work. All ships rise on a rising tide, but you have to be in a boat to start with. Many Americans are not in a boat and do not participate in the market. The market in Washington, D.C., among poor black people is not a market distinguished by people using their energy to buy themselves an education; they are buying something else.

Those problems cannot be dealt with by taking individuals alone rather than individuals who are members of communities. Professor Friedman does not take into account the great American secret: Democracy survives in America in the intermediate realm of communal associations and organizations that are neither private nor market nor the sovereign state. Intermediate organizations are where we learn citizenship, where we learn the meaning of our social identities, and where the service idea can most richly be explored. I wish we would get away from discussing the pure market and the state as if we were in the eighteenth century.

Mr. Friedman: Mr. Barber, I was just talking about all those intermediary institutions. Why was I going back to the nineteeth century to the promotion of nonprofit hospitals, colleges, and universities? Those were all intermediary institutions.

What you say about minorities not being able to find a place in the market is unhistorical. My parents came to this country as poor people without any money and without any skills, my mother, fourteen, my father, sixteen. They were able to survive and live. Why? Partly because there were voluntary organizations that were willing to help them. There were many immigrants then. The flow of immigration now is a small fraction of what it was when there was no government assistance for immigrants. The major reason minorities today have such difficulties (and they do) is not because that government is not doing enough, but because government is doing too much. What is destroying the ghettos? bad housing, bad schooling, and rent control laws. Why is schooling bad? because it is run by the government. You ought to have a voucher scheme, a scheme under which you could have the market play a larger role in schooling. The prohibition of drugs is a major factor in destroying local communities.

Please do not continue to describe me as a proponent of a narrow market with no understanding of or reference to intermediary institutions. I am saying precisely the opposite: The market has to be interpreted much more broadly.

Mr. Henderson: I have a question for you, Ben [Barber]. You were critical of "charity, where men give to others who are without what they need out of love or pity not out of duty." I agree with you about pity; I do not like pity much, but I was disturbed about what you said about love. Are you saying it would be better to help someone out of duty than out of love? Because if so, then we are not just disagreeing about means. If I understand you correctly, I also disagree with you about what is desirable.

Mr. Barber: I am not a critic of altruism, charity, compassion, or love. Those are wonderful, but if we pin citizen education on them, we teach the lesson that citizens are there to do only for others, not themselves. Professor Friedman and I agree on one thing: Human beings are deeply self-interested; they are motivated by self-interest. Our democratic citizenship is a product of enlightened self-interest. You serve yourself; you serve your freedom through citizenship. When you do not have citizenship, liberty cannot be protected. Self-interest is best served in a citizen-service program in which people see themselves not simply as helping others but as helping themselves.

Mr. Henderson: Perhaps this will help clarify matters: Who is the duty to?

Mr. Barber: Ultimately to yourself, but to yourself as a social person, a person who is a member of a community and therefore, a member of the greater community to which all communities belong, which is finally the state.

Mr. McCurdy: It would be nice to return to the days of ancient Greece, but I do not want to return to the nineteenth century. There are things we might like to take from each.

But I have to face reality. I have to go back to my constituents in the western part of Oklahoma and explain what I am trying to do. What I am telling you today is that we have a declining sense of citizenship. If you look at the statistics, you can see it. We may not have this problem at the Hoover Institution or at Stanford. But if you walk outside this campus a few blocks or go into the urban areas of the cities and ask people what is foremost on their minds, I doubt seriously that their driving force is getting other people's money.

It is something broader than that and more diverse than that. The entitlement society we have today is so entrenched that the federal government has gotten out of control and is too large. Let me tell you as someone who has been in Congress for ten years, just try to take something away that you have ever given as a government program. Heaven forbid. Ronald Reagan saw that. As a Democrat I am complaining just as loudly that the entitlement society is killing us. Look at catastrophic care; people do not want to pay for it. I have to find a system whereby we can spend a tax dollar in more than one location.

Higher education today is not delivering the services that it should or that we intended it to. That is why I am an archenemy of the high priests of the higher education lobby. When I introduced my bill, One DuPont Circle [the Washington, D.C., address of the American Council on Education, the National Association of State Land-Grant Universities and Colleges, the American Association of Universities, the American Association of State Colleges and Universities, and 25 other groups that lobby for the interests of institutions of higher education] emptied. They ran to the Hill because we challenged the very basis of their system: entitlement.

We probably are not able to take the entitlement away, but we want something in return to address social needs. At the same time we want to foster citizenship and in the long term have more productive citizens.

Are there too many people in college today? Should they not be in college, as Dr. Friedman suggests? I disagree with him. Some will flunk out, but many will return. They will have had a one- or two-year exposure to a different type of society, culture, education, and questions. Is this good? Absolutely. Such exposure is important whether you are from rural Oklahoma or from San Francisco.

I would not be here today if it were not for public education. Thus I am a proponent of public education and also of the church. Those institutions are at a risk today in this country, and I do not believe it is just the fault of government. I believe the cause is a fractionation of society and people's inability to see beyond their own concerns.

I am a believer in market forces. But back in law school in tort law class we learned that your freedom ends at my nose. To people who say, the hell with government, let me tell you something: When you smoke your dirty cigarette, you are affecting me. You are violating my rights. If you are polluting with your car, you are affecting my freedom. If you are out pursuing your buck and dumping garbage into my water, then you are violating my rights.

Mr. Friedman: No question.

Mr. McCurdy: So we have to find a way—government—to balance that.

What I am proposing in my bill is that we address some of the growing needs of this country. The high illiteracy rate in this country is real; public schools are not teaching people the right things. My wife is a psychiatrist; I was an attorney for a mental hospital. If you believe [the condition of the mentally ill] is a market success, you are out to lunch, folks!

Having cleared the field of the purely academic and philosophical, we have to focus on the reality today in the United States, on how we can make the most of our fouled-up system, and on whether we can come up with constructive proposals that we can all agree on.

3

CITIZENSHIP AND NATIONAL SERVICE

Dave McCurdy

Since January the Citizenship and National Service Act of 1989, H.R. 660 and S. 3, which Senator Sam Nunn and I introduced, has been the focus of a great deal of debate. The proposal is based on the premise that the United States must move beyond the narcissism of the Reagan years and the lingering aftereffects of Vietnam, both of which led many to ask what their country could do for them. During the last decade a generation has evolved whose members, by and large, believe they can have it all without costs.

National surveys of the attitudes and values of incoming freshmen conducted by the Higher Education Research Institute at UCLA between 1966 and 1985 reveal a large shift over that two-decade period. Among other questions, the survey focuses on life goals. The goal showing the greatest increase was *being very well off financially*; the goal showing the greatest decrease was *developing a meaningful philosophy of life*.[1]

At the same time there is a declining sense of citizenship. Spinoza asserted that "men are not born fit for citizenship, but must be made so."[2] National polling in recent years reveals that most Americans define citizenship in terms of rights and entitlements rather than of duties and responsibilities. From 1964 to 1988 the percentage of those eligible to vote declined from 67.8 percent in 1964 to only 57.4 percent in 1988;[3] too many Americans no longer view this fundamental right of citizenship as a responsibility. Joseph Duffy, the chancellor of the University of Massachusetts, asserts that, "when questioned about their understanding of citizenship, most Americans refer to freedom of speech, freedom of religion, and the right of trial by jury well before, and often to the neglect of, the responsibilities of voting, jury duty, or serving in the armed forces."[4] We must reverse this trend.

H.R. 660, has gained much attention because it is a departure from traditional service and education assistance programs. It addresses many social concerns in a direct and effective manner. This plan requires a fundamental change in the way Americans view their role in society and, most important, offers citizenship and opportunity to our young people.

National service is not a new idea, but one whose time has come, as evidenced by the national attention that the bill has received and the large number of alternative proposals that have been introduced. The American public is realizing that there are important elements missing in society today, including an increasing social deficit coupled with diminishing prospects of realizing the American dream of higher education or owning a home. Among the proposals that have been made for national service is President Bush's Points of Light. I commend his effort to bring volunteerism to every corner of the nation through exhortation and encouragement. His proposal, however, is not focused, does not outline any priorities, and does not offer the necessary incentives to address problems that, in some instances, seem almost insurmountable.

The Citizenship and National Service Act, in contrast, effectively addresses the concerns of rising postsecondary tuition costs, skyrocketing default rates on student loans, the declining pool of youth available for military recruitment, the decreasing ability of many young Americans to purchase homes, and the multitude of social needs that the government cannot meet. This country faces problems with care of the elderly, illiteracy, health care, child care, and conservation efforts, to name a few. The Citizenship and National Service Act is a way for individuals to answer those needs and earn something for themselves in return.

H.R. 660 in its present form would allow a person to perform either one or two years of community service in a citizens corps or two years of active military service. After completing the community service, participants would be eligible to receive a voucher worth ten thousand dollars for each year of service. Military volunteers would receive vouchers for twelve thousand dollars for each year of service. Those vouchers could be used to defray college expenses, to pay for vocational or job training, or to make a down payment on a first home.

After a five-year trial period participation in national service would be a prerequisite for receiving federal student aid for most students, with exemptions for recipients over 25 and those for whom national service would pose a special financial hardship. Linking national service to financial aid has been at the center of the controversy surrounding our proposal.

But I do not apologize for proposing a program of mutual obligation. Democracy is the cornerstone of our great nation, but it is not free. For each right bestowed by democratic principles, there is an obligation. Federal aid for education should be an earned benefit, not an entitlement.

Regrettably, the entrenched forces of big-government liberalism and me-first conservatism have united in opposition to national service because it threatens the status quo. Joined with them are the high priests of the education establishment who tremble at the thought of losing easy access to the $9 billion a year that the federal government provides to college students.

Critics of the Citizenship and National Service Act believe that linking national service to aid discriminates against the poor. They contend that the link would restrict federal support for higher education and reduce the likelihood of poor youths ever attending college because of the delay in entry. I would like to address some of those criticisms.

As an entitlement program federal college assistance has created a dilemma for many low-income students. From 1980 to 1986 college costs at private and public universities have risen 23 percent and 34 percent, respectively, far above the rate of inflation, whereas median family income has grown by only 5 percent. During the same period federal outlays for student aid have grown only 16 percent.[5] Simultaneously, the emphasis of federal aid has shifted from grants and work-study programs to guaranteed student loans, which account for 66 percent of all aid today as opposed to 21 percent in 1976. Since 1980 student indebtedness has increased by 60 percent,[6] creating a new class of indentured students.

There are those who argue that because the system in place is effective we need only work for changes within the existing framework of financial aid programs. In the face of budget constraints that threaten the very existence of federal educational assistance, however, it is time to seek a new solution. The current programs have basic structural flaws and inequities that cannot be corrected by simply adding to the coffers. What we need is a fundamental restructuring of the system, for the obstacles I have mentioned require more than small adjustments. National service would replace the present cumbersome, costly, complex and often arbitrary needs determination process with an equal condition—performing service—for all applicants.

H.R. 660 proposes a positive overhaul. By tying federal assistance to national service, this legislation allows students to finance their educations without incurring debt and makes educational assistance an earned benefit through service to the nation. This legislation requires a change in our fundamental perception of federal aid. It is time we make that change.

The current financial aid programs are also not reaching all of those in need. Although the percentage of minority youth graduating from high school has been rising, the percentage of minority youth enrolling in college declined by one-third from 1981 to 1986. According to the American Council on Education, black enrollment dropped from 34 percent in 1976 to 29 percent in 1986; Hispanic enrollment declined from 36 percent to 30 percent.[7]

Few students receive enough federal aid to pay for their entire education. In 1986 the average federal aid package from all sources (loans, grants, and work study) was about $2,900,[8] which covers only 61 percent of the costs of public universities and only 22 percent of private universities. Most students therefore must rely on family help, state and institutional aid, and jobs to make up the difference. To make education truly accessible, this trend must be reversed. The Citizenship and National Service Act, then, affords many individuals the chance to gain a postsecondary education who might otherwise not be able to do so and increases the benefits available for those already planning to attend.

Some suggest that this legislation would place an unfair burden on low-income youth, but a closer look reveals that low-income youth stand to gain the most from national service for three reasons. First, they would be eligible for considerably more aid than they can now obtain from federal grants, reducing the need to incur high debts from student loans. Second, participants would work in their local communities helping the desperately underserved poor. Third, national service vouchers would help correct the inequities in the way society treats America's "forgotten half"—the 50 percent of the nation's youth who never attend college.

Under the Citizenship and National Service Act, participants will earn ten thousand to twelve thousand dollars for a year of service, considerably more than they can get from federal grants, which average sixteen hundred dollars a year.[9] This would reduce the need for additional loans that these young people find difficult to repay, as evidenced by the increasing student loan default rate. (Last year [1988] student loan defaults cost the federal government $1.8 billion.)

Participants in the program would reduce America's social deficit. They would tutor illiterates, work in hospitals, care for the elderly, work in child care centers, staff drug centers and hot lines, help feed and shelter the homeless, clean public spaces, and staff a whole host of positions that during the 1980s have been underfunded and understaffed. (These are the same areas in which the poor and at-risk youth are most underserved.)

National service, unlike current financial aid, would also provide an alternative for young people that do not intend to pursue any form of postsecondary education. These students—often referred to as the "forgotten half," also have important needs that are addressed through use of the voucher as a down payment on a home. Home ownership is part of the American Dream, but for many young Americans it is no longer a reality because of its financial burdens.

From 1973 to 1988 the percentage of those under 25 who owned a home decreased from 23.4 percent to 15.5 percent. The Joint Center for Housing Studies of Harvard University, in its publication *The State of the Nation's Housing, 1989,* stated that "Over the past two decades, both the down payment and after-tax cash cost burdens of home ownership have drifted upward." This trend is preventing young people in all regions of the United States from realizing the dream of home ownership.[10] Participants in the Citizenship and National Service Act could overcome this hurdle by using the voucher (worth ten-thousand or twenty-thousand dollars, depending on one's term of service) as a down payment.

Some critics charge that because of delayed entry to college national service would reduce the likelihood of young people attending college. Community service, however, can help those at risk to develop the skills and maturity they need to succeed in college. Many national service positions would require planning, organizing, and communicating with adults and peers on a daily basis in a professional situation. These skills are essential for college and are not taught in most high schools. Today these critical skills are often lacking: In 1987 New York Telephone received 117,000 applications for three thousand jobs. Of those applying, only 57,000 were able to take the company's qualifying test and only 2,100 passed it.[11]

Opponents also argue that national service would force poor students to work for their education while the affluent would be exempt, creating a two-tiered system in higher education. Linking work to financial aid, however, is not a new idea. Most students already must work to finance their education, and linking financial aid to work is already well-established in the work-study program. About 13.5 percent of undergraduates that received financial aid in 1986 had work-study jobs.[12] (Some leaders in higher education who are critical of national service argue that work-study programs help at-risk students forge stronger ties with their university communities.)

Students who receive sparse amounts of financial aid must work to finance their educational costs; 79 percent of students who receive financial aid help finance their college costs through personal earnings. The black and Hispanic students who reach college are also the most likely to pay for their entire education through personal earnings with no financial aid or help from their families. Interestingly, 20 percent of all students pay for their educations without aid.[13]

National service participants would save more for their education because they would be compensated with a voucher for $10,000 or $12,000 for each year of service, which is much greater than what they could save while earning $6,400 per year (the average yearly income for Americans between the ages of 18 and 24).[14] National service jobs would also be more rewarding socially.

Many universities because of their escalating costs already have created a two-tiered system of education that perpetuates social inequality. Many prestigious universities are out of reach not only for poor students but also for many middle-class students. A year at Brown University costs about twenty thousand dollars, a major financial burden for even a financially comfortable family. More than 50 percent of Brown's students come from families with incomes of more than $75,000, and less than 6 percent come from families with incomes below $20,000.[15] A recent series of articles in the *Washington Post* described the current situation:

> Higher education was once envisioned as the great equalizer in American society, providing anyone who was qualified with the credential that would redress inequalities in background and birth. Today the reality is far different. The nation's colleges and universities are sharply stratified by class and race, and for many students, entry to the upper echelon is as unlikely as membership in an exclusive club.[16]

A national service voucher for $20,000 or $24,000 will make attending these private universities more of a possibility for youths from low- and middle-income families. Also, national service vouchers will allow youths to more confidently plan their college finances because they will be receiving at least the amount of their voucher each year. No longer will the fate of a student be determined by the arbitrary financial aid formulas, giving young people more control over their fates.

Furthermore, once the maturity and other gains to participants and the benefits to the community are recognized, I assert that universities will be compelled to give preference to students who have performed national service. Many universities readily offer deferments to graduate students who wish to pursue jobs, because of the knowledge and experience these students bring to the graduate programs. James B. Conant, former president of Harvard University, in 1949 recanted his earlier criticism of the GI Bill by saying that the veterans were the "most mature and promising students Harvard has ever had."[17]

Some express concern regarding the possible hardships this bill might place on nontraditional students. But remember that the Citizenship and National Service Act is flexible. Tying federal student financial aid to national service is a constructive measure that is not meant to discriminate against nontraditional students. For instance, the bill allows individuals over 25 to apply directly for guaranteed student loans without having performed national service.

There is also a provision to exempt those individuals from service deemed to have "compelling personal circumstances" or a physical or mental handicap. Compelling personal circumstances include such things as being over 25 or having a family. For instance, if an individual is eighteen and has a child, then the corporation for national service would likely deem that it would not be feasible for that young parent to live on the national service subsistence wages. This legislation does not eliminate all existing federal financial aid programs, but simply narrows the eligibility criteria for those who may receive the funds.

The estimated costs of the program have also generated concern, particularly among conservatives. The American Council of Education estimated the cost to be $50 billion annually.[18] A more thorough study done by the Congressional Budget Office, however, estimated costs ranging from $3.96 billion to $14.75 billion per year.[19] The House appropriation for Stafford Loans alone for fiscal year 1990 is $3.7 billion, more than half of which will be spent on loan defaults that do not generate any benefits to society.

In contrast, national service jobs would benefit society economically as well as socially. Several states have shown that service programs generate more than their investment: A Human Environment Center Study of the California Conservation Corps estimates that for every $1.00 spent the program yields $1.60. The Pennsylvania Conservation Corps reportedly returns $1.36 for every $1.00 invested. For the Michigan Conservation Corps, the figure is $2.00 back for every $1.00 spent.[20] On the 25th anniversary of the GI Bill, which is a model for national service programs, the Veterans' Administration noted that "the better-educated, higher-earning veterans are returning taxes to U.S. coffers at a rate expected to repay the entire government funds expended as much as thrice over the course of their lifetime."[21]

Our proposal avoids the current problems and costs associated with a federal bureaucracy by appointing an independent corporation to coordinate activities with state and local governments. State and local governments would be encouraged to utilize existing programs and agencies to help coordinate the effort. To ensure that participants would be placed in meaningful jobs, we would require private agencies to donate one thousand dollars per participant, thereby avoiding the risk of make-work jobs.

Another frequently heard criticism claims this legislation would have a negative effect on armed forces' recruiting. The All-Volunteer Force has been a success, but at an incredibly high cost. The army spent $196 million in television advertising alone in fiscal 1989,[22] and the results of the effort were discouraging. In the first six months of fiscal 1989, the army, navy, and marines had to fill ranks with individuals who scored lower on the mental category tests than did the people who took the test during fiscal 1988. Coupled with the high costs of recruitment are the high costs of the current program: a person currently enrolled in the Army College Fund program makes seventeen thousand dollars per year plus benefits.

Meanwhile, the potential benefits of this legislation for the military are enormous. As we enter the 1990s and look beyond, the armed forces will be faced with a declining pool of youth available for military service. The number of Americans aged 15 to 24 is steadily dropping. Consequently, to maintain the same number of recruits in 1991 that it had in 1989, the army will have to enlist 55 percent of the eligible eighteen-year-old males compared with 42 percent in 1981. National service will expand the pool of potential recruits and help the military draw from a wider cross-section of the nation's youth.[23]

The army wants to expand a two-year recruitment option in a way that is strikingly similar to the citizen-soldier concept in H.R. 660. The army asked for a supplemental appropriation this year to test the 2 + 2 + 4 program (two years in active duty, two years in selected reserve, and four years in individual ready reserve) in several noncombat skill categories. Army personnel chiefs believe the two-year option will reverse the new downward recruitment trend.

The Citizenship and National Service Act does not attempt to replace the armed forces' current recruiting tools. The GI Bill has worked and will continue to work well. National service will be an additional enlistment benefit option, making it possible for the military to recruit larger numbers of young people to maintain and strengthen its personnel needs.

At this point, I would like to discuss recent congressional action in the area of national service. In August 1989, Senate leaders including Senators George J. Mitchell, Edward M. Kennedy, and Sam Nunn unveiled a compromise omnibus national service bill that combines several national service bills introduced earlier in 1989. This omnibus bill includes a pilot project to test the Citizenship and National Service Act concept. The pilot project does not include the most controversial portion of the original bill, the link to financial aid. Nor does it include military service as an option for service.

The pilot project would allow states or state entities to bid for the opportunity to conduct national service test programs. The corporation for national service—created by the omnibus bill—would select participant states. Like the original bill, vouchers would be given to young people who participate in community service projects. The vouchers would be for $8,500 annually for up to two years and could be used for education or a down payment on a first home. Participants would also receive subsistence wages while in the program.

The Senate Committee on Labor and Human Resources recently [September 8, 1989] approved the bill. Full Senate action is now pending. Meanwhile, on November 21, 1989, Congressman McCurdy, along with Congresspersons Bill Gray, Steny Hoyer, Richard Gephardt, Leon Panetta, Barbara Kennelly, and Gerry Sikorski, introduced the identical bill (H.R. 3807) in the House. The Citizenship and National Service Act, like other legislation, needs to be refined, further debated, and tested on a small scale before a nationwide program is established. This pilot project is the perfect avenue to accomplish that task.

Our proposal is a progressive response to the nation's widening social deficit and to the student aid dilemma. It offers all young Americans an equal opportunity to realize the American dream of a college education or a home. It promotes civic responsibility and aims to solve many of the problems of inequality in existing financial aid programs. As an earned benefit program for all rather than another government subsidy, national service is likely to gain broad public support.

The Citizenship and National Service Act is a bold break from the status quo and as such has generated great debate. But that debate should send a signal that the traditional system is not meeting social demands in the way that Americans have come to expect. It is time to go back to a society where fulfilling the nation's needs is just as important as fulfilling our own. As Walter Lippmann said to a class reunion at Harvard in 1940:

> You took the good things for granted, you must earn them again. It is written that for every right you cherish, you have a duty that you must

fulfill; for every hope you entertain, you have a task that you must perform; for every good that you wish could happen, you will have to sacrifice your comfort and ease. There is nothing for nothing any longer.[24]

Notes

1. "The American Freshman: 20-Year Trends," The Higher Education Research Institute, University of California at Los Angeles.

2. Cited in Joseph Duffy, "Reconstituting America Through National Service," speech delivered to the World Future Society on July 19, 1989.

3. U.S. Department of Commerce, Bureau of the Census, "Voting and Registration on the Election of November 1988 (Advance Report)," Series p-20, no. 435 (February 1989).

4. Duffy, "Reconstituting America," para. 2.

5. Youth Indicators 1988, Office of Educational Research and Improvement, U.S. Department of Education, Susan Boren, "Authorization of Appropriations, Budget Requests, Enacted Appropriations (Budget Authority) and Outlays for Federal Student Financial Aid Programs Administered by the Department of Education, FY 1965 through FY 1988" (Congressional Research Service, September 11, 1987).

6. Janet S. Hansen, "Student Loans: Are They Overburdening a Generation?" (Washington Office of the College Board, February 1987).

7. Progressive Policy Institute, "National Service and Student Aid: Myth and Reality" (American Council on Education, telephone interview).

8. "Undergraduate Financing of Postsecondary Education: A Report of 1987 National Postsecondary Student Aid Study" (hereafter, NPSAS) (National Center for Education Statistics, Department of Education, June 1988).

9. NPSAS.

10. Ann Marjano, "Fewer Can Buy Homes, Study Finds: Poor Seem Trapped in Rent Cost Squeeze," *Washington Post,* June 24, 1989.

11. "When Workers Cannot Read: Bossy Businessmen," *The Economist,* August 26, 1989, pp. 21–22.

12. NPSAS.

13. NPSAS.

14. Census Bureau.

15. Barbara Vobejda, "National Service Plan; Fair to Poor, Minorities?" *Washington Post,* February 6, 1989.

16. Barbara Vobejda, "Unequal Opportunity: Higher Education in America," *Washington Post,* May 3–5, 1989.

17. Keith Olson, "The G.I. Bill and Higher Education," *American Quarterly* 25 (December 1973).

18. Pat Smith and Art Hauptman, "Subject: Nunn-McCurdy Bill" (American Council on Education memo, February 14, 1989).

19. Chuck Seagrave and Richard Curley, "Cost Analysis of Civilian and Military Corps" (draft Congressional Budget Office Report, April 20, 1989).

20. Progressive Policy Institute, telephone interview (National Association of Service and Conservation Corps).

21. "G.I. Bill of Rights 25th Anniversary: Fact Sheet for Editors, Broadcasters, Writers" (Veterans Administration Information Service).

22. Telephone conversation with Lt. Col. David L. Fredrikson, assistant director of the Office of the Assistant Secretary of Defense for Force Management and Personnel (military manpower personnel and Policy) (accession policy).

23. Democratic Leadership Council, *Citizenship and National Service;* "The Pell Grant Formula, 1989–1990" (Office of Student Financial Assistance, Department of Education, May 1988).

24. Suzy Platt, ed., *Respectfully Quoted* (Library of Congress, 1989). Quoted from a speech to the Harvard class of 1910's 30th reunion, Walter Lippmann papers, Yale University Library.

COMMENT

Tim W. Ferguson

The use of quotations such as Mr. Lippmann's is a double-edged sword: It reminds us that this debate comes around every generation or two, and it debunks the notion that there was something peculiar about the 1980s that brought us to a low ebb of public service.

I am glad that the congressman is in apparent good health after spending a month home with his constituents talking about catastrophic health care and other issues of the day. There were times probably when he suspected that his wife was not the only one in the family practicing psychiatry.

Let me also express some sympathy for his national service proposal in that he is making an effort to bring his party into what might be called the values of mainstream America, to the notion that you give as well as get. This is a bipartisan notion nowadays and is reflected in the popularity of workfare measures. This specific idea, national service, has bipartisan appeal. Back in 1981 [C.] Ron[ald] Kimberling, a Reagan official in the Education Department, in a private conversation with me said that he favored providing college loans and grants as a reward only for military service. But the idea has subsequently blossomed. There is a lot to be said for the idea that there is no such thing as a free lunch when it comes to government benefits.

I am all for extending this notion to other beneficiaries of the benevolent state. For instance, it would not be a bad thing if yacht owners were expected occasionally to collect the muck in the harbor in return for Coast Guard services. Perhaps affluent parents who benefit from sending their children to the University of California or Rutgers at a tremendous subsidy might repay it. I am heartened to learn that elderly people who receive much more in Social Security payments than they paid into the system on a time-valued basis might also be expected to give back service in return. (I used the word *service* there inappropriately. There is a distinction between the idea of merely paying back for benefits received and the larger notion of service—whether it is volunteerism or citizenship in some broader sense.)

Let me also express some sympathy for the congressman's willingness to advance a real idea, not just a proposal that is a sop to some constituency or something done for showmanship on the evening news. Such ideas are increasingly rare in Washington. The congressman's colleague Newt Gingrich is fond of saying that in Washington these days, people tend to propose solutions that are orders of magnitude smaller than the problems they are intended to deal with. In this case, we have something of meaningful size, not a petty response to a perceived problem.

What happens to ideas that are both good and bad, is that they dissolve into tentative half-steps that are prone to pork barreling. The omnibus Kennedy measure fits that description. The idea of doing pilot projects is an appealing one because they localize the effects of an experiment and reduce damage—if indeed damage is going to be done by an experiment—while you examine it. But pilot projects are similar to demonstration projects. Remember that these are what make up omnibus road bills and other pork barrel measures.

Now I will go into some specific quibbles with the piece. There has been some talk here about labor-substitution effects. I do agree that we are likely to encounter problems that are not fully anticipated. You do not want to diminish the number or the worth of the existing entry-level five-dollar-per-hour jobs by a glorified CETA [Comprehensive Employment and Training Act] or service-type program that essentially pays its recipients more, but the bidding price is steeper than you expect. Your paper cites $6,400 as the median income for the 18-to-24-year-old bracket, which is true over the entire population bracket, but when you narrow it down to 18-to-24-year-olds who are full-time employees, the median turns out to be $13,194, according to the Census Bureau. If you are aiming at people who are not going to college at present and hope to become fully employed as an alternative, that is the number you will have to bid against. Additionally, imagine the reaction of the housing and college markets to a situation in which hundreds of thousands of people are carrying around $20,000 voucher checks; the effect on prices will militate against the worth of those checks. I am more sanguine about the housing market than I am about the college market in view of what we have been reading about collusion in price setting among universities. I would expect to see a rapid increase, more rapid than we have seen, in tuition prices.

The GI Bill is a hoary example that has taken on more gloss than it had at the outset of the program itself. Successful in the same way Social Security has been successful, it spent enough money to raise millions of people above a certain low income level. The situation is different now from the time when the GI Bill was instituted. The population not attending college is different, and thus you cannot expect similar effects.

On the conservation corps, the numbers are fuzzy. I communicated with the clearinghouse for these organizations, the National Association of Service and Conservation Corps, regarding the various state programs and their success. There are, it turns out, a multitude of methods of valuing the return on every dollar spent. Each state does it differently. The [association] director, of course, is sympathetic with the programs. He told me that in some cases if it were not for the corps, the projects might not be done and thus may carry little value in the marketplace. Therefore, how you measure the return on a project requires quality-of-life evaluations about whether a tourist spot is more pleasant because a corps did its work there.

Finally, I appreciate the congressman's willingness to have the Congressional Budget Office do an exhaustive study of the foreseeable consequences of this program. But I do have to cringe somewhat. It is almost satire to think that they could quantify the various outgrowths of a program involving 700,000 to 800,000 people. Nevertheless, the effort itself reflects the fact that money matters these days in Washington. We ought to be glad about that.

My major criticism is that I do not accept what has been said about narcissism, selfishness, and Reagan's America. The facts about volunteerism suggest that the relation of income to willingness to volunteer is the inverse of what those who are arguing for a national service program say is true. The wealthier one is, the more hours one volunteers, if you separate out extraneous factors. The factors that bear on the amount of time spent volunteering turn out not to have much to do with greed on Wall Street or yuppies or cars and furs. They have more to do with place and family situation (marriage, divorce, singlehood), and no national service program is going to affect those factors. The Gallup Poll numbers paint a mixed picture: overall hours devoted to volunteer work have gone up; however, the percentage of Americans volunteering, both in the 18-to-24-year-old group and overall, has declined in the 1980s from more than 50 percent to the low forties. What is going on here, and is it necessarily negative? The indications are that those people who quit volunteering were not devoting much time in the first place because the overall hours volunteered have gone up. Perhaps the marginal people found jobs in the 1980s. If so, that is a positive development. In some cases we are not only talking about previously unemployed people, but about spouses who previously were not working and now are working.

What we are talking about here is essentially a breakdown in standards, values, and cultures in pockets of America over the last ten years. This is an externality (to use an economist's term) not of markets in a pure sense, but of a reward-seeking society that for many is without a compass in both the secular and the moral sense. It is similar to what happened to the financial institutions in the 1980s when they were partially deregulated to seek maximum return, but not fully deregulated in the sense of being held responsible for the consequences of their investments. Mr. McCurdy, Mr. Moskos, and others on the panel are trying to recreate values where they are found to be most absent; and at the same time, want to obtain a social dividend from work that is intrinsically of value, but which will produce this spin-off effect.

James Q. Wilson's work harks back to the Victorian era in America where values like temperance, restraint, respect, and responsibility were sent down from on high. The elite were expected to observe and transmit those values, and they trickled down, as it were, to others. What we have seen in recent years, however, is a failure on the part of elites to do that. The smart set got away with flaunting virtue and avoiding the costs of its indulgences because it knew how to get away with doing so. It left in its wake an underclass that was unable to escape the consequences of the values that were being transmitted.

My hope is that we can find some lessons in both sides of the debate on national service. Some will throw up their hands and say, there are basically two different types of people in the world: those who believe that a laissez-faire society is an ideal worth tolerating the excesses and abuses that attend it and those who believe that regimentation—in this case, at least at the outset, mild regimentation—is worth tolerating the excesses and abuses that accompany it. It may indeed turn out that that is where the debate leaves us. My hope is that standards and values—the moral compass that comes from work, from an exchange of effort for reward—can be distilled from the national service proposals and can be imbued in a noncoercive, fiscally responsible manner to bring back the kind of civilized society that most of us would prefer. Perhaps we ought to be encouraged by that in spite of the great differences in the approach to getting there.

DISCUSSION

Mr. McCurdy: Much of our debate today came back to the search for value standards. You [Mr. Ferguson] said there were pockets in America today where there had been a breakdown of value structures. I come from the heartland of America. We are too big to be a pocket. My district covers more than eight thousand square miles. It is right in the Bible Belt. Less than 6 percent of my constituents are black. My district has basically a white middle-class and lower-middle-class constituency. If Gallup asked the people there if they went to church, a large majority would respond that they did. Tammy and Jimmy [television evangelists Jimmy and Tammy Bakker] were big hits out in that Bible Belt, but even with all the preaching and moralizing and all the people who did not want to have sex education, we have real problems there. Oklahoma has the third highest rate of teenage pregnancy in the United States. I do not know any place that is immune today from these national problems.

One problem with our democratic way of life is its emphasis on individualism, which leads to disintegration of the family. We have seen the family as a whole give way to smaller units. A more individualistic attitude has developed. Values are not transmitted as well as they were in the immigrant families whose members had to depend on each other. There is one notable exception in this country today: the Mormon Church. The Mormons are conservative people. They have a strong sense of service and have a strong sense that members of a family should take care of each other. In many parts of the country today, that sense has been lost.

Mr. Friedman: I agree with you that the family is in decline. But it is not for the reason that you give. There is a decline in family values because government has been destroying families. One family function after another—whether it is support in old age, childcare, or schooling—has been taken away by intrusive government. The measures of the so-called welfare state are destroying family values. The absence of such measures in Asia is a major reason that has not happened there. I agree with you that we want family values restored, but let us not confuse two different matters. Individualism is not the cause of the breakdown of the family.

I would like to make one point about the Mormons. I have read many books and articles about national service, but I have never seen a reference to one of the most successful voluntary services in the world, the Mormon youth program. It works because it is voluntary.

Mr. McCurdy: If you are a Mormon and you want to succeed in that society, in that church, service is required. You do not escape service.

Mr. Friedman: It is voluntary in the sense that it is a community obligation that is not imposed by coercive government. It is not a coercive government that raises the money to pay for it. The funds for it come voluntarily from the participants' families. The Mormons do not have a policeman putting his hand in my pocket to pay for other people's missions. Yet that is what you are proposing now.

Mike Gravel, former U.S. Senator, D-Alaska: I hear constant reference to the fact that there is a diminution of civic responsibility, that families are falling apart, and that children do not listen to us anymore. That is the flip side of the good old days, which really never existed. Civic responsibility today is no worse and no better than it used to be in Greece a hundred years ago or a thousand years ago.

I am here today because I heard you would be talking about the draft and national service. I am responsible for the United States of America not having a draft today, and I am proud of that accomplishment. After I had filibustered against the draft for five or six months [May–September 1971], a deal was struck that if the liberals would vote against me to break my filibuster, [the congressional leaders] would let the draft expire [when its 1971 extension ran out in 1972–73]. So they broke my filibuster, and the draft expired.

What we see today is people coming forth with their agenda of problems: unmet social needs, the problem of education, and the problem of military service. What you are planning to do is use national service as some magic device to address those problems. But what will happen is just the opposite of what you want. History has repeated examples of this. What you will do is create an additional power structure—an oppressive and expensive bureaucracy—that will not even focus on the problems. Because we love our nation, the word *national* romanticizes the situation; *service* sounds good. But what the words really mean is that the state controls and organizes human beings to state-defined ends. That is not a desirable situation. You want to address the problems of education? Do it through the marketplace. The factor of the loan program and its defaulting beneficiaries is a whole other matter.

Let us focus on two points. The first is education. If $1,600, which is a paltry sum, will send you through higher education, borrow it. Then pay it back. You can do that without another government agency; you can do that through the private sector.

The other point, which is much more serious, is Sam Nunn's agenda. He wants to sneak the draft back in, as do the people who want to keep their one, two, or three stars by maintaining a force level that is not required. Unfortunately, we have a million too many right now; brought down to size, it would work quite well. There is nothing wrong in peacetime with paying the competitive price for the service you are getting, which is defense. Focus on the educational problem all by itself, focus on the military problem by itself, and deny the government the power to organize our youth through fear.

Mr. McCurdy: For the record, there are no proposals currently before the Congress for a mandatory, compulsory, uniformed military or service plan. There is no draft out there. No one is talking about it. There is no way in the world we could ever find jobs for the 3.5 million young people who go over that eighteen-year-old threshold. No one in his right mind today is advocating that. John McCain advocated it for awhile. But he quickly stopped because you have to make exceptions to the rules because there are not enough slots. I am not advocating that. I do not know of anyone else who is.

Robert Hessen, Senior Research Fellow, Hoover Institution: Mike Gravel raised a question that needs elaboration. We hear political rhetoric; we hear noble-sounding words. *National service* is an example he gave. I would like to come back to the phrase used nine times by Mr. Barber: *experiential learning.* It sounds terrific. What would you want out of life but experiential learning? Let us be concrete. Let us be specific. What do you mean?

Mr. Moskos gave us an example earlier of a problem that we have not properly attended to. He spoke of his late colleague Morris Janowitz, the widely respected sociologist who died of Alzheimer's disease. I pity the man, and I pity my next-door neighbor dying of the same disease. The question is whose young son or daughter is going into national service to be the companion of a man who does not recognize you, who is afraid of strangers, and will not allow his wife to leave the house because he is afraid he is going to be deserted. Let us be specific. Where are we going to find young men and women between eighteen and twenty who are willing to go into the homes of strangers? Let us say neighborhood strangers, not strangers in other cities, in other neighborhoods, of other races, cultures, or religions. Where will these people come from? What training will we have to provide? I want specifics about how people will be prepared for this service and why one assumes they will be willing to do it.

Mr. Moskos: Alzheimer's disease is the best example of what I am talking about. The true victims in that case are the spouses of these people. In West Germany, unspecialized, unskilled young people do exactly that kind of work, including work with autistic children. In the United States, the opponents of the Nunn-McCurdy bill and the DLC concept say you have to be a professional to do this kind of work. That is nonsense. Part of the liberal assault is that you have to be a trained social worker before you could handle such cases. These cases are handled now by unspecialized people, namely, the spouses. The conscientious objectors of World War II went into mental institutions and brought more humanity to that population than had ever been provided before or since by so-called professionals. These are real-life examples of short-termers performing work that the market or the government cannot deliver.

Mr. Anderson: I have a question for Mr. McCurdy. You raised a question in your paper that has been raised implicitly in other papers. You say that for each right that is bestowed by democratic principles, there is an obligation. Where is it written in the Constitution, where is it written in the Declaration of Independence that my rights as an American, my rights to life, liberty, private property, and the pursuit of happiness are conditional on doing the bidding of some bureaucrat in Washington? Where do you get this idea?

Mr. McCurdy: It is never stated as such. But the framers of the Constitution—if you read the Federalist Papers and the background on it— always made the assumption that rights entail responsibilities. There is no twentieth amendment that speaks of this quid pro quo. It is assumed in the federal government's right to raise armies and its right to tax. Maybe this is where I differ from the more libertarian philosophers. If we get to the point where you say, "Show me where it says I have to do something to live in this country. . . ."

Mr. Anderson: We are there.

Mr. McCurdy: I think we start to shatter. I think we start to tremble.
     Earlier you two [Mr. Anderson and Mr. Barber] had a minidebate on me versus we and the government. I believe that we are the government: you are the government, and I am the government. If you do not like it, that is too bad. But you are still part of the government. I get fed up with people who say, why don't you do something about this? My instinct is to say, show me your voter registration card first. Show me that you are part of the system. You are just as much the problem as I am.

Mr. Anderson: To be a citizen of the United States and to enjoy rights under the American system, you do not have to have a voter registration card. That is not a prerequisite. If an elected official asked me to show him my voter registration card, I would work to get rid of him.

Mr. McCurdy: Good, then you are a part of the system. You have just crossed the line by becoming active in the process. I do not care if you are a Democrat, Republican, or Libertarian, if you are trying to be a part of the solution, you are part of the system.

Mr. Chapman: I have a practical question I would like to ask you, Congressman, about this legislation that is changing before our eyes. What is up for consideration by the Congress of the United States? You describe the bill that the DLC proposed last year and that you and Senator Nunn, among others, sponsored. There are in my mind many problems with that legislation, one of which is that you proposed to pay people through this system more than they could make in the civilian or military sectors. The amount of money the stipends would be worth with the vouchers at the end of two years of service—in national service's military option—would be greater than that paid for the same years of service if you were a regular soldier enlisting in the armed forces. We could take that issue on, and it should be taken on.

But now the Nunn-McCurdy bill has been abandoned without much explanation. The sponsors have gone for something they call a "compromise," now embodied in the omnibus bill. Why is the military not included in the demonstration project? Why was it in the earlier project but not in the new omnibus community service bill? Why has the voucher been reduced from $10,000 a year to $8,500 a year? Why are the grants one earns from service in the demonstration project no longer the only way to get those grants? What you had originally was a proposal that shifted all the Pell money and other money into national service, so that you did not get money if you did not perform national service. You, Congressman, have defended such a principle yourself in your remarks. But now grants and loans will continue just as before. But we are going to have a second approach that says: if you stand at the first counter and do not get the free grant, then come over to us and for two years of service, you can get the same money.

First, why were those changes made? Second, what kind of demonstration project do we have if all those principles and ideas of the earlier bill have been chucked overboard? What is it going to demonstrate? Why have demonstration projects if they are not going to demonstrate what the original bill was going to do?

Mr. McCurdy: A one-word answer to your question: democracy. I introduced a bill. It was a good bill, not perfect, a provocative bill that generated debate. It had to go through a long line of committees, hearings, and so forth, before it would ever become law. My bill is not before the House or Senate because the left and the right prefer the status quo. A compromise was reached in the Senate because some principals were talking to each other. My reception in the House Education and Labor Committee was not a pleasant experience because I was challenging everything they stood for. Compromise is not fashionable in the academic community, but in government it is what happens nine times out of ten.

The pilot program as proposed in the Senate has a good chance of passing. I do not know what the House version will look like, if it passes. I am trying to get my title in the bill.

It does not have the linkage in the compromise version, the omnibus bill, because it is impossible to have linkage if you are only doing five or six states.

The idea is to see the quality and type of people who enroll, the types of jobs that would be performed, and whether or not it could work.

The second part of your question concerns the military provision. My bill, the Nunn-McCurdy bill, was the only bill that has been introduced in the Congress that dealt with the military. The other national service programs were add-on programs and are strictly community service. Sam [Nunn] and I thought it was important to look at the military because we had been in the armed services. Also the army has instituted a trial two-year program of their own in the noncombat skills area—a program that is similar to what we were proposing.

You asked, why $8,500 instead of $10,000? Quite frankly, the $10,000 was probably high. There is no magic to these numbers. It could be $7,500 or $5,500. You try to put those numbers at a realistic level. We put the provision for military service higher than that for community service because those who serve in the military should have a higher benefit than those who do community service.

Mr. Barber: Congressman, let me ask you a specific question about the most controversial feature of your bill—which is its financial impact. I agree with you that service would and could benefit the poor and the disadvantaged. I do not have a problem with it that way. My problem is that it exempts the well-off. You said that higher education used to be a great equalizer and that it is not anymore. The last equalizer we have in our nation is citizenship. If citizenship is not the equalizer, I do not know what is. The problem is that the Nunn-McCurdy bill creates a two-tier system of citizenship. Some people become citizens and pay their debts to society because they cannot afford not to. Others, who in fact do benefit from society in a variety of unseen ways, do not have to pay for that benefit. I would hate to replicate on the civic level the economic two-tier system we already have by creating a system of incentives that forces the disadvantaged to become citizens, but exempts the other part of the population.

Mr. McCurdy: That is a danger. In contrast to the senator [Mike Gravel], many of the people who were opposed to the draft criticize this program as not promoting equality because one segment of the society is getting off free while others have to serve. There is a two-tier system out there, whether we like it or not. There is a two-tier system in education, and in much of society. I cannot change that. What I attempted to do was to mitigate its impact by extending opportunities and benefits to those who are really disadvantaged. If those people serve, they will benefit.

4

NATIONAL SERVICE: WHO BEARS THE COSTS AND WHO REAPS THE GAINS?

Walter Y. Oi

> *If now—and this is my idea—there were, instead of military conscription a conscription of the whole youthful population to form for a certain number of years a part of the army enlisted against Nature, the injustice would tend to be evened out, and numerous other goods to the commonwealth would follow.*—William James[1]

The proposition that citizenship entails an obligation to serve is warmly embraced by those who endorse military conscription and national service. Conscription (compulsory national service) is nothing more than an in-kind tax, an appropriation of labor services at below market rates of pay. This fundamental nature of the inequity of compulsion was recognized by Benjamin Franklin, who wrote,

> But if, as I suppose is often the case, the sailor who is pressed and obliged to serve for the defence of this trade at a rate of 25s. a month, could have £3.15s, in the merchant's service, you take from him 50s. a

I wish to thank Professor John Warner (Clemson University) and Dr. J. Hosek (The RAND Corporation) for data and Ms. E. A. Schacher for research materials. Research and clerical assistance was provided by S. Carboni, J. Saul, and J. Oi. The responsibility for facts and opinions is mine.

month; and if you have 100,000 in your service, you rob that honest part of society and their poor families of £250,000. per month, or three millions a year, and at the same time oblige them to hazard their lives in fighting for the defence of your trade: to the defence of which all ought indeed to contribute, (and sailors among the rest) in proportion to their profits by it; but this three millions is more than their share, if they did not pay with their persons; and when you force that, methinks you should excuse the other.[2]

The costs of compulsory military service were high not only to those who were forced to serve, but also to those who incurred substantial costs to escape the draft.[3] In the late 1960s national service—whereby a young man might satisfy his service obligation by entering the armed forces for two years or by enrolling in a national service program for a term of three years—was proposed as an alternative to the draft. This plan, which would have sharply increased the social costs of involuntary servitude, was never adopted. Instead, Congress substituted a lottery draft that allegedly resulted in greater equity. Conscription was abolished in 1973. Our armed forces are presently staffed by volunteers, young men and women who have exercised their freedom of occupational choice by selecting a military profession. Although no longer touted as an alternative to the draft, national service is still alive. Compulsion, which used to be an integral part of the models of the late 1960s, has been replaced by voluntarism.[4]

In this paper, I first review the advantages claimed for national service and then its budgetary and social costs. Next, I analyze the implications of a large federally funded national service program proposed in the Citizenship and National Service Act of 1989 (H.R. 660 and S. 3).

AN UNEASY CASE FOR NATIONAL SERVICE

Voluntary contractual agreements are mutually advantageous to both the buyer and the seller. The party that supplies a national service job is demanding the labor services of a participant whose efforts will promote the goals and objectives of the employing organization or agency. On the other side of the market, the youth who volunteers for national service believes that the time devoted to the program is worth as much as the time allocated to the next best use in civilian, military, or academic pursuits. In addition to the direct gains to the two parties, national service may generate externalities to the community, the higher education sector, or the nation.

Providing Needed Social Services

If we ignore costs (and no economist would), we could find a wide range of activities that could use more labor resources—taking care of children, the sick, and the aged, tutoring in literacy programs, protecting the environment, joining the Peace Corps or Volunteers in Service to America (VISTA), and so on. On the domestic front alone, Eberly claimed that there were 5.3 million jobs that could be staffed by national service participants.[5] The labor that can be supplied by raw, untrained youths is, however, of questionable value. When the term of service is only one or two years, an employer has little incentive to invest in training. Additionally, short-timers are hard to motivate because they have no opportunity for promotions or pay increases. The draft was criticized because it encouraged waste; that is, if more soldiers can be conscripted, why should the army worry about efficiently using uniformed personnel? A similar concern was voiced by Eli Ginzberg, who wrote, "the more manpower there is, particularly the more manpower there is paid for by somebody else, the less effectively it will be utilized."[6] Indeed, one can imagine a situation where the output of a service agency might actually decline because it received too many youths.

Training and Education

Youths will allegedly obtain useful training and education from the jobs created by national service. Many teenagers, especially blacks, are unemployed and have difficulty accumulating work experience.[7] National service will presumably reduce teenage unemployment rates, thereby easing the transition from school to work. I have already noted that there is little to be gained from training someone who will be gone tomorrow. Ginzberg argues that effective development requires effective supervision: a ward nurse or a firefighter assigned to a national service youth may not have the qualifications or inclination to serve as a trainer. Ginzberg says that if there is a conflict between training and getting work done, the former almost always loses. Some work discipline may be learned, but is it worth the cost?[8]

Interruptions: Benefits or Costs?

The period following high school is sometimes a turbulent one. An interruption in a structured environment (for example, national service) may prove to be beneficial for at least two reasons. First, an individual has time to establish priorities about what she wants to do for the rest of her life. Second, he will be a more mature person after a tour of national service duty and thus get more out of college.[9] If national service were compulsory, the interruptions could be costly. The mean working life of a running back in the National Football League is under three years. Ginzberg suggests that a majority of youths are not off the track and that for them disruptions are *not* beneficial.[10]

Shaping Attitudes and Values

The national service experience, which is generally not available to most youths, exposes them to the problems of the needy. They can then derive the satisfaction that comes from helping to solve those problems. Urban service and youth conservation corps familiarize them with important public policy issues. The national service experience will, some claim, shape their attitudes and values, giving them a stronger sense of social responsibility and strengthening their obligation to public service. Others, however, worry about the fuzzy boundary between shaping and manipulating young minds.

The proponents of national service have identified other benefits of their program. The aspects I have discussed here—expanding the supply of much-needed social services, providing opportunities to get job skills and training, offering an interlude from formal schooling to establish priorities and to become more mature, and, finally, exposing them to job experiences that will shape their adult values and attitudes— are some of the more important benefits that support an uneasy case for national service.

BUDGETARY AND SOCIAL COSTS

It is important to distinguish between compulsory and voluntary national service programs. If youths are forced to participate at below market rates of pay, the budgetary costs will be less than the social costs, which are the sum of (1) the opportunity costs incurred by program participants, (2) the administrative program costs, and (3) the avoidance costs. In his analysis, Charles Benson assumed that the opportunity cost, OC, was the difference between the i-th individual's civilian earnings or wages, W_i, and his national service stipend, S: $OC_i = (W_i - S)$. This is a valid measure if the disutility of the civilian job is the *same* as that of the national service job. Although Benson estimated the cost of fringe benefits, supervision, and training at sixteen hundred dollars per participant, he refused to develop an aggregate estimate for the real costs of national service.[11]

There is, in principle, a shadow wage, $\hat{W}_i$, which would induce the i-th individual to take the national service job. Individuals who have strong aversions to national service will have higher shadow wages, which give us the correct social costs of youth labor. In a compulsory program the opportunity costs placed on youths will be the sum of the differences, $\hat{W}_i - S$, which are simply conscription taxes.[12] In a voluntary program the total compensation of NS youths that appears in the budget may include a stipend, S, fringe benefits, B, and possibly a postservice voucher, V; full pay is thus $F = (S + B + V)$. If the program is universal and open to all, the budgetary and social costs of labor will probably coincide. If, however, the program is limited and oversubscribed (meaning that full pay exceeds shadow wages, $F > \hat{W}_i$), budget outlays will exceed social costs. National service workers will receive economic rents resulting from a transfer of resources from taxpayers to program participants.

Administration and supervision are costly. In some models part of these costs are shifted to existing host agencies or volunteers; these "donated" supervisory and clerical services should be included on both sides of the ledger. The implicit cost of a volunteer (and hence his contribution) is thus the shadow wage that the Corporation for National Service would have paid to hire this volunteer. The social costs of program administration therefore include the implicit costs (contributions) of donated services. These are substantial and cannot be found in the budgets analyzed by the Congressional Budget Office.

The jobs that can be filled by untrained youths ordinarily command low wages. A large national service program might create 500,000 to 750,000 public sector jobs that would compete with public and private jobs for unskilled adult workers. Teenage unemployment might be reduced, but the cost could be a higher adult unemployment rate. This indirect cost was recognized by the authors of the proposed legislation as discussed below. Finally, if a balanced budget is truly a binding constraint, the allocation of resources to national service entails an opportunity cost of fewer funds for other federal projects.

THE CITIZENSHIP AND NATIONAL SERVICE ACT OF 1989

"The purpose of this bill is to (1) encourage Young Americans to serve their country and each other . . . and (2) insure that these Americans get the basic financial support to aid them in their future lives." The authors of this bill (Dave McCurdy, [D-Okla.] and Sam Nunn [D-Ga.] describe it as a new GI Bill. Youths will be asked to serve, but will be adequately (some might say generously) remunerated. In this section, I sketch the features of the bill, examine the data on the transition from school to work, and analyze the implications of the act.

An Outline of the Act

To qualify, an individual must have completed high school with a diploma or its equivalent. A volunteer to the Citizens Corps serves for one or two years for a subsistence wage of one hundred dollars a week plus health insurance valued at eleven hundred dollars a year. One can work in approved social service agencies (including hospitals, schools, public safety facilities) or in an existing national service program such as VISTA or the Peace Corps. Under this act, youths can enlist in the armed forces for two years of active duty for which he or she will get two-thirds of basic military compensation. (The details of this option will be developed by the Department of Defense.) Local national service councils, staffed mainly by volunteers or members of the senior corps, will be responsible for recruiting and placing volunteers. A Corporation for National Service will be established in Washington, D.C., to develop guidelines whereby the states can audit and monitor the program. This corporation will be eligible to receive private donations.[13] The voucher is perhaps the most important component of the compensation package. For each year of service, a volunteer in civilian service will receive a ten-thousand-dollar tax-free voucher that can be used (1) to finance an education, (2) for vocational or job training, or (3) as a down payment on a home. A two-year stint in the armed forces entitles the volunteer to a $24,000 tax-free voucher. After a phase-in period of five years, virtually all federal funds for student aid will be tied to the Citizens Corps; that is, national service will be a prerequisite for receipt of student aid.[14] In scenario one the program will begin in fiscal year 1991 with 60,000 volunteers and level off in 1995 at an enrollment of 280,000. Scenario two assumes an initial corps of 120,000 volunteers (100,000 in civilian service) leveling off at 760,000. It is a sizable program with significant budgetary and employment implications.

Target Population—Youths in Transit

In 1987 the U.S. population included 3.63 million eighteen-year-olds, which is 16 percent below the peak cohort of 4.32 million in 1979. The proportion of this cohort completing high school reached a high of

.771 in 1969, fell to .714 in 1980, but recovered to .733 (see panel B of table 4.1).[15] The number of general equivalency diplomas (GEDs) increased from 340,000 in 1975 to 479,000 in 1980. Roughly a third of the GEDs are issued to youths under 20 years of age (see the *Digest of Education Statistics, 1988*, n. 15, table 70). If we include GEDs issued to youths, the high school completion rate in 1985 climbs to just under .77. As adults acquire GEDs, this completion rate will eventually reach .85.[16]

A majority of high school graduates go directly to college as full-time freshmen. For males this college entry rate (panel D, table 4.1) was .627 in 1970, the height of the Vietnam War. It fell to .534 in 1978, but rose to .586 in 1985 despite the rapidly rising costs of attending college. The female college entry rate (.474) was below that of males in 1970, but has risen (.608 in 1985). In table 4.1, panel E is the fraction of the eighteen-year-old cohort whose principal activity is that of a full-time college student: .424 for men and .452 for women in 1985.

Unemployment in relation to the labor force is a somewhat mislead-

TABLE 4.1

HIGH SCHOOL GRADUATES AND FULL-TIME FRESHMAN ENROLLMENTS, 1970–1985

	1970	1975	1980	1985
A. High School Graduates (in thousands)				
Men	1,430	1,542	1,491	1,323
Women	1,459	1,591	1,552	1,360
Total	2,889	3,133	3,043	2,683
B. High School Graduates (proportion of eighteen-year-old cohort)				
Men	0.7612	0.7246	0.6997	0.7233
Women	0.7767	0.7477	0.7283	0.7436
C. Full-Time Freshman Enrollment (in thousands)				
Men	896	942	862	775
Women	691	821	887	827
Total	1,587	1,763	1,749	1,602
D. College Entry Rate (C/A)				
Men	0.6266	0.6109	0.5781	0.5858
Women	0.4736	0.516	0.5715	0.6081
Total	0.5493	0.5627	0.5748	0.5971
E. Ratio of Freshmen to Population				
Men	0.477	0.4427	0.4045	0.4237
Women	0.3678	0.3858	0.4162	0.4522

ing measure when so many young people are in college. An alternative measure of labor utilization published by the Bureau of Labor Statistics (BLS) is the civilian employment, E, to population, P, ratio, shown as E/P in panel A of table 4.2. These data exclude employment in the armed forces, which I approximate by the ratio of seventeen- to eighteen-year-old enlistments to the total size of the cohort, AF/P*, shown in panel B. Enlistments were high in fiscal years 1970–1973 because of the war and the draft so that AF/P* averaged .097. With the smaller All-Volunteer Force, this ratio averaged .056 in 1985–1987. The relative demand for women in the armed forces has increased, accounting for the upward trend in AF/P*; more than 12 percent of total enlistments in fiscal year 1987 were women. I next calculated a worker-to-population ratio by adding armed forces employment of eighteen-year-olds, AF, to both the numerator and the denominator.[17] This adjustment raises the ratio of gainfully employed persons to population by 2.3 percentage points for white men and 4.2 points for black men. The behavior of E/P and W/P is shown in figure 4.1. The unemployment rate of 35–44-year-old men, UR40, is also shown to indicate the business cycle. The data suggest that when the aggregate level of economic activity is high (a low value for UR40), the teenage worker–population ratio is high. There is some reason to suppose that when the size of the cohort is large, it is harder to find employment. These two variables—population, P*, and UR40—were included in a regression to explain the time series behavior of W/P over the period 1970–1987.

$$(W/P)_t = .529 + .0007p^*_t - 1.955(UR40)_t. \qquad [R^2 = .8763]$$
$$(3.08) \qquad (9.87)$$

TABLE 4.2

EMPLOYMENT IN THE CIVILIAN SECTOR AND ARMED FORCES, 1970–1985

	1970	1975	1980	1985
A. Ratio of Civilian Employment to Population, E/P, Ages 18–19				
Male	0.577	0.572	0.594	0.566
Female	0.459	0.472	0.522	0.519
B. Ratio of Armed Forces to Total Eighteen-Year-Old Population, AF/P*				
Male	0.0877	0.0896	0.06	0.0595
Female	0.0031	0.0055	0.0071	0.0068
C. Worker to Population Ratio, W/P*				
Male	0.6141	0.6103	0.6184	0.5918
Female	0.4607	0.4749	0.5254	0.5223

FIGURE 4.1

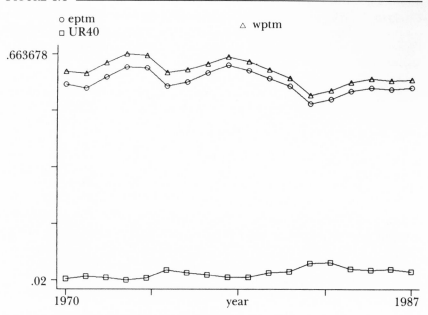

The figures in parentheses are *t* values, and the adjusted R^2 is shown in brackets. The corresponding regression for women is

$$(W/P)_t = .515 - .00001P^*_t + .194(UR40)_t. \quad [\text{females, } R^2 = -.1141].$$
$$(0.20) \quad\quad (0.41)$$

The cohort size, P^*, has the wrong sign for men, but the negative coefficient on UR40 suggests that work and college are substitutes. When the college entry rate was related to these variables, however, there was no relation. Finally, the regression for females omits the strong secular trend in female labor force participation rates over this period. When a time trend is included in the regression, both P^* and UR40 become highly significant.[18]

Estimates of the annual costs of attending college (tuition, room, and board), which are reported in the *Digest of Education Statistics, 1988* (table 193), are reproduced in panel A of table 4.3. Adjusting for price inflation reveals that these costs in constant 1987 dollars (panel B) increased by around three hundred dollars per year through 1981 and then climbed sharply for the next six years. The real costs of attending a public four-year college exhibited a slower rate of growth. In panel C

TABLE 4.3
COLLEGE COSTS AND SELECTED EARNINGS DATA

	1970	1975	1980	1985
A. Annual Costs of College				
A.1. Private University	$3,163	$4,467	$6,566	$11,110
A.2. Four-Year Public College	1,206	1,657	2,420	3,750
B. Annual College Costs in Constant 1987 Dollars				
B.1. Private University	$9,261	$9,434	$9,055	$11,732
B.2. Public College	3,531	3,500	3,337	3,960
B.3. Ratio (B.1/B.2)	2.623	2.696	2.713	2.963
C. Ratio of Annual College Costs to Mean Earnings of Male High School Graduates				
C.1. Private University	0.539	0.543	0.524	0.799
C.2. Public College	0.205	0.201	0.193	0.270
D. Mean Year-Round Earnings of 18–24-Year-Old Men				
D.1. High School Graduates	$5,871	$8,234	$12,527	$13,907
D.2. College Graduates	7,591	10,646	14,182	18,484
D.3. Ratio (D.2/D.1)	1.293	1.2929	1.1321	1.3291
D.4. High School Graduates in Constant 1987 Dollars	$17,190	$17,390	$17,275	$14,686
E. Annual Entry-Level Pay				
E.1. Enlisted, E-1, Basic Pay	$1,596	$4,128	$5,388	$7,440
E.2. Enlisted Reg. M1. Comp.	2,445	6,318	8,276	11,745
E.3. Officer, 0-1, Basic Pay	5,016	7,608	9,924	14,268
E.4. Officer Reg. Mil. Comp.	6,922	10,499	13,828	19,815
F. Ratio of Military, RMC, to Civilian Earnings				
F.1. Enlisted	0.416	0.767	0.660	0.844
F.2. Officer	0.911	0.986	0.975	1.072

annual college costs are related to the mean year-round earnings of male high school graduates. In 1985 one had to work nearly 0.80 of a year to finance one year at a private university, but only 0.27 of a year to pay for a year at a public college. Despite the sharp rise in college costs, the college entry rates climbed from 1982 to 1987 (see table 4.1). This can be explained in part by the rise in the rate of return of a college education, indicated by the rise in the ratio of college to high school earnings shown in panel D. The transition from school to work is arguably harder when there are fewer opportunities for full-time work and schooling. National service, which creates public sector jobs, can facilitate this transition. The data indicate that the need for such a program was substantially greater in the late 1970s; in the mid-1980s, more youths are finding jobs and places as full-time college students.

The Citizens Corps—Winners and Losers

An ideal national service program should be open to all, irrespective of their skills, abilities, or backgrounds.[19] It is useful to review the guidelines for paying volunteers as set down by Donald Eberly because they are indicative of the aims of national service:

> If all young people are entitled to serve, the stipend must be sufficient so that no youth is kept out of UYS [universal youth service] because of payment below subsistence level. On the other hand, payments should not be so high as to be competitive with salaries for comparable jobs in the open market either in the public or private sector. A third criterion which would be consistent with the service ethic would be to have no payment differentials based on the jobs done or on the qualifications of the participant. ("Universal Youth Service," p. 156.)

The Citizens Corps proposed in the Citizenship and National Service Act of 1989 violates these guidelines in two ways. First, enrollments are restricted to those who hold a high school diploma or its equivalent. Second, pay and benefits are higher for those who select the military option. The financial rewards of serving in the Citizens Corps are likely to attract opportunistic youths in search of a quick nest egg. If the size of the voucher is reduced, the corps will probably experience recruitment shortfalls. The social costs are high, I contend, and far exceed any benefits that may redound to participants or to society as a whole.

National service is also likely to harm those individuals who work in the low-wage labor market. Service in the Citizens Corps entitles the volunteer to (1) a subsistence allowance of one hundred dollars a week, (2) health insurance worth eleven hundred dollars a year, and (3) a tax-free voucher for ten thousand dollars for each year of service. This subsistence allowance is below that of a VISTA volunteer.[20] If the voucher is discounted for six months at an annual interest rate of 10 percent, it is worth around $9,500 in the after-tax earnings stream. Assuming that the typical volunteer faces an average income tax rate of 15 percent, I calculate that the full annual pay of a citizen corps volunteer would be around $17,500 a year.[21]

The full pay of $17,500 exceeds the mean annual earnings of a year-round worker by 18.8 percent for males and 43.7 percent for females. (Earnings data for young high school graduates were obtained from the Current Population Report, series P-60; see table 4.4.) If we assume a 40-hour workweek and ignore the pay for time not worked (holidays, sick leave, and vacations), the hourly wages for full-time work are $8.41 for the Citizens Corps compared with $7.08 for men and $5.86 for women in the civilian labor market. These wage gaps are even larger when full pay is compared to mean earnings of all employed high school graduates with full- and part-time jobs. If wages are log normally distributed, I estimate that around 73 percent of male and 80 percent of female high school graduates who were full-time employees in 1987 earned less than the $17,500 that will be paid to members of the citizens corps.[22]

If the Citizens Corps is kept small (less than 100,000 youths, which is less than 4 percent of the graduating class), it is likely to be oversubscribed. Rules will have to be established to ration the available positions. When nonprofit organizations face similar situations, they allocate the spaces to those individuals whose characteristics yield the highest perceived values to the managers of those organizations. Self-interest goes a long way in explaining, for example, the criteria for admitting students to Harvard, Stanford, and the University of California at Berkeley. The rhetoric goes that efficiency calls for good students to be matched with good faculty; however, it is also easier and more fun to teach bright, inquisitive students who will probably go on to earn higher incomes and become better alumni.[23] In a small Citizenship and National Service Act program, where local national service councils are responsible for recruiting and assigning volunteers (often by negotiating suitable internships with social service agencies, hospitals, universities, and police, fire, and sanitation departments), well-paying positions are likely to be given to youths from the upper middle class. (To the extent that some agencies

TABLE 4.4 _____

MEAN EARNINGS IN 1987 OF 18–24-YEAR-OLD HIGH SCHOOL GRADUATES
(BY SEX AND WORK EXPERIENCE)

	Full Year	Part Year	Total
Males with Income	2,342	2,613	4,955
Mean Earnings, 1987	$14,732	$5,833	$10,039
Females with Income	1,807	2,897	4,704
Mean Earnings, 1987	$12,180	$4,214	$ 7,274

may practice reverse discrimination [for example, the Buddhist church may prefer Asians], minority representation in the program could be controlled by a central authority such as the Corporation for National Service.) Who gains from a small program? Individuals who meet the criteria set by the host agencies are more likely to secure positions in the Citizens Corps, thereby entitling them to the stipends, health insurance, and tax-free vouchers. Some might object to my assumption that a volunteer will get the full, tax-free face value of ten thousand dollars at the end of his or her term of service. The cost analysis by the Congressional Budget Office assumes that most of the vouchers will be redeemed over a period of two or three years as students charge college costs against their vouchers. But why should they wait? Remember that the voucher can also be used as a down payment for a home. I can imagine a situation wherein a real estate agent sells an apartment for $80,000, but promises to buy it back a month later for $79,000. The holder of a voucher can get nine thousand dollars in cash within a month, and the agent receives one thousand dollars for laundering the voucher through the apartment. Citizens Corps members will, on balance, be overpaid and enjoy economic rents. The plan thus violates Eberly's guideline whereby "payments should not be so high as to be competitive with salaries for comparable jobs in the open market." The host agencies will benefit by obtaining labor services at the prescribed donation rate of one thousand dollars, less than 50 cents an hour, well below the wage of comparable employees. The losers are the taxpayers, who must bear the burden of the budgetary program costs, which are far in excess of the social costs. The host agencies may also be losers because they may incur the implicit costs of invidious income comparisons; the full pay of $17,500 for an untrained high school graduate may in many instances be higher than the annual wages of regular agency employees, some of whom hold bachelor's and advanced degrees.

A large program that creates jobs for as many as 700,000 youths raises at least three questions: (1) Will enough youths volunteer? (2) What are the social costs of allocating so many resources to national service? and (3) What are the implications for third parties?

The reservation wage, $\hat{W}_1$, was earlier defined as the sum needed to attract the i-th individual into national service in preference to college or an alternative civilian job. The distribution of reservation wages, f(W), along with full pay, F, thus determines the supply of volunteers, V.

$$V = \int_0^F f(W)dW.$$

If national service entails no net disutility (that is, at the same pay, youths are indifferent between national service and civilian jobs), f(W) can be replaced by the distribution of full-time civilian wages. Given the assumption of no net disutility, the Citizen Corps should be able to attract 700,000 recruits a year. A ten-thousand-dollar tax-free voucher dangles a lucrative incentive that will induce many youths to postpone college or normal work careers for a year. Much of the voucher costs represent transfer payments from taxpayers to a subset of youths lucky enough to get into the Citizens Corps. Recall that at its height, the corps will recruit 700,000 youths a year from high school graduating classes ranging in size from 2.6 to 3.0 million students. The authors of the bill envisage a scenario in which the size of the Citizens Corps will expand over a five-year phase-in period during which federal appropriations for Pell grants and student aid for higher education will be successively reduced. Participation in the Citizens Corps will become almost a prerequisite for federal aid to attend colleges and universities. The sponsors of the bill seem to believe that the voucher incentive will be most attractive to those individuals who are most likely to attend college and who have the greatest need for financial aid. The option to use the voucher as a down payment on a home greatly increases the voucher's liquidity, making it especially valuable to present-oriented youths who have no intention of attending college. Given the size of these vouchers, the program is likely to result in income redistributions from taxpayers to national service volunteers.

Transfer payments can be neutral if they incur low administrative costs and have little or no effect on work incentives. Proponents of national service claim that the one-year interruptions needed to capture these transfers will, on balance, generate net social benefits. I am of the opinion that large-scale interruptions will entail positive social costs. When nearly 45 percent of each cohort presently enroll as full-time college students and another 30 to 40 percent obtain full-time year-round jobs in the civilian labor market, we need to question the wisdom of creating 700,000 well-paying, short-term public sector jobs.

The main concern of third parties is the impact of the Citizens Corps on wages and employment in the civilian labor market. If we include workers in publicly operated hospitals and schools, there are some 16 to 18 million public sector employees, the vast majority of whom are skilled or semiskilled workers; at most, only 20 percent (3 to 3.5 million employees) occupy unskilled positions that might be competitive with national service jobs. The Citizenship and National Service Act of 1989 recognizes the potential threat of creating 700,000 new jobs and includes provisions that are summarized as follows:

In placing members . . . the National Service Council shall assure that placement does not result in (1) the displacement of any currently employed worker or position or result in the impairment of existing contracts for services or collective bargaining agreements or (2) a national service volunteer filling a position in an organization when an individual is on layoff from that organization; or, the employer has terminated the employment of a regular employee or reduced the workforce with the intention of filling the vacancy with a national service volunteer.

Enforcement of such provisions is difficult, especially when there is no mention of wages or recruiting efforts. There will be no worker displacement if the positions stay vacant because the Parks Department, for instance, will only offer the jobs at the minimum wage. The incentive to raise wages to attract a regular employee is nil if the position can be filled by a Citizen Corps member whose full pay is $17,500, but whose cost to the Parks Department is only $1,000 a year. The creation of 700,000 unskilled, public sector jobs has to depress the market for unskilled adult workers.

The Military Corps in an All-Volunteer Force

A provision in the act requires that within 60 days following enactment, the Department of Defense must develop plans for a Military Citizens Corps wherein youths will serve for two years of active duty at two-thirds of "basic military compensation." At the end of this tour he or she is entitled to a tax-free voucher of $24,000. "Basic military compensation" could mean either (1) basic pay, which for an E-1 (enlisted pay grade one, a private) in 1987 was $7,896, or (2) regular military compensation, RMC, which in 1987 was $12,401.[24] If we take the larger figure, a person who volunteers for the Military Citizens Corps takes a pay cut of $4,134 in her first year of service compared with what she would have received in the regular active duty forces. Assuming that RMC will rise by 15 percent, the pay cut in the second year will be $4,754. In return for this reduction in pay of $8,888, the Military Civilian Corps participant will be entitled to a tax-free voucher worth $24,000.

The payment of volunteers in the military and civilian sectors violates the guideline "to have no pay differentials based on the jobs done or on the qualification of the participant." The military corps receives an average subsistence allowance of $170 a week compared to $100 for the civilian corps. The tax-free voucher is larger by two thousand dollars per year for military service.

The more important pay inequity is between the military corps and regular enlisted personnel. The former gives up one-third of her regular military pay, but at the end of two years, she is entitled to $24,000 for a tax-free voucher. To establish a nest egg of $24,000 at the end of two years, assuming an annual interest rate of 10 percent, one would have to save $911.32 per month, which is equivalent to a before-tax earnings of $1,072. But the military corps volunteer has to give up only $370 a month for this entitlement. The military corps thus realizes a *full pay* that is 63 percent higher than that of a regular enlistee.[25] Three implications for the armed services follow: First, it will be harder to obtain regular enlistments from the top three mental groups (I, II, and IIIA corresponding to the top half of the test score distribution). Second, individuals have to be discharged from the active duty forces to get their tax-free vouchers. Knowing this, the armed services are unlikely to assign military corps members to the long, highly technical training courses. Third, turnover is likely to increase and may adversely affect force effectiveness. The Military Citizens Corps will increase the costs of national defense not only in terms of the budget, but also in the design of efficient recruitment and human resources utilization policies. A military citizens corps is a bad idea that ought to be forgotten, especially when the Montgomery GI Bill already provides generous educational benefits to regular enlistees who choose that option.[26] The size of the military corps would be set by Congress, whereas the services control the size of the GI Bill program depending on manpower needs.

Up to now, I have devoted considerable space to the high costs of the Citizenship and National Service Act. How is my assessment affected by reducing the act's budgetary costs? If the size of the tax-free voucher were cut from ten thousand dollars to six thousand dollars, it would eliminate most of the economic rents. However, the Citizens Corps would probably confront recruitment problems, especially for the big scenario of 700,000 members. My conclusions about the value of training and interruptions are unaffected by the size of the voucher. Finally, I suspect that, dollar for dollar, society can get a larger output of "needed" services by means other than hiring high school graduates for one-year tours of duty.

CONCLUDING REMARKS

Its proponents intend national service to provide youths with an opportunity to serve and, in the process, facilitate the transition from school to adult life. In the Citizenship and National Service Act, at least half the youths in the Citizens Corps will be placed in existing agencies—hospitals, social service agencies, schools, parks, police and sanitation departments, and so on. Other volunteers will be put into an urban service corps or a youth conservation corps that entail substantially higher administrative costs. The value of the training received by youths depends on the kinds of jobs they hold as well as on the quality of the supervision supplied by the host agency. Advocates of national service contend that a year's break will, on balance, result in net social benefits because these young people will get the time to sort out their thoughts and to mature. I am inclined to agree with Eli Ginzberg that a majority of our youths are not off the track; for this majority, the interruption, whether coerced or induced, will be costly. In rebuttal, the advocates point out that participation in the Citizens Corps will be *voluntary*. Two possibly tangential remarks can be offered. First, if money is what motivates a young man to enlist in the army, some people would call him a *mercenary*. What do we call someone who enrolls in a national service program to get a large, tax-free voucher that can be easily converted into cash? The issue is further confounded if in five years, participation in the Citizens Corps is the only way to get federal student aid. Second, the budgetary costs of the Citizenship and National Service Act are high. In addition to the administrative program costs, vouchers and stipends entail an annual cost of sixteen thousand dollars per person, a figure well above the mean earnings of high school graduates. A secondary aim of the proposal is "to assure that these Americans get the basic financial support to aid them in their future lives," but the full pay that yields this financial support is well above the opportunity costs of youth labor. Additionally, this support will only be provided to those who elect to serve or who are chosen to serve. More important, the social costs of national service will almost certainly exceed the value of any public services produced by the program, including the ancillary benefits realized by participants.

It is alleged that needed social services are not being supplied because we, as a society, are not devoting the requisite funds. When national service is fully operational, the Citizens Corps will house 250,000 members in its small scenario and 700,000 in its big scenario. Outlays for stipends and vouchers alone will exceed $10 billion, and to that we have to add the costs for administration, transportation, and materials. (A full accounting should include the implicit costs of volunteer labor and the losses in government revenues due to the nontaxable feature of the vouchers.) This input-driven policy tries to expand the output of socially needed services by injecting large quantities of untrained labor. We could pursue an alternative strategy wherein more federal funds could be appropriated and distributed to agencies and organizations that agree to provide the needed services. Each agency would be free to choose the way in which to produce the services, be it delivery of food stamps to the poor or cleaning up dump sites, but would not be obliged to demand an input mix consisting mainly of young high school graduates who have to postpone college or a regular job for a year or more.

My observations and reading over the last 25 years lead me to believe that the individuals who promote national service usually exhibit a fundamental distrust of the free market and a substantial amount of utopian thinking. William James, for example, said, "I devoutly believe in a reign of peace and a gradual advent of some sort of socialistic equilibria."[27] The maintained and untested hypothesis is that American youths either lack the opportunities to serve or are uninformed about the satisfaction that comes from serving others. Young people thus have to be coerced or bribed into taking the kinds of jobs that will expose them to the right experiences and teach them the values that will make them better citizens. William James put it as follows: "To coal and iron mines, to freight trains . . . will our gilded youths be drafted off according to their choice to get the childishness knocked out of them and to come back into society with healthier sympathies and soberer ideas."[28]

National service is, in short, a youth policy that rejects the outcomes of free choices made by young persons who are endowed with different abilities and interests and who sometimes reject attempts to control their behavior and actions. It strives to homogenize the population into sharing the values and exhibiting the behavior patterns that conform to the model designed by the social planner. The principal winners are the social planners. More resources will be allocated to the public sector not for national defense or public goods, but rather under the guise that these resources will improve the well-being and attitudes of a minority of young Americans. Remember that even in the big (700,000) scenario, only one in every five young Americans will serve in the Citizens Corps. The losers will be those who attach a high value to freedom of choice and who want a smaller role for government in the allocation of our scarce resources.

NOTES

1. William James, "The Moral Equivalent of War," in J. J. McDermott, ed., *The Writings of William James* (Chicago: University of Chicago Press, 1967), p. 669.

2. Cited in *Report of the President's Commission on an All-Volunteer Force,* Thomas S. Gates, chairman (Washington, D.C.: U.S. Government Printing Office, 1970), p. 24. The principal author of this report was William H. Meckling, the executive director of the staff.

3. Under the selective service system, deferments could be obtained by remaining in college, holding a critical job (farming was at one time classified as a critical job), fathering a child, or being the principal provider for a household. During the Vietnam War, some young men left the United States, while others incurred substantial costs to obtain medical deferments. These avoidance costs can properly be regarded as part of the costs of collecting taxes. Put in this way, the conscription tax was an especially inefficient tax because it entailed such high collection costs. Estimates of these latter costs were developed by L. Sjaasted and R. Hansen, "The Distributive Effects of Conscription" in K. E. Boulding and M. Pfaff, eds., *Redistribution to the Rich and the Poor: The Grants Economics of Income Distribution* (Belmont, Calif.: Wadsworth Publishing Co., 1972) pp. 285–308.

4. See "A Universal Youth Service," in D. J. Eberly, ed., *National Service* (Rochester, N.Y.: John Alden Books, 1988) (hereafter, Eberly [1988]), pp. 151–57.

5. His list is as follows:

Source of Employment	Job Potential in Millions
Medical institutions and health services	1.20
Educational institutions	1.10
National beautification	1.30
Welfare and home care	0.70
Public protection	0.35
Urban renewal and sanitation	0.65
Total	*5.30*

These figures were taken from the report of the National Commission on Technology, Automation, and Economic Progress, February 1966. He presents these data in: *National Service and Manpower,* D. J. Eberly, ed. (hereafter, Eberly [1968]) (New York: Russell Sage Foundation, 1968), p. 4.

6. "Manpower Dimensions of National Service" in Eberly (1968), p. 55.

7. In March 1988, the unemployment rates of 18–19-year-old men were 12.4 percent for whites and 31. 7 percent for blacks. The duration of unemployment in the transition from school to work is considerably longer for black youths; confer Richard B. Freeman and David A. Wise, "The Youth Labor Market Problem: Its Nature, Causes, and Consequences" in R. B. Freeman and D. A. Wise, eds., *The Youth Labor Market Problem* (Chicago: University of Chicago Press, 1982) pp. 1–16.

8. In "National Service, An Issue for the 1980's," Eberly (1968), Eberly cites the experience of the Seattle Program for Local Services (PLS). The unemploy-

ment of participants in this program fell from 70 percent to 18 percent some six months following completion of the program. The post-PLS youths are, however, two or more years older than the pre-PLS job applicants. Even if they had not participated in PLS, their unemployment rate would have declined.

9. According to Eberly, "National Service in the 1990's," in Eberly (1988), the GI Bill showed us that the break caused by wartime service whetted the appetite for more education. But freshmen enrollment rates in the late 1940s, even with the GI Bill, were only a third of the rates today.

10. According to Ginzberg, "there are a large number of people who should not be interrupted and delayed unnecessarily. . . . After all, Mr. Pitt was prime minister of Great Britain at the age of 21." Eberly (1988) p. 53. (In my encyclopedia, William Pitt was born in 1759 and became prime minister in 1783.)

11. He assumed that one supervisor/administrator would be needed for every twenty youths, which seems low to me. In his summation, Benson wrote, "I therefore conclude that the efforts to calculate the real costs of national service in the conventional accounting framework are probably not worth serious effort," p. 26. He wants instead to substitute a system of human resources accounts that can better reflect the values for our social priorities. See Charles Benson, "The Real Costs of National Service," in Eberly (1968), pp. 15–27.

12. The importance of the nonpecuniary aspects of employment was discussed by Alfred Marshall and amplified by Simon Rottenberg. See Alfred Marshall, *Principles of Economics,* 8th ed. (New York: Macmillan Co., 1920) and Simon Rottenberg, "On Choice in Labor Markets," *Industrial and Labor Relations Review* 9, no. 2 (January 1956); 183–99.

13. I cannot determine whether the bill places a cap on the proportion of such donations that can be used for fund raising. It would seem prudent to write such a cap into the enabling legislation.

14. This outline of the act was taken from a summary of H.R. 660 by Dave McCurdy, "A Quid Pro Quo for Youths," *New York Times,* June 26, 1989, and Chuck Seagraves and Richard Curley, "Cost Analysis of the Citizens and Military Corps" (Washington, D.C.: Congressional Budget Office, April 1989). The military service option includes a scenario for the selected reserve. The federal-state cost-sharing arrangements and mandatory donations of host agencies are omitted in this outline.

15. Data are from the U.S. Department of Education, *Digest of Education Statistics, 1988* (Washington, D.C.: U. S. Government Printing Office, 1988), Table 69. The fraction who earned a high school diploma was only .020 in 1870, .064 in 1900, and .508 in 1940. Females outnumber males in the postwar years.

16. Diplomas and GEDs are imperfect substitutes. The armed forces have found, for example, that judged by attrition rates in training courses, diploma holders do better than GED recruits. The Citizens Corps is likely to increase the demand for GED because they satisfy the entry requirement.

17. Let $P^* = P + M$ denote the total population, the sum of the civilian

noninstitutional population, P, plus members of the armed forces, M. The worker to population ratio is W/P* = (E + M)/P*. It is related to the civilian employment to population ratio, E/P, as follows: W/P* = (E/P) + (AF/P*) [1 − (E/P)]. These ratios are presented in panel C of table 4.2. When nearly 6 percent of each cohort is employed in the armed forces, one has to adjust both the numerator and the population base. The adjustment is more important for black youths.

18. The expanded regression for eighteen-year-old females is
$$(W/P)_t = .342 + .00008P^*_t − 1.493(UR40)_t + .0073t.$$
$$(R^2 = .9454) \quad (5.68) \quad (10.35) \quad (17.08)$$
The inclusion of a trend, t, sharply increases the goodness of fit. UR40 is highly significant, but the cohort size, P*, still has the wrong sign. When a trend was included in the male regression, it was insignificant. The results for black males and females were similar to those for the total of all races.

19. Donald Eberly emphasized in his "A Universal Youth Service" that useful jobs could be designed for everyone: "For example, persons with few skills may do well in environmental conservation camps where they can serve with college-educated environmentalists and receive necessary training" (p. 154). The language suggests life arranging that is reminiscent of what utopian thinkers proposed to do in their communities. An amusing example is described by Charles Fourier. In his phalanx the division of labor is determined by individual preferences. When a question arose about how certain odious tasks would be performed, Fourier wrote,

> The madness for dirt which prevails among children is merely an unculti-vated germ, like wild fruit . . . repugnant occupations will become games having indirect composite attraction. . . .
> There is nothing therefore left for children to do but to take over the field of unclean work. . . . [These little hordes] are always on foot at 3 o'clock in the morning, even in the depth of winter, attending to the animals, working in slaughter houses.

Gray commenting on Fourier goes on to say, "The little hordes also repair the highways, turn out in any emergency, kill reptiles and vipers, and do all the things that boy scouts dream of doing." These excerpts can be found in Alexander Gray, *The Socialist Tradition: From Moses to Lenin* (London: Longsman, 1963), p. 189. The quotation from Fourier was taken from *Oeuvres Completes*, vol. 5, cited in Gray, *Socialist Tradition*, pp. 158–62.

20. A *VISTA* volunteer is entitled to a monthly subsistence allowance varying with the cost of living. Based on a phone conversation with ACTION (August 8, 1989), I learned that this allowance is presently $487 a month in Rochester and $513 in New York City. (The cost-of-living differential for New York City seems to be too small.) The Citizenship and National Service Act subsistence allowance is only 89 percent of that for Vista and 46.3 percent of the average poverty income cut-off for a nonfarm family of four, $11,232 (see U.S. Bureau of the

Census, *Statistical Abstract of the U.S., 1988,* [Washington, D.C.: U.S. Government Printing Office, 1988], table 713). It is hard to see how one can pay for rental housing on $100 a week. The Citizenship and National Service Act program will presumably follow VISTA, namely the subsistence allowance will be taxable, but it will not be counted as "substantial gainful activity" for purposes of the earnings tests for Social Security, Disability Insurance, Supplemental Security Income, or Aid to Families with Dependent Children.

21. Recall that full pay is the sum of the taxable stipend, S = $5,200, plus the before-tax equivalent of the tax-free health insurance of $1,100 and the voucher worth $9,500. At a tax rate of t = .15, the full pay, F, works out to be $17,671, which I have rounded to $17,500.

22. Let f(x) denote the distribution of annual earnings with mean m and variance s^2. If X is log normally distributed, then Y = lnX has a normal distribution with mean M and variance S^2. The two sets of parameters are related as follows:

a. $S^2 = \ln[1 + (s/m)^2]$

b. $M = \ln\{m[1 + (s/m)^2]^{1/2}\}$

For full-time year-round workers, I assumed that the coefficient of variation (s/m) was bounded by 0.8 < (s/m) <1, whereas for all employed persons, I assumed that 0.8 < (s/m) <1.2. Notice that the larger the s/m, the smaller the log of the geometric mean, M. The values of m were taken from the current population report data on the mean earnings of 18–24-year-old high school graduates. The log-normal distribution is described in J. F. Kenney and E. S. Keeping, *The Mathematics of Statistics, Part II* (Princeton, N.J.: D. VanNostrand and Co., 1951), pp. 122–23.

23. The nonprice rationing of positions in the freshman class was analyzed by James M. Buchanan and N.E. Devletoglou, *Academia in Anarchy* (New York: Basic Books, 1970), pp. 34–61. On pp. 60–61, they reproduce an excerpt from A. A. Alchian, *Pricing and Society* (London: Institute of Economic Affairs, 1967) on just who would end up with designer dresses if the couturiers were forced to work for nonprofit firms and were hence denied the opportunity to sell their original creations for profit.

24. RMC is the sum of (a) basic pay, (b) basic allowances for quarters and subsistence, BAQ/BAS, and (c) the tax advantage. Military personnel enjoy a tax advantage because they are not taxed for BAQ/BAS. The ratio of RMC to mean year-round earnings was .841. (Remember that fringe benefits, especially medical care, are excellent for the uniformed forces.) At entry, newly commissioned officers, pay grade 0-1, received basic pay of $15,132; RMC, $20,697. Relative pay in relation to college graduates was $20,697/$22,255 = .929. I am indebted to Professor John Warner for these data.

25. These calculations assume a monthly interest rate of 0.798 percent and an average income tax rate of 15 percent. Military pay was assumed to be that of an E-1 in the first year, $12,401, and 15 percent higher in the second year, $14,261. The implied pay premium is even higher if the volunteer citizen-soldier

has to give up only one-third of his basic pay of $7,896 for an E-1. If basic pay is, on average, 20 percent higher in the second year, the implicit costs for the volunteer are $2,632 + $3,158 = $5,790, or only $242 a month.

26. Under the Montgomery GI Bill, a regular enlistee has to declare his or her intention to participate near the beginning of the first term of service. A deduction of one hundred dollars a month is contributed toward the fund during the first twelve months of service. At the end of two years of active duty service, a soldier is entitled to educational benefits worth $7,800. (This sum is increased to $9,600 if the enlistment term is three or four years.) Under the Army College Fund, an individual can qualify for additional educational benefits of up to eight thousand dollars by enlisting for certain critical occupations. But, and it is an important difference, the GI Bill voucher can only be spent for education and training, whereas the $24,000 military corps voucher could be used for a down payment on a home. Suppose that a soldier signs up for the Montgomery GI Bill, serves for two years, and enrolls in college after discharge. If she later drops out of college (nearly half of all freshmen never earn a bachelor's degree), she may never get all of the $7,800 due to her. If, however, she had been a member of the military citizens corps, dropping out entails a smaller opportunity cost because the remainder of the voucher can be recovered as a down payment. In short, there is less risk associated with the latter voucher.

27. James, "Moral Equivalent of War," in *Writings of William James,* p. 667.

28. Ibid., p. 669.

COMMENT

Peter L. Szanton

Some years ago there appeared in the *New Yorker* a cartoon that was a drawing of a display case in a fancy department store in which there were four bottles of perfume. The first three were small and had lovely sinewy shapes. The first was labeled "Passion"; the second, "Sultry Night"; and the third, "Ecstasy." The fourth bottle was a little larger but was square and klunky looking, and the label on it was "Reasonable Expectations." I was looking forward to Walter Oi's paper because what this debate over national service badly needs is "reasonable expectations." It is a subject on which passions have been aroused and doctrines deployed. I looked forward to it as well because I am conscious of the extraordinarily important contribution that Professor Oi made to the debate on the draft. When I opened that fourth bottle of Professor Oi's paper, however, what I found was not a perfume of any kind, not one of reasonable expectations, but rather a liquid which seemed to be an antidote to a passion to which none of us is subject, namely a passion for military conscription. Therefore, I have a number of quite critical comments to make about the paper. As Don Eberly will tell you, I am not one of the band of devoted advocates of national service. If I sound like a defense counsel, I regard myself as forced into the role.

What might a paper do that was devoted to reasonable expectations on the question of who pays and who gains from national service? It might discuss who pays and who benefits in the proposal now before the country that had the best chance of being adopted. Given that national service is an elastic concept, it might discuss the costs and benefits of alternative proposals. It might, because so many alternatives are to be looked at, set out the principles to be followed and the caveats observed in calculating the costs and benefits for any such proposal. In doing any of those things, it ought to display knowledge of the recent debate over national service. Even more important, it should show an understanding of what can be learned from the recent experience with service of various kinds. What has been distinctive about the last decade, especially the last five years, is not the re-emergence of this old debate in familiar terms, but that all over the country experience with various forms of service has emerged. There is much to learn from this. Little that you have heard so far, including Professor Oi's paper, profits from that experience. In my view, none of the objectives I have set forth are met by Professor Oi's paper. Let me then turn to what it does do.

There are four sections. I will take them one at a time. The paper begins with an extended non sequitur: The first two and a half pages deal with the inequity of the military draft. I concede that; I am not prepared to concede that that is a useful way to begin a discussion of national service. The defining characteristics of the military draft are, first, that it is involuntary and, second, that it exposes those affected by it to hardship and potentially to danger. Neither is characteristic of national service as it is now being discussed. National service is not a stalking-horse for a return of the draft. The Joint Chiefs of Staff have opposed national service schemes from the beginning and still do. Its intention is not to provide manpower for the military nor, in the minds of most of its proponents, to return to the draft. Second, section 1 tries to provide a sense of the potential scale of national service by citing Don Eberly's estimate of 5.3 million jobs. The estimate was path breaking in its time and useful, but it is half again as large as careful and more recently published estimates that are not cited. [Richard Danzig and Peter Szanton, *National Service: What Would It Mean?* (Lexington, Mass.: Lexington Books, 1986), p. 41.] Section 1 then goes on to arguments that I find unpersuasive. Let me give you an example from page four:

> The labor that can be supplied by raw, untrained youths is, however, of questionable value. When the term of service is only one or two years, an employer has little incentive to invest in training. Additionally, it is hard to motivate individuals if they are "short timers" with no opportunity for promotions or pay increases.

What that ignores is that the largest potential sources of service positions are in conservation, the environment, child-care, school tutoring, and health care. Many such jobs require little training. What it also ignores is that the experience of the last decade shows that youth given high-quality supervision—including underprivileged, illiterate, undisciplined youth—in only short periods can do effective work in a variety of areas. The notion that only dollars and chances for promotion can motivate eighteen-year-olds is simply wrong. Anybody who has coached a soccer team knows that, as well as anybody who has looked at the better service programs now out there. The section ends with a return to the argument about compulsion, which is irrelevant: "The period following high school is sometimes a turbulent one. An interruption may prove to be beneficial. . . . First, the individual has time to establish his or her priorities. . . . Second, she would be a more mature person. . . . [But] if national service were compulsory, the interruptions could be costly." Right. But we are not talking about compulsion. No one is talking about compulsion. There is no bill currently in Congress that is compulsory. Even the Nunn-McCurdy bill, which though not formally compulsory provides powerful incentives to serve, has had its incentives reduced following discussion of their feasibility.

Section 2 consists of only two pages on resultant social costs. It makes the right and important but not novel point that social costs may exceed budgetary costs. It does not make the reciprocal point that social benefits may exceed the benefits to participants and the measurable benefits of the work performed. For example, the experience of national service might enlarge the civic participation of those who served. It might give them, as it gave those of us who experienced military service, a sense that they had paid their dues to society and were fuller and more complete members of society than if they had not done so. It might, therefore lead them to participate more fully in that society. It might not. But those benefits, if they exist, belong in the formula.

There are other hard-to-measure benefits. One that particularly intrigues me is this: In any large-scale program, national service participants would work in large bureaucratic institutions—hospitals, schools, nursing homes, social service agencies. The staffs of those institutions tend to organize their work more to suit their own convenience than to benefit their patients or clients. The passage through those institutions of large numbers of persons not dedicated to the profession would open the institutions to public scrutiny in a way that does not now happen. It may not be a large benefit. It may not happen at all. But it is worth listing among the potential benefits. The larger point here is the point that Amitai Etzioni was trying to make this morning, namely, that, at least potentially, there are combined benefits of national service. Even though no single benefit justifies the cost, the sum of the benefits may more than justify the cost. Knowing that, I say that there is danger that games will get played as proponents argue that if it does not meet this condition, it meets another. The discipline is to do the analysis, not to ignore the arguments.

Section 3, the extremely valuable heart of the paper, shows that the Nunn-McCurdy proposal is generous and that if performed on a large scale it would not only create labor substitution problems, but produce a large number of low-value, meaningless jobs, flooding the system with more volunteers than we can use. If performed on a small scale, it would create equity problems between those who were admitted to this generous program, and those who were not. The value of that analysis is compromised by the fact that the Nunn-McCurdy bill is no longer likely to be adopted. Nunn-McCurdy has been chosen as the object of attack by most of the people who are uncomfortable with national service because it is the most vulnerable of the proposals, not because it is the most likely to be adopted.

Another virtue of section 3 is that it comes down hard on a problem that is often overlooked, namely, the difficulty of ensuring that national service positions do not displace employed persons. All national service proposals purport to deal with the displacement problem; few of them deal with it effectively. They do not deal with ensuring that people now employed will stay employed or the even tougher problem, as Professor Oi points out, of depressing the wages of those in jobs that are competitive with the positions that would be occupied by national service personnel.

The last section, section 4, makes essentially three arguments. One is simply a summary of the objections to Nunn-McCurdy. The others seem to me to be more problematic:

> Advocates of national service contend that a year's break will, on balance, result in net social benefits because youths will get the time to sort out their thoughts and to mature. I am inclined to agree with Eli Ginsburg, namely a majority of our youths are not "off the track," and for them, the interpretation will be costly. In rebuttal, it can be pointed out that participation will be voluntary. Two possibly tangential remarks can be offered. First, if money is what motivates a young man to enlist in the Army, some people would call him a mercenary. What do we call someone who enrolls to get a large tax free voucher?

I have two problems with that analysis. First, in the six years that I have been tuned into the national service debate, I have heard the argument that it will help ghetto kids make a clean break from their current poisonous environments. I have heard the argument that it will provide the experience of collective action in service of common, constructive goals, especially in the company of youths unlike themselves. I have heard the argument that it will enable youths to pay their dues and to earn their citizenship. I have never heard the argument that it will help them "to sort out their thoughts and to mature."

Second, the fact that the participation will be voluntary is a complete response. The fact that there is payment involved does not undercut this at all. After all, voluntary transactions in the marketplace often involve transfers of money.

The paper ends with what I think is the real motivation behind it: "National service is, in short, a youth policy that rejects the outcomes of free choices . . . [and] strives to homogenize the population into sharing the values and exhibiting the behavior patterns that conform to the model designed by the social planner." The winners "are the social planners. . . . The losers will be those who attach a high value to freedom of choice and who want a smaller role for government in the allocation of our scarce resources."

The problem here is one of exaggeration. I would start with Justice Holmes's response to the comment that the power to tax is the power to destroy. His response was "not while this court sits." Almost any course of action if carried to an extreme is an evil. One should not judge a course of action in terms of its extremes. National service may give some fraction of the population a similar set of experiences, perhaps in the same way military service does. This is a society that is a long way from homogeneity. As to sharing values, that is deemed important by the democratic majority. What does public education do? What does the tax code do? If it is legitimate for some public institutions to foster shared values deemed important by the majority, why is it illegitimate for service to do so?

DISCUSSION

Mr. Oi: I have several comments I would like to make. One is on the value of the training: Its value is minimal.

With respect to the point that Mr. Szanton made that there are multiple benefits: I remember a class in early 1954 in which someone said, why do I have to pay for the shoestrings when I buy the shoes? I have a friend whose left foot is one size bigger than the right. Why does he have to buy two pairs of shoes and throw the opposite ones away? The question here is if these other benefits are valuable, and they very well may be, in a competitive labor market they are going to be reflected in the wages. If you are going to get that management training position, go [to work] at a lower salary. That position should call for you to do harder, direct work. From that viewpoint, the benefits will be reflected in the total value and in the supply prices of these people.

We then come to the issue of how valuable are these services and is this is an efficient way of providing those services? We are providing a big voucher, a lucrative one. I agree that if we reduce the size of that voucher we will reduce much of the transfer and income redistribution. In the course of twenty years we have persuaded a fair number of the national service proponents that happiness will not buy money, and therefore, we ought to make money. In our present set of circumstances, I agree there is nothing wrong with being remunerated for what you do. But shouldn't we ask, is this the most efficient way to teach values—to dangle these things before people?

If you look at the jobs and look at the programs, it is not true that a majority of these positions will be in the environment, conservation corps, etc. A large number of these positions will be menial. These jobs are negotiated between local service councils and host agencies that pay a thousand dollars. The federal government pays in excess of sixteen thousand dollars—if you include the tax advantage now, then seventeen thousand dollars; the question is, is this an efficient way of allocating the resources? Are we going to politicize service? I think the dangers are great that we cannot help doing so.

Mr. Etzioni: I would like to make a point on the problem of the two Adam Smiths. Too many people have read the *Wealth of Nations,* and too many have forgotten the *Theory of Moral Sentiments.* If Adam Smith was big enough to recognize that human nature was more complicated than simple self-interest, it should be allowed in these halls too.

I suggest that a volunteer should be paid less. I agree that if volunteers are paid a high wage and are tax exempt, it would kill the whole purpose. I favor a system in which people are given subsistence wages and no more. The opportunity to do volunteer service, if it is a meaningful job, does allow people to exercise and strengthen that part of the Adam Smith in them—the nobler part that makes people do things for the community.

The ultimate misapplication of the notion that the only thing that drives people is lining their own pockets is to apply it to the designers of programs like national service and suggest that they are out there to make a profit. If you are going to go that route, then you have to ask, what do the people opposed to national service get out of it? This is really not an acceptable argument. Let us drop the idea of examining the payoffs to the proponents or opponents of the program and stick to analysis.

Is there a problem? Can national service help it? Is human nature richer than self-interest and does it look for opportunities of community service? Would national service make a difference or not?

Mr. Oi: If a study allows for national service to improve the well-being of the community, it should also allow for deterioration as well. By enacting this program we could make things worse.

You ask why people want power? Why do ministers want bigger flocks? Bigger flocks increase the income of the minister, we know that. Irrespective of that, most ministers would want bigger flocks. They have a message. That is clearly one of the gains from it.

Robert Burkhardt, director, San Francisco Conservation Corps; president, National Association of Service and Conservations Corps: I have some profound disagreements with you, Professor Oi.

I would like to advise you of two events that are going to happen next week that shed some light on the relatively academic discussion that is going on about "what might happen if." On Tuesday morning [September 12, 1989] a crew of inner-city, high-risk, low-income kids from San Francisco will go to Yellowstone National Park to spend a month in the back country. They will be one of sixty some crews from around the country in a cooperative venture of the National Park Service, the Student Conservation Association, and the National Association of Service and Conservation Corps. There will be crews from Florida, Maine, Minnesota, and so on for three months this summer into October. They will help repair fire damage and the erosion resulting from the fire, putting in water bars and things like that. Many of them have never been on a plane before. Many of them will experience a snow storm for the first time. This is experiential education at its best.

On Thursday [September 14] at a press conference in Washington, a group of us will announce the Urban Corps Expansion Project, which will create fifteen urban conservation corps in major metropolitan areas around the country. We got together with several national foundations, who have a sense that if they can supply seed money, the mayors of many cities—all of whom are strapped for funds—will help find a way to meet the needs of young people, community needs, and so on. We invited 150 cities to send representatives to Philadelphia in late July 1989. Eighty-two showed up, 52 submitted applications, and now we are down to the 25 whose proposals have put together the open-entry, broad-based coalition of mayoral, corporate, clerical, and scholastic-based support that is necessary to help address many of the problems that you see when you walk down the street in Newark, New Jersey, New Orleans, Portland, or San Francisco.

There has to be a way to provide diversified opportunities for young people to move through the rites of passage, to be exposed to some of the values that will give them the free choices that Professor Oi is saying may not exist in opportunities like this. I know kids who are not doing crack anymore and who have good jobs in the private sector as a result of six months, eighteen months, in a conservation corps program, whether it is in the rural areas of Pennsylvania or downtown Oakland.

Mr. Anderson: That is an interesting example of how relatively small programs are working. It raises a question as to the necessity for a national program.

One thing has always bothered me. Several months ago I asked Will Marshall, executive director of the Democratic Leadership Council, about it, and you [Mr. Szanton] raised the same point. You said that all these people, millions of young people, young boys and girls are going to be working mostly with institutions. I asked Marshall, "You are going to pay people a hundred dollars per week; how are they going to live; how can they buy food, pay rent?" He said they are all going to live at home. I accepted that, now then you [Mr. Szanton] say they are going to work in institutions. How can they all live at home and work in institutions? Don't you have a fundamental problem of logistics? My question is for the people who have been involved in designing and studying the programs for many years, how will the logistics work with several million young boys and girls? Where will they live? Where will they eat? Who will supervise them?

Mr. Szanton: The problem is real. The logistical problem is underexamined. Are you talking about residential programs such as the old CCC [Civilian Conservation Corps] where you take the kids out into the woods? Are you talking about programs where they will live in their own communities?

Mr. Anderson: I was talking about the program where they will work in institutions.

Mr. Szanton: With most of those, you are not following the CCC model. The kids are living in their own homes, working in institutions in their own community.

Mr. Anderson: But you will find a mismatch between where these people live and where the jobs are you want them to do. Has anyone even looked at that problem?

Mr. Eberly: About a quarter of the people in national service will be in conservation work. Most of them will be in Yellowstone and other such places. The arrangement there would be as it was in Young Adult Conservation Corps ten years ago. The stipend would be reduced by the amount of food and shelter provided.

About three-quarters would work in the cities, largely out of their homes, as the people in the San Francisco Corps do now.

I still consider the Seattle program the best test of national service. Some young people lived in their homes to save money. Some of the others chose to share apartments, three or four together.

We will not have several million people right away. Today, including the Peace Corps, VISTA, the San Francisco Conservation Corps, and the other several dozen state and local programs, there are only about nine thousand full-time, year-round 18-to-24-year-olds in service. ["Surveys Show Strong Teenage Interest in Civilian Service as Full-Time Service Openings Grow Slowly," *National Service Newsletter,* no. 55 (October 1989), p. 2.] We will not have several million overnight. We would build up gradually over the years.

Mr. Anderson: It would help the people who have concerns about national service programs if the people proposing them could be more specific and tell us how would it be built up, how they would take care of 100,000 or one million young people, where they would live, how much they would be paid, how much would it cost. In the many years that this has been studied, this has not been addressed. This leads me to believe you have a serious problem here.

Mr. Henderson: Walter [Oi], I liked the paper generally, but I was unclear about something. You said the labor would not be used well. But in another place you said it would displace other relatively high valued labor. I presume the people in national service would be doing the job that high valued labor did. This sounds as if the labor would be used relatively well.

Mr. Oi : It would not be used efficiently. If you have 700,000 positions, that could easily affect the market for another 200,000 positions. You are injecting a sizable number of positions and that could affect other positions, but not on a one-to-one basis. It would not displace 700,000 jobs.

Mr. Henderson: To the extent that it does displace, those people are used in relatively high value pursuits.

Mr. Oi: No, not high value. It is going to be low-wage labor.

Mr. Henderson: By high, I do not mean $20 an hour. I mean $7 an hour instead of $3.50.

Mr. Oi: Yes.

Catherine Milton, director, Haas Center for Public Service, Stanford University: For the last five years I have been working with students, running programs that enable students to volunteer. At Stanford, about two thousand students a year are out in the community volunteering. I also have been working with colleges around the country through an organization called Campus Compact. I would like to go back to what Amitai [Etzioni] said, that it is important to figure out what the problem is. In the last five years a grass-roots movement has started. Young people are concerned about the issues and are out there volunteering on their own. Something is going on that is new and did not exist before. It is important that whatever is done does not hurt that by putting in a bureaucracy that harms or destroys it.

I would like to make a point about something we have learned by running school-based programs. You just cannot place the students out there without considerable thought or you will harm the community. If you have students tutor, you cannot just send them out there. We tried it. I know from hard experience if they go out there without the right kind of training, without the right kind of structure to place them, the logistics will get in your way. The students will go to tutor, and the kids will not be there to be tutored. Things like that happen. You have to have a good staff who can take care of training and logistics. If you are going to worry about values, you have to have people who can encourage the young people to reflect on what they are learning so they learn positive things and are not turned off. If you do not do a good job, you will have the opposite effect. One thing that concerns me about the national service program is that it is starting things too fast. We need to start things in a small way and build incrementally.

Mr. Szanton: You are right that good programs require high overhead expenses. Good service programs that recruit students, train them, supervise them, and evaluate what is going on are not cheap. That point is often fudged by the advocates. That is not to say the costs outrun the benefits.

Mr. Moskos: Some people have been talking about waving a magic wand to have mandatory service. Others here might like to wave a magic wand and have no government. They cancel each other out. I was talking about a concrete issue. If the program became so successful that the citizens wanted a mandatory service program, I would be happy to cross that bridge when we get to it.

Peter [Szanton], if I may make a few more addenda to your point about local lessons for national service. Several other lessons might be stressed that might answer your question more directly.

There is a problem of stigmatization in local programs, especially large ones. It is a recurring problem to get middle-class kids into them. The New York City Volunteer Corps is a prominent example. The other thing we have learned is that voluntary agencies use people less effectively than government agencies.

I may have misheard Professor Oi, but the citizen-soldier gets less pay than does the regular soldier.

Mr. Oi: I include the voucher.

Mr. Moskos: I hope that in future comments on the all-volunteer force and the payoff from citizen-soldiers, you [Mr. Oi] pay some attention to reserve forces and how reserve forces do or do not dovetail with the use of short-termers as active duty personnel. It changes the budget situation considerably.

Mr. Oi: The concept of pay has to include something more than what you get at the end of the week. The concept of cost must include opportunity cost. James Buchanan has a book called *Cost and Choice* that points out the distinction between these various concepts of cost and what social cost is. [James M. Buchanan, *Cost and Choice: An Inquiry in Economic Theory* (Chicago: Markham, 1969)] I looked at the appendix to your [Mr. Moskos's] paper; you are looking at what comes in the paycheck, not cost.

5

NATIONAL SERVICE: SERVING WHAT?

Richard John Neuhaus

The subject is national service, and my argument is service yes, national, maybe. The question is, service to what? Without engaging in excessive Hegelian flights, there is something necessarily antithetical about a definition of the *what:* What it is that one is serving, to what end, what goal, what common good, what agreed-on purpose, what—to use an old-fashioned term—national interest defines this service. There must be something against which the purpose receives its definition.

Theologians have argued—as have philosophers of a less theological bent—that the fall of humankind was in some sense a fall into humanity, a fall into the human condition. Only by virtue of the knowledge of good and evil, by virtue of the consciousness of the conflict between the thesis and antithesis, did human beings become human and thus contestants toward something—some things to be served and some things not to be served. The centrality of contestation is certainly true of U.S. history.

Consider the idea of national interest. Presumably people are to serve the national interest, and certain varieties of conservatism want to revive national deliberation and debate about how that national interest

Editor's Note: This is an edited and revised transcript of a speech delivered September 8, 1989.

should be defined. Historically, national interest has always been defined in conflict. Certainly in the early American period—the preconstitutional period, the Puritan period—there was no doubt that the errand into the wilderness had a high sense of moral intentionality (the light on the hill and so on). The constituting period can only be explained as a powerful carryover from that period. Witness on the back of every dollar bill *Annuit Coeptis Novus Ordo Seclorum*, a new order of the ages.

A new order of the ages as opposed to what? the old order—the tyrannies, the corruptions, the decadence, and the degradations of Europe. It was possible then for free men and free women to talk about national purpose. In a manner reminiscent of Aristotle, free persons (of course they said free men) deliberated the question, how ought we to order our life together? That it is a moral question is evidenced by the word *ought*, but the new thing, the *novus* in *Novus Ordo Seclorum*, was that the state was not to define the points of reference by which the *ought* was to be determined.

In early America, then, the purpose was to exemplify a new way in which people could order their lives together. It had a biblical, Hebraic dimension to it and a classical dimension: people were engaged in politics in the Jeffersonian mold.

In many ways it was a paradoxical venture, strange and unprecedented in human history and, in world historical terms, as new and audacious in 1989 as it was in 1776. But it was only in contrast to something else—the old versus the new—that the idea of a national purpose that could give meaning to national service was developed or emerged. *The redeemer nation* (recall Tuveson's marvelous book)[1] is a powerful myth, not in the sense of falsehood but in the sense of compelling story, a way of putting reality together, of seeing how progress and history moved as the sun moved, ever West. This was not simply Greeley's "Go West young man," but a deep, rich, historical, literary, religious, spiritual set of sensibilities. Without subscribing to any of the deterministic historical theories about the frontier, what happens when a nation has gone so far West now that it now encounters the old East? It seems that things have come full circle. To many it is highly problematic now to talk about a national purpose that can be defined only as opposed to that which is to be repudiated for the sake of the *novus*, the new.

At other times in U.S. history national purpose could enlist and even mobilize people to a declared end, supported democratically in a consensual manner. In our history as a nation that was articulated most eloquently, persuasively, and profoundly by Abraham Lincoln in the Civil War, when he talked about a nation so conceived and so dedicated.

Those are the premises on which people can be galvanized not only to a common purpose but to a common destiny—something external to our own decision making, schemes, and desires, something that engages God's providential purposes.

Never in American history has that been so compellingly articulated as by Lincoln, America's greatest public theologian. But again, it was in a time not only of crisis but in which the nation had failed the crisis facing it. It was a time in which a nation so conceived and so dedicated could not, in Aristotle's terms, deliberate about how to order its life together within the bounds of civility, but had to have recourse to arms in the bloodiest conflict in the history of this nation. But there was inspiration, there was purpose, there was something that made sense of a term like *national service*—something that answered the question, service to what?

There have been other such times in U.S. history. Woodrow Wilson envisioned making the world safe for democracy, not only, as in the constituting period, resisting the decadence and the oppressive, tyrannical forms of the old world, but going beyond that by saying that America could be the catalyst, the agent for the transformation of world historical change. We could not only make the world safe for our democracy, but make the world safe for everybody's realization of their aspirations and their approximation of the democratic idea.

It was grand and sweeping—many people think reckless—but nobody can deny its compelling character or that it illuminated a period of world historical change. People had what the sociologist Alfred Schutz called an "Aha" experience. They saw the world in a different way. The world *could* be this way; it does not have to be the old way. America was the key to it! It was wonderful, and it was morally ambiguous; and in retrospect most us have ambivalent feelings about it.

Since the 1930s other antitheses have helped us to answer the question, service to what? Fascism, national socialism, and, above all, communism have served as points of reference by which sane human beings and a minority of intellectuals perceived the great contests in the world for the last near half century.

What brought such people together? We knew there was a truly horrible alternative—a totalitarian alternative that was aggressive, articulate, and had powerful allies within the key institutions, ways of thinking, and control centers of culture and public life in the West. We knew this, and maybe we still know it. But that reality is changing, and we do not know what it will mean in terms of defining American purpose and "service to what."

There was a cold war. A large number of people who for the last 45 years denied that there ever was a cold war or that there should have been one are now congratulating and pinning medals on themselves and their buddies because we have won the cold war. This is truly a wondrous thing: veterans of a war that never was congratulating one another on their victory. But for those of us who know that there was and may still be such a war, there are many unanswered questions. Nonetheless, something major has changed.

The definition of the word *national* in national service is tied to a sense of national worth, purpose, destiny. That definition has been shaped in the past almost always in antithesis with clear and threatening alternatives mainly in the context of war.

William James talked about the "moral equivalent of war." William James is in my pantheon of intellectual and spiritual figures. He is a person not only to be respected but respected in a manner bordering on reverence. But even Homer nodded from time to time, and William James was not exempt from having his bad days.

There is no moral equivalent of war. There is war. War is the only moral equivalent of war, and we shouldn't want there to be moral equivalents of war. A long tradition in Judeo-Christian thought deals with just war. There are criteria by which, in extreme circumstances when all other resorts have been exhausted and when about five to seven classical criteria have been met, we may—reluctantly, sad-eyed, of necessity—say that war is morally justifiable.

But it is never something we would choose. There is no moral equivalent of war. We should even be suspicious of "drug wars" and "wars on poverty" and the rhetoric involved in similar campaigns. Yet what do we do when the antithesis is fudged, when it has lost its sharp edge?

In the summer of 1989 considerable discussion took place about an article in a journal, not incidentally called *National Interest,* on the end of history.[2] Leaving aside its Hegelian flights—to be a Hegelian is not necessarily a fault, but this article was somewhat excessive—there is much to be said for the argument that we have arrived at the end of history in the sense that a certain way of defining the contests that have shaped modern world historical change has come to an end.

What is wrong with the argument is that it is altogether too political a definition of reality that wants to find the meaning for human existence in political contestation. In the Judeo-Christian tradition the word for that is *idolatry.* It is salvational politics, and, unfortunately, our society, our political culture, and our religious culture are riddled with salvational politics.

Especially in this century in the United States, what have we seen but the churches taking over the business of the government and the government taking over the business of the churches. The churches taking over the business of the government is evident enough, especially among what used to be called the mainline churches, now the old-line churches, and fast becoming the sideline churches. In their view, the agenda of the world is social and political change. It is the dominant item shaping the institutional life of the churches. It is sad; it is a form of idolatry.

But the flip side of that is the move by the government to assume that its responsibility is essentially that of the churches—character formation, the transmission of the civilization's traditions, values, dreams, aspirations, and understandings of virtue, public and personal. That governmental expansion has happened in large part because there is a vacuum left by the default of institutionalized religion in American life. The expansion of this governmental ambition creates proposals such as some proposals for national service.

The questions of character formation and whether we make sense of our lives, the questions of why we are here and whether we have fulfilled or failed that purpose are the ultimate questions. The questions of politics are at best penultimate questions and most of the time prepenultimate.

The great lines of Dr. Johnson in his gloss on Goldsmith:

> How small, of all that human hearts endure,
> That part which laws or kings can cause or cure!

are followed by lines which are not as often quoted:

> Still to ourselves in every place consigned,
> Our own felicity we make or find."[3]

Salvational politics—French 1789 politics as distinct from American 1776 politics—does not believe that. The politics of 1789 wants to find salvational meaning, interest, purpose, destiny, fulfillment in the public arena in the exercise of power by some over the power or powerlessness of others.

The American experiment was radical because it said that the most important questions of life are not the government's business. The radicalism of the American proposition is that a John Adams, and even a Thomas Jefferson in his more sober and less antireligious moments, could say candidly that this whole enterprise depends on virtue and that virtue depends on religion. Having said that the whole enterprise depends on religion, they went on to say something that seems not to follow at all and seems absolutely contradictory. They said that religion is not the government's business and that the formation of virtue is not the government's business. Our constitutional order presupposes that we distinguish between the spheres of the political, precisely understood, the cultural, and the economic. The economic takes care of itself for the most part, although the government might tinker with it somewhat. We can without too much trouble define the limits of the political. But it is in the cultural sphere where people ask the meaning questions of their lives, where they form the communities of ultimate allegiance and transmit the values by which they hope to live. The cultural is a sphere that we must work at keeping distinct.

Now you may say, oh, well, yes, that is how it was originally envisioned, but that was a long time ago, not 1989; whether we like it or not, 1989 is much closer to the vision of 1789.

There is something to that. There is no doubt that the default of the cultural forces in society has created a vacuum, for which I hold two clusters of institutions primarily responsible: first, the church and second, higher education. The vacuum is in shaping culture and character, molding lives, inviting the successor generation to a grand adventure requiring high virtue, both personal and public. This vacuum will be abhorred by governmental power. Just as nature abhors a vacuum so the opportunity to exercise power abhors a vacuum. You have probably detected by now that I am modestly skeptical about proposals for national service.

Recently, in connection with another project, I was rereading William McNeill's *The Rise of the West,* which goes back through all the empires—from the Sumerian to the Egyptian to the Mogul—and all the changes—economic, mythical, and religious—finally arriving at the triumph of the West. In the vanguard of the West is the United States, for better or worse. All of this McNeill said in 1963.

There are some interesting parallels with the current discussion about the end of history and the national interest. McNeill asks at the end of his reflection, where does this leave us now? and although he does not use the Hegelian terminology, he is asking, what now is the antithesis? The Industrial Revolution and its permutations have carried the field; the democratic revolution, the democratic idea have clearly carried the field. Some of us would not have been quite that confident in 1963, but we may be modestly confident in 1989. Reasonable people now believe that the great achievements of the West have prevailed, and in what is basically a mopping-up operation, the marginal historical experiences of other people's cultures will be incorporated into the circle of the achievements of the West.

McNeill asks, what is going to happen now? Interestingly, he does answer his question. What may come now, he writes, is a "safe conservatism of routine [that] make[s] modern bureaucracy potentially capable of throttling back even the riotous upthrust of social and technical change nurtured by modern science." So even modern science and technological change will no longer, McNeill says, be the catalyst for world historical development that he thinks the West has been in the past:

> Consequently, as the corporate entities of government bureaucracies grow and mesh their activities more and more perfectly one with another, both within and among the various "sovereign" states of our time, use and wont . . . may become, bit by bit, an adequate surrogate for social theory. By sustaining an unceasing action, administrative routine may make rational definition of the goals of human striving entirely superfluous.[4]

Now this is a dour view of the future. As opposed to it, people would rather say that we need to raise up a grand vision, to get this country moving again, to have some J. F. Kennedy–like sense of a new frontier, a new adventure. Except in doing that and advancing that, would we not require precisely the deadening, bureaucratizing routine that McNeill describes as precluding the very purpose for which it would be brought into existence? What an excellent paradox that what we bring in to remedy the perceived spiritual deflation becomes the instrument of ever-deeper deflation.

I do not know how we get out of this. I believe that Dr. Johnson was right when he said that our felicity we make or find in those places to which we have been consigned in what many dismissively refer to as the private sphere. But the private sphere is public in its nature and its way of asking Aristotle's most public question, how ought we to order our lives together?

Most people answer that question in ways that are not usually perceived of as political, and yet that does not mean that the answers are not political. Politics is going on through the mediating structures—the family, the church, the neighborhood, voluntary associations, and face-to-face institutions in American life. That is the vibrant heart of the polis, and we must not believe those people who tell us that what is going on there is not political in a morally significant sense or that activity is not public unless it is governmental.

The great confusion—a confusion that goes back to the beginning of the common school movement and the repression of educational freedom in America in the nineteenth century and that became particularly manifest during the New Deal—arose when the word *public* became synonymous, in many people's minds, with *governmental.* A public school was a government school; a public purpose was a purpose governmentally defined, funded, and administered.

Public life—the vitalities, the vibrancies of human beings ordering their lives together, dealing with the res publica—is in no way synonymous with governmental life. We need to release all the energies of American life through those mediating structures that stand between the autonomous, isolated individual on the one hand and the megastructures of the society on the other hand. Such megastructures include not only government, but the control centers of the elite culture, as well as education, big business, organized labor, and others.

Those mediating institutions are where most Americans are answering the question, how ought we to order our lives together? Those are the institutions that need to be strengthened, particularly when we think about service. The Mormons' two-year mission for all their young men and women shows us that something like national service can be done within a church; it cannot be done by a nation. Religious orders did this in the past, never well, and real heroes and heroines are always rare. The church cannot produce many Mother Theresas, and there can be no international program for the manufacture of virtues like hers.

What can be done is to create a context of freedom and spheres of free discourse and vision in which human beings pursue ideas of how to live nobly together and how to serve. The institutions that can do that are failing today, but it would be a great sadness if we respond to that failure by saying, let us have recourse to the government.

When we talk about service, we are really talking about virtue, character, and morality. If you ask where we might find the sources to restore public virtue in American life, would any sane person suggest that we should go to Washington? I do not think so; and most thoughtful people in Washington do not think so either.

One thing that makes this question urgent is the development of an underclass that is predominantly black—the bottom third of black America. That is where I spent all seventeen years of my pastoral ministry.

Some of my thinking about this issue is impressionistic. In the 1960s, the war on poverty had many service corps, and I was party to expending hundreds of millions of dollars in New York City. We were often asked whether the money was being well spent and not squandered. I, like others, used to answer in a facile way that in retrospect, I am ashamed of. No, we said, we cannot account for every dollar, but what we are doing is democratizing the corruption, letting the poor in on it. That struck me as a cute answer in the late 1960s, but it gave people many wrong ideas about what it means to succeed in America and what it means to serve.

At Saint John the Evangelist, a large, black, low-income parish in Williamsburg and Bedford-Stuyvesant where I was pastor, we had summer programs, year-round programs of various sorts employing young people in various kinds of community service work. We had supervisors (volunteers to begin with) who started getting paid well.

After we had been running these programs for about two years, I began to realize that these kids were not working and many showed up only to get their checks. Some of them felt bad about it.

I talked to the regional director of this program, a fine person that I thought I could confide in. "I have been looking at this program," I said, "and I have been talking to the supervisors we have on staff here. They are worried; no significant work is being done. These kids are not really working. They are getting a false idea of what it means to work. We are doing something bad here."

She said, "Pastor, look, I don't think your supervisors should push this issue of work product because if they do that, pretty soon I am going to have to start pushing them, and somebody is going to start pushing me about it. Pretty soon this whole program won't exist any more." This seemed to suggest that the whole program operated on the premise that nobody was going to ask serious questions about work. What did this communicate to the kids? They were being told falsehoods about what it means to be a productive participant in the community.

This is anecdotal. I admit that, and I do not want to put much weight on it. Neither would I deny that it has a bearing.

We do not have a national purpose. We do not have a leadership cohort in American life capable—except in times of war—of democratically defining a national purpose that can be legitimated according to our constitutional system. There is no moral equivalent of war, and nobody wants war.

What we need is not national service but a hard look at the ways in which what was morally best in the New Deal era can now be fulfilled. That era did expand our sense of public responsibility for human need; its error was to identify public responsibility with governmental programs.

American life may be entering a period in which we can empower the institutions by which people engage in their most intense and ennobling political activity—ordering their lives together—by the government getting out of their way and also creating incentives that encourage freedom and diversity.

The purpose of America is to sustain many purposes; the purpose of national interest is to sustain many interests. This requires taking seriously what it means to be a pluralistic society and repudiating grand longings for some kind of coherent and comprehensive national consensus. Call it a civil religion, call it a governmentally defined public philosophy, by whatever name, if it is imposed across the board, it will inevitably stifle all those particular points of initiative, those mediating structures. That would be a deadly way to go, but it is the way that is at least implicit in some proposals for national service.

The other way is to exalt the diversities. Government has a role in this because government has moved into those cultural-forming vacuums created when what should have been the culture-forming institutions in our society abandoned their task. Government as well as other institutions must understand that service is altruism. We should be skeptical of service premised on incentives, for such incentives become enticements, which quickly become nearly irresistible pressures on young people to conform—pressures backed by government power.

Certainly the single most critical domestic problem in American life is the underclass in impacted urban areas such as Bedford-Stuyvesant, Williamsburg, the South Bronx, and South Chicago. In 1988 in Bedford-Stuyvesant, the largest black community in New York City, 83 percent of all the children were not simply born out of wedlock, but born without men who would publicly accept responsibility for them.

Never in human history have we witnessed a significant population in which the institution of the family, however structured, has simply collapsed, but it has happened here to a sizable population. Depending on how you count it, there are 5, 10, or 12 million American kids who not only do not have fathers, they do not know what it is to have a father—an adult male who accepts open-ended, long-term responsibility for his children. The family, that most elementary factor in the ordering of our life together, has disappeared in this population. Because this has not happened before, we do not know whether the institution of the family can be revived.

The intergenerational consequences of this are sobering, especially if you have personal involvements with these families and these children. This is the most heart-wrenching thing in American life. If there is an answer—short of a spiritual renewal, a great awakening, a movement of the spirit in our time—it is going to come through retrieving what is left of the indigenous structures of these communities. This means that the church must assume again its virtue-evoking, character-forming mission.

This will not happen, however, if to mobilize the young people of the underclass, we set aside what the Founders had in mind as a free society. I have great ambivalence about this. During the 1960s, I, along with Father Daniel Berrigan and Rabbi Abraham Joshua Heschel, headed Clergy and Laity Concerned, the largest sustaining anti–Vietnam War organization in the country at the time and indeed for about a decade. While I was at Saint John's and actively involved in civil rights as well as opposing the war in Vietnam, I was keenly aware that one of the best things that ever happened to some young men was military service.

You can imagine what the congregation and I went through. One week we held a service of turning in draft cards to protest the war, and the next week we had Donny Bradford's funeral, who came back from Vietnam a hero to the people of that community because he pulled his life together with the help of the military.

What would be required to make community service comparably effective for these Brooklyn young people in pulling their lives together, comparable, that is, to what I saw happen with young men going into the military. It would require a radical, self-conscious thorough abandonment of the idea of a free society or the conscious development of two nations, one free, the other unfree. That price is too high. But what can we do for those William Julius Wilson termed the *radically isolated.*[5] They are radically isolated from what most of us deem to be the normal channels of opportunity and obligation in American life. I do not know, but I do know that nothing can be done without revitalizing those institutions that are indigenous to those communities, beginning with the church.

Nothing can be done without the broader revitalization of those many mediating structures through which Americans have discovered their sense of unity. This sense of unity comes from their pluralism— not their conformity, not their agreements. This pluralism gives them the freedom to engage one another in disagreements and to find their ultimate felicities, which is to say their ultimate meanings, in institutions beyond the control of government. When that happens, when the mediating structures are revitalized and America discovers again that its national purpose is to sustain many purposes, then we will see a flowering of that *Novus Ordo Seclorum* that the Founders believed was their legacy to a history I am inclined to think is far from over.

NOTES

1. Ernest L. Tuveson, *Redeemer Nation: The Idea of America's Millennial Role* (Chicago: University of Chicago Press, 1968).

2. Francis Fukuyama, "The End of History?" *National Interest,* no. 16 (Summer 1989): 3–18.

3. Samuel Johnson, lines added (1763–1764) to Oliver Goldsmith, *The Traveller, or A Prospect of Society.*

4. William H. McNeill, *The Rise of the West* (Chicago: University of Chicago Press, 1963), p. 803.

5. William Julius Williams, *The Truly Disadvantaged* (Chicago: University of Chicago Press, 1987).

Discussion

Mr. Ferguson: Because we heard about incentives to encourage these institutions earlier today, I am curious about what you had in mind. Are these something the state would provide by getting out of the way?

Mr. Neuhaus: As I indicated, getting out of the way is important. When Peter Berger and I did the Mediating Structures Project [a 1976–1979 project of the American Enterprise Institute], we talked about a minimal proposition and a maximal proposition. The minimal proposition was to redesign government policies so they get out of people's way or out of the way of institutions that are important in shaping people's lives. The maximal was, can legitimate public purposes be advanced by government policies that utilize these institutions? In the four years that we had the various panels—on criminal justice, education, health, and so forth—working on this study, we became increasingly skeptical about the maximal proposition and more enthusiastic about the minimal.

That is not to say that I became a libertarian. But I did come to have a profound appreciation of how the law of unintended consequences works overtime in governmental policies. The best intentions cannot appreciate the nuances that are required for the way in which people make or find their felicities. Anybody who is going to advance what is right in the welfare state will have to humbly and modestly underscore the welfare part of it and downplay the state part of it.

Milorad M. Drachkovitch, Senior Fellow, Hoover Institution: What is your reaction to President Bush's famous vision of a "thousand points of light"?

Mr. Neuhaus: It is rhetorically valuable. I do not mean that in a demeaning sense; public discourse is to a large extent the struggle to elevate the level of rhetoric by which people understand themselves. It is an important metaphor and a valuable one. Mr. Chapman's paper says that basically it is something different from national service. That is probably the case.

Mediating structures are politically interesting. In 1976 or 1977, Joe Califano—head of Health and Human Services, then called HEW [Health, Education and Welfare], in the Carter administration—was enthusiastic about mediating structures. Studies were done, and task forces went to work. But they ran into the megastructures—particularly organized labor in the public sector and education—which cooled their ardor in short order. In the Reagan administration, there was initially much interest and discussion; I do not see any difference in the Bush administration.

Let's face it, they have perhaps one-third of it right. They have the Charles Murray side of it right, which is an important thing to get right. Charles Murray's *Losing Ground* obviously has not convinced everybody, but it was the two-by-four that made everybody look seriously at the way in which well-intended programs aimed at helping the poor, in fact made life much worse for the poor. [Charles Murray, *Losing Ground: American Social Policy, 1950–1980* (New York: Basic Books, 1984).] The administration basically got that message.

But where is the alternative? What are the policies that will free and encourage, if not use, the mediating structures? That has not been given the systematic attention it requires. I do not see it being addressed in the "thousand points of light" program of this administration. I hope that will change. But it is possible that the administration's main approach to America's chief domestic problem—namely, the radically isolated poor—will be through its drug policy. I find that worrying because it backs into the problem of the poor in a strange way without being clear about what can be done.

Mr. Moskos: Pastor Neuhaus, you began with a point of view opposed to William James and then ended up on his side. Basically you do not want the military because you do not want war, which is exactly James's position. At the same time you were ambivalent because you shared James's belief that military service shaped up men. Where you and

James have it wrong is that it is not martial values that make military service do what it does.

In a democratic society military service is a form of civic obligation. James did not understand that we do not have an army to mature young men and women; it serves other purposes. Neither should we have civilian structures to mature young men and women. Only when service is presumed in the secular civic sense does the military do the good things that you described. The question is then, to both you and James, why not have civilian structures as well as military structures that can perform that function? And the military is not a mediating structure; it is a national structure.

Mr. Neuhaus: I would agree with you on that last point. The other thing in James's defense is that there was, at the time when he said that, a certain understood cultural consensus and an elite that reinforced and effectively transmitted that consensus with regard to moral purposes— an elite that does not exist in American life today, for better and for worse.

But I do not know what can be done for the kids on Maujer Street between Grand and Bushwick avenues in Brooklyn. What is required is a community of discipline and shared purpose that would make community service something dramatically different from what [the anti-poverty service programs of the 1960s] I described earlier. But I cannot see anything doing it other than a radical regimentation and exertion of governmental police power comparable to what is the case once you have entered the military. Today this is a voluntary decision. But once you have entered the military, there are things that you are in for—in their most rigorous form in the Marine Corps—and I cannot see anybody making that decision for the kids at the Williamsburg housing project or at Saint John the Evangelist.

Are they making poor decisions about their lives? Yes, many of them are, not all of them by any means. It is important to underscore how many heroic young people are resisting the destructive siren songs that are so powerful in their communities. They have to be lifted up. That is a key thing that institutions in that community have to do.

But, no, I do not see a civilian parallel to that military experience, unless we are prepared to say, "Here is a sector of American life in which the constituting vision of a free society is now suspended." And you cannot do that with a sector of American life without doing it across the board. Even if you could, you should not do it with that sector no matter how much they are messing up their lives.

Mr. Barber: I have considerable sympathy with your argument about mediating institutions. They have been underexploited as sources of citizenship and community. But as opposed to the anarchist vision of a Nozickian cafeteria where there is no law, Aristotle was right when he said that there is a sovereign association. [Robert Nozick, *Anarchy, State and Utopia* (New York: Basic Books, 1974); Aristotle *The Politics* 1252a4-6.] The sovereign association is the state. What makes it sovereign is that it sets the rules and regulations for all those intermediate associations and allows our pluralism to function in an orderly fashion.

That sovereign association is in trouble, quite aside from what is happening in the ghettos of America. Citizenship is in trouble; national citizenship is in trouble. Only half the country votes. Many people who do not vote are poor. We cannot get people to do jury duty in many places. It is hard to constitute a sense of the democratic polity at the highest level. The people who are concerned about national service are concerned about democratic citizenship in the highest, the sovereign association. Without a democracy at that level, I do not see how your mediating structures can remain free. I do not see how this nation can retain the freedoms that are required to make those mediating institutions work. What I miss in your analysis is a concern with the maintenance of citizenship and democracy in the sovereign association. These are preconditions of freedom and pluralism.

Mr. Neuhaus: Ben Barber and I have been going around on these questions for a long time. Not having a large voter turnout is not a big problem. One could make a plausible case that this may well indicate voter satisfaction. Or it may indicate a mix of voter satisfaction and robust cynicism about not encouraging the S.O.B.'s. As the saying goes, don't vote, it only encourages them. There is something healthy, vibrant, and independent in spirit about that, which Tocqueville admired and which I admire. Jury duty is another matter. There are other reasons jury duty is failing.

Ben, you put nicely what you said about the sovereign power. But the American proposition is that the sovereign power is not the government, the sovereign power is the people, "We the people." We have a political life apart from the power of the state. Sovereignty rests outside the state. Earlier I related some of the remarkable statements of the Founders about what the whole enterprise is founded on, which is beyond the purview of the state.

The American enterprise was a radical departure from Aristotle, who saw a continuity with the gods. Despite the secularizers of Aristotle's thought, he thought not simply in terms of a utilitarian use of religion, but in terms of a metaphysical transcendent dimension in which the polis found its order in a continuum of authority.

The constituting American vision was quite different, even as captured in something like the pledge of allegiance. In 1954, Congress put the phrase *under God* in the pledge. Many people wanted it there to indicate that America is the chosen nation, exempt from corruption and the moral ambiguities of other nations. Those are poor reasons for having it there. But if one understands, as I do, that *under God* means under judgment, this nation-state, this political structure, is not finally sovereign. It is held accountable to sovereignties over which it has no control and those are borne primarily by the mediating structures in American life. They, above all, the religious institutions and the family, are the ones who speak for those sovereignties.

6

POLITICS AND NATIONAL SERVICE: A VIRUS ATTACKS THE VOLUNTEER SECTOR

Bruce Chapman

Proposals for government-operated national service, like influenza, flare up from time to time, depress the resistance of the body politic, run their course, and seem to disappear, only to mutate and afflict public life anew. Unfortunately, another epidemic may be on the way. The disease metaphor comes to mind not as an aspersion on the advocates of national service because, with good-natured patience, persistence, and seemingly relentless political invention, they mean well, but from the frustration of constantly combating the changing strains of a statist idea that one thought had been eliminated in the early 1970s, along with smallpox.

Why does the national service virus keep coming back? Perhaps because its romance is so easy to catch, commanding a nostalgic imagination and evoking times when Americans were eager to sacrifice for their country. Claiming to derive inspiration from both military experience and the social gospel—if we could only get America's wastrel youth into at least a psychic uniform we might be able to teach self-discipline again and revive the spirit of giving—it hearkens back to William James's call for a "moral equivalent of war." But at the end of the twentieth century should we be looking to war for moral guidance?

True service is one of the glories of our civilization in the West, especially in the great independent (or volunteer) sector of American society. Inspiration for service in the West comes from the Bible in parable and admonition and is constantly restated in the long historical tradition of Judeo-Christian faith. Personal service is a freewill offering to God. This is very different from performance of an obligation to government, which is a tax on time or money.

True service, then, has a spiritual basis, even for some outside the Judeo-Christian tradition per se. Fulfillment of an obligation to government, in contrast, has a contractual basis unless it is founded on an outright commitment to a coercive utopianism. Either way, it is not true service. Nor can enrollment in a government-funded self-improvement project or acceptance of a government job be called true service. Indeed, when coercion or inducements are provided, as in the various national service schemes, the spirit of service is to that degree corrupted.

In practice the service in a federal program of national service would be contaminated by governmental determination of goals, bureaucratization of procedures, and, inevitably, government insistence on further regulating the independent sector with which it contracted. National service would tend to demoralize those citizens who volunteer without expectation of financial reward and stimatize the honest labor of people whose fields were invaded by stipened and vouchered volunteers.

Government intervention is always a potential threat to the voluntary sector. When totalitarians have come to power in other Western countries, they have sought to absorb this sector, conferring official sponsorship on certain organizations and scorning others, thereby inculating in the citizenry the government's valuation even on use of free time. Although in the United States totalitarianism is not a current danger to our liberal democracy, coercive utopianism is always a legitimate concern.

Alexis de Tocqueville saw in our own early history that the genius of voluntary association was America's superior answer to the leadership energy provided in other societies by aristocracies. But government, he warned, may seek to direct the voluntary sector in the same way it erroneously seeks to control industrial undertakings:

> Once it leaves the sphere of politics to launch out on this new task, it will, even without intending this, exercise an intolerable tyranny. For a government can only dictate precise rules. It imposes the sentiments and ideas which it favors, and it is never easy to tell the difference between its advice and its commands.[1]

National service proposes to organize the voluntary sector efficiently and render it more fruitful. Can one imagine a political scheme in this field that purported to do otherwise? But is the voluntary sector so weak that it needs this unsolicited assistance? On the contrary, it is at least as robust as ever. According to the Gallup Poll, American adults contribute an average of two hours a week of service;[2] more than 23 million Americans (according to the umbrella association Independent Sector) give more than five hours a week in service.[3] Financial contributions to charity have risen 30 percent (adjusted for inflation) in the 1980s.[4]

Some volunteer sector leaders, perhaps failing to anticipate the spirit-killing cost of government paperwork and second-guessing, eagerly solicit government funding, and during the 1960s and 1970s such funding grew steadily. Interestingly, during that same period the value of private sector charitable giving was relatively stagnant. By 1980 the independent sector was relying on government contracts for more than a quarter of its funds.[5] Experts on philanthropy using the same data differ as to whether the government's share of funding in the volunteer sector shrank or remained the same thereafter. In either event, however, some administrators of volunteer associations would like to see more federal money.

But although federal contracts for services may represent an advance over governmental operation of certain programs, one has to worry about any trend that makes the independent sector more beholden to the government and thus less independent. When volunteer association leaders complain that the government cannot expect the much smaller volunteer sector to do the government's job, they must be heard. But they need to recognize in turn that the volunteer sector should avoid the temptation of accepting more and more federal funds to do the government's job. In this, national service represents the greatest peril.

Government's undue influence and controls on the volunteer service sector are especially dangerous to the country's religious institutions. The largest share of the money (46 percent)[6] and likely the largest share of service activities in the volunteer service sector come from churches and synagogues. Government cannot tread in this field except with big feet, and the ground is filled with the landmines of the separation-of-church-and-state issue. As government intervenes in the roles of religious institutions, it diminishes them. Worse, it may chose to play favorites, providing paid volunteers for the service activities of one church because its activities are considered constitutional (for example, day care) while denying them to another (for example, day care where religion is part of the schooling). "Without intending" it, in Tocqueville's phrase, the government's use of tax monies in this way can distort churches' choices, tempting them to follow the government's money rather than their own consciences.

In countries where churches receive public subsidies, faith typically is weaker than where, as in America, churches are not taxed but also are not tax supported. With the trend toward government support for the voluntary service sector, especially with prospective national service (or community service) contracts for paid volunteer programs, religion has the most to lose. Either it will find the government outbidding it with financial inducements for volunteers, or it will find the competition for government funds pitting one church or synagogue activity against another and one denomination against another, with money taken from the people as a whole. The claim, then, that a federal program of national service will be a boon for the existing volunteer sector could not be more insidious.

But the claims that national service would help solve certain practical societal problems also prove fallacious on inspection. The romantic impulse of national service is not genuinely connected to any worthy public need that cannot better be met in other less disruptive and less costly ways. To the extent that we want a highly motivated military and affordable college tuition, housing, hospital maintenance, or job training, government employment subsidies are not the most efficient or fair way to get them. If, for example, we want to support students, we might adopt the idea used in other countries of offering more scholarships based on old-fashioned scholarship rather than on the government's idea of service. Or we might provide a tax credit for working students. What we do not need to do is start a war, as it were, and then try to justify it by creating a GI Bill.

To the extent that we lack the human resources to staff menial jobs in hospitals, we should raise pay, pursue labor-saving technology, allow more legal immigration, or all of these rather than overpay high school graduates as short-term workers and thereby cause bad feelings among permanent workers who are paid lesser amounts to do the same jobs.

To the extent that we want to see the private sector as a whole expand, it makes no sense to engage a federal bureaucracy, let alone a host of little federal and local bureaucracies, to orchestrate the movement. Under such terms it is government, not the voluntary sector, that will be expanded. Douglas Besharov, Research Scholar at the American Enterprise Institute, has suggested that reducing existing government regulation of the voluntary sector, especially the liability for personal suits, would invigorate voluntary associations. Independent Sector would like an improvement in tax breaks that were reduced in 1986, such as tax deductions for nonitemizers.[7] To expand the role of service in society, government can also exhort, inform, recognize, and praise, which President Bush is doing in his Points of Light initiative.

National service is a poor answer to concrete problems, then, because it is barely cognizant of the problems themselves. Instead, government-directed national service is advanced a priori as the answer to almost any public ill, from ravaged forests to overcrowded prisons, to poverty, to illiteracy, to graffiti on buildings, to overtaxed border patrols.[8] Presented almost as a panacea, what we have in the national service cosmogony is the concept that millions of potential volunteers exist whose own problems, whatever they are, can be solved by putting them to work meeting the needs of the rest of society, whatever those needs are, and that this concatenation can occur only by the magic hand of government.

National service proponents also want us to believe that work performed by all people called *volunteers* is free. In fact, the labor of national service volunteers represents an opportunity cost, a hidden expenditure of time that could be used in other ways more useful to society, as well as to the national service volunteers themselves. For many youth, their serious career contributions would be delayed by time in government-directed service. Arguably, we already have too many older teenagers earning entry-level pay at fast-food emporia (often for pin money, not tuition) instead of studying.[9] It is a mistake born of inexperience to think that such work is ennobling, whether financed by Colonel Sanders or Uncle Sam. In Japan, with whom we must compete, students typically do not hold down jobs but concentrate on their studies.

Moreover, the national servicers propose to load down their volunteers with untaxed government stipends and postservice financial rewards. This provision, which is unfailingly coupled with a requirement that only government-approved service be funded, thus reveals national service as a disguised government jobs program like the long-abandoned Comprehensive Education and Training Act (CETA) of the 1970s or any number of its wasteful and often corrupt predecessors. National service doesn't save time or money; it squanders both.

But if the desire for national service lacks an object (if, indeed, it is a passionate desire in search of a public need), it is a desire with at least superficial political appeal. The Gallup Poll of December 1987 showed that 83 percent of the populace favored the national service concept. Because the particulars of the concept are vague and changeable, politicians can identify with national service without raising many objections, meanwhile associating themselves with warm and gushy—if indistinct—humanitarian sentiments. Backers therefore have been at pains to find political purposes worthy of such sentiments and to attach their passionate desires to them.

In the mid-1960s national service was promoted as a politically acceptable way of curing the manifest inequities of the draft by, of all things, expanding the draft. The hope was to unite supposed national service idealism with what was perceived as the grim necessity of conscripting soldiers for the armed forces. Morale would surely go up if everyone, one way or another, had to serve. This assumed, of course, that young people could not tell the difference between serving in the library at home and getting shot at overseas. Regardless, social engineers were happy to employ military conscription to fulfill their own societal designs.

Some political figures in the 1960s, such as Defense Secretary Robert S. McNamara, subscribed to the national service rationale.[10] But most leading congressmen, such as House Armed Forces committee chairman L. Mendel Rivers (D-S.C.), decided to stand by the selective service system. National service advocates were not gratified when a volunteer military proved feasible in the 1970s, thereby removing the draft as an available vehicle for national service. (Those of us who resisted national service then suspect that obligatory service for all young people is still the long-term aim of most of these national service backers). In the years after the draft ended little was heard of national service. But the germ was kept alive in sociology department equivalents of the petri dish and nurtured on a culture of foundation grants until the late 1980s, when the virus was again let loose. This time it invaded two connected public issues, the rising cost of higher education and the rising expense to the federal government of educational grants and loans. Why not keep and even expand the loans and grants, national service backers reasoned, but require some government-approved form of service from each recipient? This would give the government something in return for its money and institutionalize national service at last; moreover, military service could be combined with the program.[11]

Its backers undoubtedly hoped that this new strain of national service would prove politically contagious, infecting wide numbers of patriotic conservatives, pay-as-you-go moderates, and idealistic liberals alike. The Democratic Leadership Council (DLC), which was the locus of study on the proposal, surely thought national service might help this group gain prestige within the Democratic party and, in turn, help the party attract support within the electorate, especially among college students and their parents.

Early on, however, the drafters of the DLC proposal became aware that because many youth do not aspire to college, the national service plan could be seen as discriminatory, a way to assist well-off and upwardly mobile youth to go to college while the underclass and the working poor remained largely "under" and "working." How could youth who are not college-bound, and the sizable political constituency behind them, be attracted? Because housing costs are rising faster than college costs, why not allow national service vouchers to be used to purchase a first home? Because not all youth are thinking ahead to home ownership, why not make job training another optional use of the funds? To avoid the charge that national service would create a large, new federal bureaucracy, why not add the elderly to the program, mainly as part-time administrators? This would hold down overall costs (less pay, no retirement), put money into the pockets of senior citizens, and add yet another political constituency to the burgeoning army of supporters the national service drafters anticipated assembling.

Under the DLC plan[12] "volunteers" would plant trees, empty bedpans, tutor children, and assist librarians for one hundred dollars a week, tax free, plus medical care. With a tax-free ten thousand–dollar voucher payment at the end of each year (usable for college and so on), the volunteers would make a wage comparable to seventeen thousand to eighteen thousand dollars a year.[13] Mind you, most of those would not be college graduates, unlike Peace Corps volunteers, who presumably have good outside employment prospects and who are thus making a genuine economic sacrifice. Instead, unskilled seventeen- and eighteen-year-olds, some not even high school graduates and many saving money by living at home, would be doing better financially than civilians with the same kinds of jobs or taxpayers working for a living and perhaps supporting families. The national service volunteers entering the armed forces also would make more than regular military recruits.[14] Government not only would be showing financial preferment in this jobs program for its own chosen workers, but would be setting them up as morally superior, thanks to the misleading honorific title, *volunteer*.

The DLC plan also anticipates a complicated process by which the government would sanction some service jobs and not others; that is, bureaucrats and politicians could use public funds to support some volunteer sector activities while denying support to others, thus effectively resetting priorities in this sector. Further, the plan would regulate such activities at a level of government interference that the voluntary sector has never before seen. Some bureaucratic concerns may be legitimate, such as the desire that national service not displace existing workers, but they all entail red tape and provisions for prosecution.

It was this proposal, nonetheless, that came out of the DLC in 1988 and that Congressman Dave McCurdy (D-Okla.) and Senator Sam Nunn (D-Ga.) later introduced as the Citizenship and National Service Act. But other members of Congress were developing their own national service proposals, some entailing less of a time commitment for students to earn grant monies, others with different organizational structures, and all requiring less public funding.

Meanwhile, President George Bush had his own idea of service: it should be strictly voluntary, should involve all citizens (though emphasizing youth), and should not stake its success on government funding. His sizable White House staff supported him in developing this approach, and on the White House stage he exhibited nearly unlimited examples of successful programs of true voluntary service, the moral concept encapsulated in his "points of light." The Bush administration made it clear that although its initiative would require the initial expenditure of some $25 million for a public foundation to promote voluntary service (to be matched by $25 million in private support), it did not support the expenditure of billions of federal dollars on any coercive or bureaucratized process of government-approved service. By the summer of 1989 the White House had begun to back away from even using the term *national service* because of the divergence of approaches at opposite ends of Pennsylvania Avenue.

More discouraging to national service planners supporting the DLC bill was the political opposition from education lobbies who saw national service as a meddlesome complication of federal scholarship and loan plans. Additionally, some minority group representatives saw the bill as one more obstacle to disadvantaged youth seeking educational aid. Such opposition from normally liberal sectors of society was far more threatening politically than the Bush administration's rival proposal to mobilize unstipended volunteers or the competitor national service plans proposed on Capitol Hill. Conservative and libertarian opponents might be defeated or forced to compromise; congressmen with competitive plans could be co-opted, but opposition from some of the very quarters where national service was supposed to be most popular did not bode well. The absence of enthusiasm for the national service proposal from parents of college students or the students themselves did not bode much better.

The Pentagon was less than enthusiastic and politely but firmly testified to that lack of enthusiasm on the Hill, which dealt another blow to the political appeal of national service. The all-volunteer force is well regarded by defense officials, thanks to longer retention rates for personnel, higher educational levels for inductees, and better morale than under the old draft. The relatively small age cohort of eighteen to twenty-one-year-olds now in the population and the sustained good performance of the economy, however, have created a labor shortage in the United States, a problem exacerbated by the failure of military pay in the late 1980s to keep pace with wages in the civilian sector. Accordingly, the armed forces are having trouble meeting their recruitment quotas, and the education levels of recruits have recently dropped somewhat.[15]

National service competition with military higher-education incentive programs would make matters worse, especially because the DLC's national service plan, which offers military service as an option, would entail a shorter-than-normal enlistment commitment. Enactment of national service might ultimately help bring down the all-volunteer armed forces and bring back the draft, thus finally fulfilling the national service objective of the late 1970s—a two-year obligation for all, some in the military, others not. This might be a happy prospect for many national service backers, but not for the Pentagon or many prodefense legislators.

Finally, the deficit problem was the last straw for the DLC plan of national service. In a time of continuing public demand for deficit reductions, the Nunn-McCurdy, née DLC, bill would have added $11–$13 billion to the federal budget for a program that lacked a highly motivated constituency and that had failed to gain the support of lawmakers on its merits. Congressional support for the idea, strong on the level of generalities, tended to fade once the particulars were known.

By late spring 1989 one might have assumed that such widespread indifference and skepticism had defeated the national service virus once more. Senator Nunn, among others, set aside the original plan and began speaking of a trial demonstration project for the plan he and Congressman McCurdy backed, although it is hard to understand how a fair demonstration could be given a program whose rationale depended on some form of universality. National service seemed doomed.

Soon, however, the doughty devotees of national service concocted a formula to instill life in the demonstration project, neutralize education and minority opposition, win over liberal competitors by embracing their plans, and remove some of the Pentagon's anxieties. Crucial to this further development was Massachusetts Democrat Edward Kennedy's Senate Labor Committee, that great stove of government expansionism where many a pot of old liberal porridge is kept on the back burner until it can be brought forward and presented as nouvelle cuisine.

In this case, the new recipe for national service called for throwing everything into one kettle: the demonstration project for educational aid (recommended especially by Chefs Sam Nunn and Barbara Mikulski [D-Md.]), a similar demonstration program for youth conservation (à la Senator Christopher Dodd [D-Conn.]), a competitive grants program to states to spark youth and senior citizen volunteer projects (a Kennedy *spécialité*), a community service work-study program for students (pleasing to the palate of Senator Dale Bumpers [D-Ark.], among others), plus engorgement of the Volunteers in Service to America, Retired Senior Volunteer, Foster Grandparent, and Senior Companion programs.

Too many cooks spoil the broth. But that wisdom probably reflects the critical tastes of potential customers, and not necessarily the views of the cooks, especially if they are senators. (Of course, the House sponsors also were busy contributing ingredients to the stew.) Although the bill that resulted might be unwholesome glop, the assorted chefs were happy and the restaurant pushed the dish hard. An aroma of patronage was in the air.

The proposed National and Community Service Act, reported out of the Senate Labor Committee in July 1989, was an opportunity to organize more people in government service, not in volunteer service. Although the new omnibus bill's financial commitment is a mere $300 or so million compared with the original $11–$13 billion of the DLC plan, the original plan's incongruities threaten to grow worse under the new version. Now the double standard on employment—whereby only some menial workers, called *volunteers,* get preferential government payments—would be joined with another double standard on education, giving grants gratis to some students, while others, regardless of need, would be obliged to do service to qualify for aid. This bill is the kind of omnibus where some citizens pay to sit in the back, while others ride free up front.[16] Nonetheless, if funded by Congress, it could prove a good vehicle for a full-scale national service plan later, which is why it has the united support of the DLC plan's authors and those of other forms of national service.

But could national service in such a highly politicized and opportunistic form exert enough appeal to get adopted? The charitable and philanthropic community, even those who had confidence in the earlier national service proposal, seemed less than convinced about the omnibus bill. The Bush administration also seemed ill-disposed in the fall of 1989 to substitute any of it for the president's Points of Light initiative.

Senate Democrats nonetheless hoped to have the omnibus bill up for a vote. An extensive roll of supporters in higher education was assembled when it became clear that national service awards would *add* to the existing grants and loan programs for higher education rather than replace them. Other associations and societies and councils also lent their names. The military became silent because it no longer was included in the national service demonstration project, though the assorted stipended volunteers surely would not help military recruitment efforts. But the new bill had been poorly researched and scarcely ventilated in public, except for the original DLC plan, which persisted only in adumbrated form. The only handle national service backers had on the White House to prevent a veto, moreover, was power to stop the Bush Points of Light initiative, but this tactic might backfire politically, since that proposal had no important opposition.

Indeed, Points of Light was not a typical, me-too, scaled-down imitation of a big-spending federal program, but an independently developed plan with different ideological antecedents from those of the national service scheme. Points of Light would build on the traditional American commitment to an independent service sector and rejoice in its recent growth. The opposition of Points of Light to federal funding for programs reflected the hostility that conservatives and liberals alike feel for federal strings that go with federal money. It would not stigmatize volunteers with stipends and vouchers.[17] If this encouragement for voluntary service could prevail over the coercive designs of national service, it would be a victory for all who believed in both service and its integrity.

In late 1989, however, it seemed that even Points of Light could become objectionable if the White House gave in to congressional Democratic pressure to add to the initiative's scope or to involve the proposed independent Points of Light Foundation in brokering federal funds for volunteer sector projects. Such ambitions would open Points of Light to the national service disease and damage its political base of support.

The outcome of this particular phase in the saga of voluntary service versus national services is not yet known. The hopes of those who oppose national service were high, even though they knew that defeat of the utopian virus would not kill it. But another temporary defeat would assure that, for a while at least, millions of knee-socked national service youth performing works of supposed civic content would be mobilized only in the imagination of their progenitors and that the "moral equivalent of war" would be fought only in the sociological petri dishes of academe.

NOTES

1. Alexis de Tocqueville, *Democracy in America*, vol. 2, book 2, chap. 5, J. P. Mayer (New York: Doubleday and Co., 1969).

2. Gallup Organization (for Independent Sector), "Giving and Volunteering in the United States," 1988.

3. Brian O'Connell, "What Volunteer Activity Can and Can't Do" (Washington, D.C.: Independent Sector, 1989).

4. "Issues and Concerns," *Philanthropy*, July–August, 1989. The article analyzes new figures reported by the American Association of Fund-Raising Counsel in *Giving U.S.A.*, a publication of Independent Sector. "Adjusted for inflation,

giving during the 1980s rose by a hearty 30 percent, following a decade of hardly any growth at all."

5. O'Connell, "What Volunteer Activity Can and Can't Do."

6. Gallup, "Giving and Volunteering in the United States."

7. O'Connell, "What Volunteer Activity Can and Can't Do."

8. See, for example, Democratic Leadership Council (DLC), *Citizenship and National Service* (Washington, D.C.: DLC, 1988) and Charles C. Moskos, *A Call to Civic Service: National Service for Country and Community* (New York: The Free Press, 1988).

9. Brad Edmondson, "Harvard or Hardees?" *American Demographics* (March 1989).

10. Robert S. McNamara, speech, Montreal, Canada, May 18, 1966; cited in *New York Times*, May 19, 1966.

11. DLC, *Citizenship and National Service*.

12. Ibid.

13. Subsistence payments would total $5,200 yearly. I have valued health care at approximately $1,200 a year, a typical group rate. The $10,000 balloon payment would bring the yearly compensation package to $16,400—tax free. Charles C. Moskos's estimate is $16,500. A civilian single person would pay approximately $1,700 in federal taxes alone on that amount; adding that in, $18,100 is the approximate total value of compensation for a national service job. Add another $2,000 for a national service military job and $300 more in light of its tax-free status for a total of about $20,400 in comparable private sector income.

14. About sixteen thousand dollars, according to the U.S. Army Recruiting Office, Indianapolis, Indiana.

15. George C. Wilson, "Military Faces Shortage of Qualified Volunteers," *Washington Post*, July 29, 1989.

16. *Congressional Record*, July 27, 1989.

17. Points of Light Initiative fact sheet, the White House, Washington, D.C., June 22, 1989.

COMMENT

Amitai Etzioni

I would like to start with the question of need and suggest that every society—society not government—should worry about the balance between individual rights and the needs of the commons.

There are both logical and moral reasons for concern with the balance between rights and needs. No society can assume that an invisible hand will automatically secure a proper balance. Studies find that young people say they would like to have the right to be tried before a jury of their peers; at the same time, when they are asked if they would be willing to serve on a jury, they say—in other words—that they are busy and that some unemployed person, older person, or minority person could serve. Logically, if you want a jury of your peers and you refuse to serve, it creates a certain unbalance. If people want defense, but do not want to pay for it, you have a certain deficiency. The same is true if people want services and want to avoid taxes. Society requires that if people want rights, they have to balance them with duties. There is legitimate argument about the scope of those: some would like to have a minimal scope and some a broader scope, but nobody can deny that there is a need for balance.

On the moral side, the issue is the deficit, which is not just an economic issue but a moral issue. I sometimes think the economists are preaching to us because the technicalities are weaker than the force of the moral argument. The question is should we or should we not spend the resources of future generations? That is a fair moral question that deserves consideration.

In that context data indicate that there is a growing imbalance in the United States today compared with the 1950s. If you use the 1950s as a baseline, *The Confidence Gap* [Seymour Martin Lipset and William Schneider, *The Confidence Gap: Business, Labor, and Government in the Public Mind,* 2d ed. (Baltimore, Md.: Johns Hopkins University Press, 1987)] and many other studies suggest that there has been an increase in apathy and narcissism and a significant diminution in service to the commons. This derives not from the individualism of individuals, but rather from special interest groups and the explosion of their power in Washington and in state capitals. Every special interest claims that it is acting in the public interest.

Recently some people advanced the argument that there is no public interest, only special interests. This is the ultimate conclusion of the argument that does not even recognize the commons.

If one accepts that there is a need for a balancing and a strengthening of the commitment to the commons, national service will not answer that need. It is overselling to argue that a national service—whether a "thousand points of light" or three million people drafted to serve— would completely or even largely answer that problem. But I do suggest that certain forms of community service can make a contribution to that problem and to some others that come under the category of restoring the moral order. They will provide a shared experience across classes, agendas, and races and would render other services in the process. A good policy idea can serve several goals simultaneously and complementarily.

A community needs some measure of consensus on what its values are; they do not come to us naturally. In France, for instance, a shared school system teaches all the children the same set of values from textbooks chosen by the government, what you might call a forced consensus. In other societies the people share a joint experience. The United States in its early history had a shared frontier experience.

These days an American child born in the South or in a northern ghetto has few opportunities to develop a shared moral framework—a shared sense of values. Almost the only thing all children share is "Captain Kangaroo" and other nationwide television programs. This does not justify the government imposing a set of values, but does justify creating opportunities where people can freely come together, as they did in settling the country, to work next to each other. Shared assignments would provide opportunities for people from different backgrounds to get together in a constructive environment. The [San Francisco] Conservation Corps is a fine example of such an opportunity.

I have learned at this conference that it is not productive to talk about community service as if there were only one kind. Some I find increasingly objectionable, but I have not heard a compelling argument against the other kind.

Those who confuse tricycles and tanks and then suggest that we do not need community service do not deserve credit for their confusion. The tricycles are those fine people who give two hours a week reading for the blind; they are useful and should be encouraged. But they are different from people in the conservation corps who spend 50 weeks up in the Sierra together in a total environment. These things are radically different.

A serious challenge has been raised about the cost. Two points should be made. First, the incentives here [in the Nunn-McCurdy bill] are, in my judgment, too high. It robs service of its content, of its opportunity to sacrifice, if you say that you will do something for your community if you are highly paid. I would like to say to my liberal friends that they should not overload the program with other goals because this will destroy the program and not serve their goals. If we want to reallocate wealth—if that is the purpose of a high monetary reward here—I think it will not serve either this goal or the program. The program should be one of service, not redistribution.

The other thing I do not believe in is coercion. There might be a way of minimizing coercion—you cannot avoid it completely—if the program were run not by a government corporation, but by a coalition of existing volunteer associations.

During the year I spent in the government, 250,000 Cubans suddenly decided to move to the United States. Nobody was prepared. Victor Palmieri [U.S. coordinator of refugee affairs in the State Department, 1979–1981] proposed another bureaucracy to aid in their resettlement. I suggested that we call in the three main religions—the Catholic Charities, the National Council of Churches, and the American Jewish Congress—and the Salvation Army, and create a National Emergency Coalition and turn the problem over to it. I asked the leaders of all those associations, and for their own reasons, they were delighted.

That was a different situation. Emergencies make the juices flow better than routine work does. But I have heard no single reason why we could not turn service over to a national coalition. Most questions about who would be qualified for public funding could be handled by requiring matching funds: if you can raise matching funds then you can participate in the national coalition. There might be some other limitations: separation of church and state, of course, and no political organizations. Otherwise any voluntary organization that either raises matching funds—or, for those who do not have money, matching volunteers— could participate. I do not see why national service could not be run by such a coalition. And what service was to be performed would be determined by the local community. In short, where there is less rhetorical posturing and more willingness to look at the genuine need, a program can be designed that will answer many of the fair objections that have been raised.

You should not ignore the opportunity costs. As Peter [Szanton] said, you should study the opportunity costs, but that does not automatically mean the costs will be too high for the program to qualify. One opportunity cost that could be cut into is the large amount of television watching that is done by the group we are targeting: from six hours a day to perhaps five. That is an opportunity cost that we could survive. We can argue about other activities. I could accept people working less for McDonald's and more for the conservation corps. Each community should make the judgment. But I do not think the term *opportunity costs* should be a conversation stopper.

As to the military, I am happy to hear that they are having second thoughts about national service. If you take kids from either the cozy suburbs or from the crack neighborhoods and put them for a year in the conservation corps, they would make better soldiers. I would think this consideration would not be lost on the military. If that necessitates paying someone more to go into the military, that is another cost that should be calculated.

DISCUSSION

Kim Grose, Stanford undergraduate: I have a question for all of you on the panel. When was the last time any of you asked young persons what they thought of national service or what their values were? What are their thoughts on serving? We have talked in the last day and this morning about values, education, a military draft, bureaucracy, and economics. We are missing one crucial point: namely, what do young people want? This issue is not like child care where the parents have to make the decision because the three-year-old does not know what he or she wants. We are voters. We have opinions. It is important to include us in whatever debate is going on on this issue.

Mr. Henderson: First, of all, Kim, touché; I have never asked, I will admit that right up front. Because of the importance of asking people, I want to emphasize that everyone here has agreed that whatever emerges (I am hoping it is nothing) should be voluntary not in the sense of the funding—Milton [Friedman] is right on that—but in the sense that no one will be sent to prison who does not go along. The ultimate in not asking people is to impose a system—even if many students want it—where you send those who do not go along to prison.

Mr. McCloskey: I would like to respond to the question because in 1979 I had a national service bill in Congress. It provided four alternatives: If you enlisted in the regular armed forces for two years, you got four years of college benefits. If you enlisted in the reserves for six months, you got one year of college benefits. If you volunteered for civilian service in your local community, you received no benefits. If you did not volunteer for anything, you went into the draft pool, where you were available for service in the event the army did not get the 400,000 people it needed and the reserve did not get its 400,000.

Mr. Bandow: Then you went to jail.

Mr. Henderson: For up to two years.

Mr. McCloskey: If you did not opt for any of those, you would come under the *Holmes* case, which went to the Supreme Court, that said that to preserve the morale of the military, you could be required to do some civilian service. [*United States v. Holmes,* 387 F.2nd 781 (1968). Certiorari to the U.S. Supreme Court denied, 391 U.S. 9361 (1968)].

We took a poll in two successive classes of Washington Workshops, which were made up of groups of about 400 students who were in the top 10 percent of their high school classes who came to Washington for two weeks. Forty-five percent of those kids said they would volunteer for two years in the military, some clearly to get the college benefits. Only 10 percent said they would volunteer for the reserve. Forty percent said they would volunteer for the civilian service, and only 5 percent said they wanted to go into the draft pool. Most said they wanted to volunteer. But 55 percent, including women, said they were willing to go into the military. Since 1979, I have never found that to change. As a rule, young people want to serve.

Mr. Etzioni: Yes, you and other young people should be asked. The polls cover young people, but there should be other mechanisms. But some people here are kidding you to suggest that everything we do should depend on the veto of the young. Certain things are of merit and should be done. I would not coerce anyone to participate in national service. But as a parent I would set forth certain things as right. Then I would try to convince the young that they should avail themselves of that opportunity. I would not give them complete veto power over everything that we should do. It would be inappropriate.

Mr. Anderson: Your [Ms. Grose's] question is interesting, and everybody should be embarrassed that we have not asked it. The last time I recall that it was asked directly and discussed with a representative cross-section of youth was when Don Eberly and I were at the White House Conference on Youth in 1971 in Estes Park, Colorado. If I recall correctly, after serious discussion for a number of days, the idea was rejected. [See *Report of the White House Conference on Youth,* April 18–22, 1971, Estes Park, Colorado (Washington, D.C.: Government Printing Office, 1971), pp. 25–28.]

Mr. Eberly: Personally, the answer [to Ms. Grose's question] is yesterday.

At the Estes Park, Colorado, conference there were ten panels. Out of the ten panels, five of them, in their respective ways, endorsed resolutions supportive of national service. The education panel, for instance, supported service learning. Coming out of the environmental panel, there was support for a conservation corps. I was on the draft panel; as I recall there was a one- or two-vote margin after a heated debate. You may be right as how that particular vote came out. But half of those ten panels supported the kind of national service most of us are talking about today. ["Youth Conference Supports National Service Concept," *National Service Newsletter,* no. 18 (May 1971), p. 2.]

The final piece of good news in reply to Kim is that we are going to get better data than we have had before because the Gallup people did a survey this last summer that asked detailed questions about national service. [See "Surveys Show Strong Teenage Interest in Civilian Service as Full-Time Service Openings Grow Slowly," *National Service Newsletter,* no. 55 (October 1989), p. 2; "Surveys of the Attitudes of Teen-agers Towards National Service Proposals," press briefing presented as background to the September 21, 1989 remarks of Robert Bezilla, director of the Gallup Youth Survey. Issued by the George H. Gallup International Foundation, 100 Palmer Square, Princeton, NJ 08542.]

The results will be announced September 21 at the East Coast national service conference being sponsored by the American Veterans Committee and a dozen other groups. ["Dialogue on National Service," Washington, D.C., September 21–22, 1989.]

Mr. Barber: One reason that I have advocated school-based and college-based programs of service, whether mandatory or voluntary, is that students can be brought into the process of planning whatever programs are developed. In answer to your [Ms. Grose's] question, I spent last year talking to about 150 students from Rutgers University who were planning the current program. Campus Compact and COOL [Campus Outreach Opportunity League]—two organizations that are made up primarily of students and schools and colleges that are interested—also have been doing this.

Mr. Wycliff: I wanted to ask Mr. Chapman: Are your objections simply to a federal service program or would you also object to local and state programs?

Mr. Chapman: I would oppose a federal program, especially a coercive federal program. I am agnostic on local programs. There are some good programs even at the federal level that operate on a temporary basis. For example, the enormous summer intern programs in the federal government, some of which involve conservation, are terrific. I do not know enough about the California situation to comment. The question of inducements—whether there is really a sacrifice involved— is important. The question of coercion is decisive. You do not have to worry about coercion at the local and state levels.

   We have four young interns working at the Hudson Institute, and I vetted this paper and another paper on this subject with them. Of course, speaking to a few young people does not mean speaking to all young people. It might be useful if there were a national conference or local conferences where young people could get together to discuss this. When they do, I hope they will distinguish between the different kinds of programs—whether they are coercive programs, whether they have financial inducements, or whether they are the sort of general service projects that we all support.

Mr. Friedman: I find Mr. Etzioni's comments tantalizing. I agree with almost all of them, and yet every now and then he goes off the track. I agree fully that you cannot give any one group, whether it be the young, the old, or the in-between, a veto power over what society should do. We do have parental functions; we do have community functions. On the other hand, he talks about opportunity costs as if the only opportunity costs are the costs to the people who voluntarily choose the more attractive jobs offered to them under so-called voluntary service.

   I did not hear anything about the opportunity costs to the people who provide the money. I did not hear anything about what the taxpayers might do if they could spend the corresponding amount of money according to their values instead of according to your values. That is the question you have to face.

   You say you do not object to sacrificing television. Neither do I, but perhaps other people do not agree. Who am I to tell them how to spend their time? The same thing goes for you. You say you do not mind sacrificing McDonald's. That is not a problem for you and me to decide. That is a problem for the people who eat at McDonald's, or the people who work at McDonald's, or the parents who pay for the McDonald's hamburger. Throughout this you have a double standard.

I agree that it is desirable to develop a sense of community. No society can exist without shared values. The question is, how do those shared values come about, and how do you preserve a society that has shared values?

To preserve a community with shared values, do not stretch those shared values too far. The less consensus you require, the more room you provide for diversity and individuality and the less likely you are to get terrible disputes within the community. The single most important argument for limited government and primarily voluntary market arrangements is that they minimize the area over which values must be shared for a community to live together in peace.

There is a law of conservation of common values: Every time you try to impose another program on society, you impose something to which a group objects. That is what happened with the draft. The young objected, and I do not blame them. They were right; the older people were trying to reduce their burden by imposing it on the young. The same thing is true with our subsidization of higher education. We impose costs on the poor to send the children of the rich and the middle class—my children, your children—to school.

There was not a single thing you said about opportunities that required the government to enter into this. The Boy Scouts of America, which is comparable to what we had in the Civilian Conservation Corps, was established without any government money. The Boys' Clubs were established without any government money. On what grounds do you think that government money is an essential ingredient? Not only government money, but government decisions about who should qualify? How can you justify that interference in the lives of people?

Mr. Etzioni: We have been hearing for two days and for the last 50 years that the market is voluntary. It is time for those of us who see things differently to get a minute. The voluntariness of the market is like the majestic equality of the law, which, as Anatole France pointed out, forbids the rich and poor alike to sleep under bridges; it is just that one of them does not need to do it often. The market is "voluntary"? General Motors recently told its suppliers that next year they will be able to increase their charges by N percent; if they do not like it, they can go fly a kite. There are several thousand small suppliers for whom General Motors is their only outlet. In the free market that some dream about— but that has never existed historically—where, every unit is small and truly competitive, some of those virtues may be realized. In American society, there is little voluntary about the market. It is full of powerful units screwing their victims.

As to imposing the program, to bring up the draft in this context is not fair. I do not want to impose anything on anybody. Why do I have to keep answering questions on imposing service?

As to the taxpayers, it never ceases to startle me; economists are willing for everyone to choose in the marketplace what they want, but not what government service they want. You have the right to buy a can of beans—some people even say illicit drugs—but do you not have a right to vote for the public services you want? The government buys the things the people want it to buy. If the people want to pay for public service, that is their right.

Finally, I agree that there is a danger of stretching the commonality too far. But it is my considered judgment that the commonality is so thin that it desperately needs reinforcement. Therefore, I think American citizens are wise when 83 percent of them are willing to allot their hard-earned dollars to programs that—if properly designed and carried out by voluntary associations—could strengthen the moral fiber of the young and the old. I recognize the right of taxpayers to vote on how they want to spend their money. In response to that, the government should allocate some money to volunteer activities. If Boy Scouts and Girl Scouts did their job, we would not need it, but they do not.

Mr. Friedman: I agree that the market is not fully voluntary. There are great imperfections. But do you really think that the taxpayers as a whole vote to have the price of sugar three times as high in the United States as in the rest of the world? Do you really think that the taxpayers vote to keep prices of agricultural products high and subsidize producers up to twice their net income? I could go down the list.

The problem is that you have government failures as well as market failures. The problem with the government system is that you vote for a package. You talk as if you think you are going to be able to get to vote on your particular project. The government system of voting is an unfortunate necessity, but you cannot pick and choose. The great virtue of the market is that you can pick and choose and vote for each item separately. Of course, it is an imperfect world. The market is imperfect, but the government is more imperfect.

This is not a market economy. Government spending is 45 percent of total national income. There are federal, state, and local controls way beyond that—immigration controls, the tariff, minimum wages and hours. Half the economy is government controlled. Moreover, most of the worst features of the government-controlled economy were pro-

moted by businessmen. I have said over and over that the greatest
enemies of the free market are businessmen on one hand and my fellow
intellectuals on the other. You talked about General Motors. Do you
think that the voters voted that General Motors and its fellow domestic
automakers should be able to induce the government to impose an
embargo on Japanese cars? Was that my vote? Your vote? The consumer's
vote? Let's not kid ourselves.

Now let me go one step further. This has to do with the future.
Suppose you, Mr. Etzioni, or your friends could get the program
adopted that you think is perfect. I guarantee you that within five years
you would be opposed to it.

Why? Because every time a pot of money is put there by well-
intentioned people for well-intended purposes, less well-intentioned
people come into the arena. They grab the pot and use it for purposes
that you and I would object to strenuously. That happened when irate
consumers decided that the railroads were charging too high prices.
They formed the ICC; the railroad industry took it over. You can go
down the line with every government program. If each of you separately
got the program you wanted enacted tomorrow, you would end up
getting the opposite.

Once at the end of a *Newsweek* column dealing with the law of
unintended consequences—the fact that government programs generally produced the opposite of what was intended—I asked for people to
suggest a name for that law. One suggestion came from a fellow who
was then a professor of economics and is now a member of Congress. It
was "the invisible foot of government." [laughter]

Mr. Etzioni: I agree that the market is full of failures and that the
government is full of failures. None of them is perfect. But I do not
accept the proposition that all government programs get perverted.
Head Start has done well, and I can list others. We should not blindly
say that just because all too often government programs get perverted,
we cannot consider a new policy. We have to go back to examining each
program on its own merits. We should take special pains to build in
protective mechanisms to reduce the ease with which they get perverted.
That is why I suggested that voluntary associations—a sector that needs
strengthening—run the program. That is why I suggested local decision
making. I am happy to have a law that sunsets [automatically repeals]
national service after five or ten years if it is not successful. We should
not stop all consideration of new policy ideas because some government
programs get perverted.

Finally, if we were concerned only with the market and nothing else,

I still would argue for this particular policy because the market rests on a moral community. It is not self-sustaining; it requires respect for a set of values and for the rules of the game. Those are not borne by the Boy Scouts either. Anything we can do to strengthen the moral community is in the end beneficial for the market.

7

CIVILIAN SERVICE AND MILITARY SERVICE: HOW WELL MIGHT THEY MESH?

Sue E. Berryman

INTRODUCTION

Finding powerful and persuasive arguments on both sides of the national service issue, my main objective in this chapter is to urge those on both sides of the debate to look empirically, not ideologically, at the behavior of institutions and individuals. The success of a national service program—whatever the version—will depend partly on the fit between its objectives and those of the institutions (in this case, the military) with which it interacts and through which it must operate.

I am not arguing that national service should (or should not) include military service. If a national service program does include military service, however, the fit between the objectives of that program and military service becomes an issue. Three deeply rooted characteristics of military service thus pose both a threat and an opportunity for national service:

- The historic role of the military in transforming the status of those who have served when they return to the larger civilian society
- The historic recruitment patterns of the enlisted force—the segments of the society from which it traditionally draws

- The historical influence of the political process on military personnel policy

The opportunity lies in designing a national service that takes advantage of military traditions; the threat lies in ignoring these traditions, thus imperiling the national service–military institutional relationship.

Military Service as a Status Transformer

If one objective of national service is to confer political, social, and adult legitimacy on young people, then the national service version of military service must respect the grounds on which the military confers this legitimacy.

The U.S. military trains young people, employs them, and matches the money that enlistees spend on schooling; by providing these opportunities, it echoes private sector employers or major domestic youth programs, such as the Job Training Partnership Act and postsecondary school financial aid programs. However, military service is unique in offering opportunities that are best thought of as status transformations—changes that provide legitimation for a young person's political, social, and adult statuses.

Specifically, the military

- *Transforms boys into men.* This theme appears in early enlistment advertisements such as Join the Army, Be a Man; The Army Will Make a Man out of You; or the Marine Corps' We Take Only a Few Good Men.[1] Several characteristics of military service reinforce this image. The enlisted force relies heavily on individuals from youth to adulthood. As an institution, the military controls raw "masculine" power. Although only about 15 percent of today's military jobs are combat jobs, the military role is still seen as that of a warrior. Enlistment standards stress physical fitness, and the rigors of basic training echo the hardship rituals associated with the manhood rites of passage of many tribes and social groups.
- *Enfranchises the politically disenfranchised.* As Theodore Roosevelt noted, "Universal service and universal suffrage go hand in hand."[2] Ever since the Republic was founded, especially during times of war, the U.S. government has offered citizenship in exchange for military service. As James Jacobs and Leslie Hayes point out, "The idea that one who fights for the United States is entitled to become a citizen is deeply embedded in our traditions. Millions of immi-

grants have entered the societal mainstream, legally and socially, by serving in the armed forces."[3] From 1945 to 1977, 3.9 million persons were naturalized. Of these, about 190,000, or 5 percent, achieved naturalization on the basis of military service. In sum, as Mark Eitelberg notes, "entry into the American melting pot has first meant proven loyalty, sacrifice, and, frequently, some price-in-blood."[4] Michael Novak observes that "it is no accident that acceptance into the society has been preceded by large losses on the battlefield—the Irish in the Civil War; the Poles, in World War I; the blacks, in Vietnam."[5] It is also no accident that Congress lowered the voting age to eighteen at the end of the Vietnam War.

• *Provides a legitimate career for those from groups with marginal social and economic positions.* The military not only enfranchises politically, but also integrates socially and economically. The social reputation of the military varies, increasing during popular wars and declining during peacetime and unpopular wars. In general, however, military service represents a legitimate and sometimes highly honored occupation. Its legitimacy arises from its basic function, defense of the nation; its potential honor, from the possibility that its members will give their lives for the common good. The military's concentrated, raw power reinforces its status, as does the fact that some military activities can be transformed into respectable civilian careers.[6] John Butler thus describes military service for blacks: "Within the black community military participation has consistently enjoyed a certain amount of prestige. During the days of complete forced segregation, the military occupation, along with service occupations, teachers, and ministers, were significant positive role models for youth. Within households the picture of a 'son in uniform' indicated that he was doing well. He and his family were enjoying a quality of life unknown to the great majority of black Americans."[7]

• *Transforms provincials into nationals.* Individuals from diverse local and regional traditions are exposed to common experiences in a national institution.

• *Provides a legitimate moratorium.* The major alternatives for young people who leave high school are civilian work or college. Military service represents a legitimate activity outside these two options. As such, it provides a socially acceptable and productive niche for those who are not yet prepared to make the choice between work and college.

The power of military service to confer political, social, and adult legitimacy on its members rests on an implicit contract between the individual, the armed forces, and the society. The military's legitimating function is contingent on the military person *giving to the nation*. Specifically, the contract presumes that the military person (1) contributes to, not takes from, the institution, as in financial aid and other youth welfare programs, (2) contributes to a higher good (the nation), and (3) offers to the nation the most priceless gift (human life). National service can confer legitimacy on young people only if the national service version of military service fulfills these conditions.

Historic Recruitment Patterns

If supporters of national service want military service to integrate socially marginal youth into the mainstream society, they will be limited by the military's historic recruitment patterns. Even in World War I, but especially from World War II through the Vietnam War and the All Volunteer Force (AVF) years, the military has kept the most disadvantaged out of its ranks. Deeply entrenched recruitment patterns for the military's enlisted force have prevailed across centuries, in war and peace, and under volunteer and draft conditions, but are not widely understood. More selective when composed entirely of volunteers and less representative under a draft than many assume, the military draws in a fairly consistent way from the upper-lower and lower middle classes.

First, I will describe these patterns for the current enlisted force, the AVF; second, for volunteer forces of the nineteenth and early twentieth centuries; and, third, for draft forces in the Civil War, World Wars I and II, and the period from 1947 to 1973.

The All Volunteer Force

To assess the composition of the AVF, I used the 1979 National Longitudinal Survey of Labor Force Behavior, Youth Survey (1979 NLS), which sampled youth between the ages of fourteen and twenty-one in the civilian and military sectors, thus making it possible to compare active duty enlistees with their nonmilitary age mates. This survey covers a period when the military unintentionally violated its own enlistment standards in that young enlistees in the survey entered military service under miscalibrated versions of the Armed Services Vocational Aptitude Battery (ASVAB).[8] Because the Armed Forces Qualifying Test (AFQT) measurement failure allowed individuals who would have been ineligible under a properly calibrated test to enlist, the survey's military sample has a larger share of those from the lower end of the youth talent distribution than the enlistment standards intended.

I classified male respondents between the ages of seventeen and twenty-two by their main activities at the time of the 1979 NLS interview: in the military, on unemployment in the full-time civilian labor force, in a two-year college, or in a four-year college.[9] The data incontestably show that the enlistees did not come from the most marginal groups on any of three dimensions: family socioeconomic status,[10] measured verbal and quantitative abilities, and educational achievements. For this period, then, the military was not an employer of last resort for those who enlisted, even though this was a period when enlistment standards were inadvertently violated.

For each measure of parental socioeconomic status, youths in four-year colleges came from families with the highest status scores, followed by those in two-year colleges. Families of those in two-year colleges had higher scores than those in the military, who, in turn, came from families with higher scores than youth employed fulltime in the civilian labor force. Unemployed youth came from families with the lowest socioeconomic status scores. Thus, on average, the military drew from families with a higher average socioeconomic status than did civilian employers. For blacks and Hispanics in the enlisted force, the military moves up in rank order.[11] For each measure of parental socioeconomic status, youths in four-year colleges again came from families with the highest status scores. They were followed by two groups who tied for family status scores: those in two-year colleges and the military. Families of those in two-year colleges and in the military had higher scores than those of youth employed full-time in the civilian labor force. Unemployed youth came from families with the lowest socioeconomic status scores. For blacks and Hispanics, then, the military and two-year colleges were drawing from socioeconomically similar families.

Measures of verbal and quantitative abilities and educational attainment show similar results. White enlistees and the white civilian youth population had about the same median AFQT scores and percentage scoring AFQT 50 and above. Although the 1980 male white population had a somewhat higher percentage of high-scoring members than the white male enlistee group (46.5 versus 38.9 percent in AFQT categories I and II), it also had a higher percentage of low-scoring members than the military accepted (22.4 versus 13.9 percent in AFQT categories IV and V).

Black and Hispanic enlistees' median scores were almost double those of the black and Hispanic civilian youth populations, and more of the enlistees scored AFQT 50 or above. Black and Hispanic male enlistees had about the same percentage of high-scoring individuals as black and Hispanic male civilian youth (9.3 versus 7.5 percent in categories I and II for blacks; 15 versus 17.2 percent for Hispanics). The military, however, accepted a much smaller percentage of low-scoring males than existed in the total population (45.8 versus 72.8 percent in categories IV and V for blacks and 36 versus 55.6 percent for Hispanics).

The educational attainments of enlistees were about the same as those of their counterparts in the full-time civilian labor force and higher than the other out-of-school groups. Black and Hispanic enlistees had higher average educational attainments than their racial and ethnic counterparts in all other out-of-school groups. Relative to the other out-of-school groups, the active duty military group had a smaller percentage of high school dropouts. The rate even for males in the full-time civilian labor force was about double. The military group also had a smaller percentage of those with one or more years of college.

Another way of learning where the military got its enlistees in the 1970s is to look at enlistees' pre-enlistment participation in federal youth programs. The 1979 NLS asked respondents if they had participated in any federally sponsored training and job programs such as the Comprehensive Employment and Training Act (CETA) Summer Program, In-School Work Experience, Job Opportunities in the Business Sector, Public Service Employment, CETA training, Job Corps, or Jobs for Progress (all of which are often seen as welfare programs and their participants as coming from the bottom part of the social structure). Although this participation was originally used as an indicator of socioeconomic status, it also has implications for how different racial, ethnic, and socioeconomic groups might interact with a voluntary national service program if it is perceived as a training and employment program.

Enlistees' participation rates were second only to those of unemployed youth. These data seemed to imply that the military was drawing from the least employable of the youth cohort; however, further analyses showed that participation in government training and job programs was distributed more broadly across the youth cohort than one might expect. For whites, one in ten active duty military youth versus one in twenty four-year college enrollees had participated in such programs. For black and Hispanic youth, the military and four-year college groups had smaller differences in rates of participation: for blacks, 4.5 of every 10 members of the AVF versus 3.4 of every 10 enrollees in four-year colleges; for Hispanics, 3.1 of every 10 members of the AVF versus 2.5 of every 10 enrollees in four-year colleges.

Using father's occupation, father's education, mother's education, and reading in the home to measure socioeconomic status, I found that participation in federal job and training programs had penetrated the higher socioeconomic families, especially in the black and Hispanic communities. For white youth, participation decreased as family socio-economic status increased, but participation was still at about 10 percent (the rate for whites in the military) in the middle ranges of all four socioeconomic status indicators. For black youth, participation was fairly evenly distributed across different levels of father's education, father's occupation, and mother's education, but increased as reading in the home scores increased. For Hispanic youth, participation declined some-what as family socioeconomic status increased. Differences in rates of participation between lower and higher socioeconomic levels, however, were not as pronounced as for whites.

In sum, family socioeconomic status and participation in federal youth programs were negatively related, but the relationship was not as strong as generally presumed, especially for black youth. Thus, partici-pation did not necessarily signal a family at the bottom of the nation's socioeconomic distribution. In conjunction with other data about AVF youth, these participation data may indicate that upwardly mobile indi-viduals are making use of opportunities.

The Nineteenth- and Early Twentieth-Century Volunteer Enlisted Forces

Just as popular images of the AVF's social composition seem to have been distorted, historical images of volunteer enlisted forces have rarely been accurate. The U.S. military has been more selective under volun-teer conditions than commonly presumed.

Compositional images. Before and after the Civil War the officer corps commanded social esteem, but the enlisted forces had negative social images. For example, Tocqueville's countryman Guillaume Tell Poussin concluded that "The [American] recruits are generally men, who, as laborers and mechanics [would] receive much higher compen-sation than in the military service. They must, therefore, be infected with some moral infirmity, which renders them unfit for a useful and laborious life."[12] The image of the post–Civil War regular army was not much better.[13]

Are these views of the nineteenth-century enlisted forces valid? For the answer, let us look at some social facts. First, nineteenth-century soldiering was physically demanding and relatively unskilled, but so were the majority of jobs in nineteenth-century America. Second, since the founding of the Republic, Americans have distrusted the centralized power inherent in a regular standing army; for example, in the late eighteenth and nineteenth centuries they preferred militias under the control of the states. Distrust of an institution biases people against its members. Third, the peacetime U.S. military image has always suffered, public esteem varying in direct proportion to the geographic or temporal proximity of hostilities.[14]

Fourth, those who recorded impressions of our nineteenth-century enlisted forces were literate, which placed them at least in the middle and more likely in the upper-middle and upper classes. The U.S. military has always reproduced the class structure of the larger society: the officer corps represents the professional and managerial classes; the enlisted force, the low-level white-collar, blue-collar, and laboring classes. The differential regard accorded the officer corps and enlisted forces may say less about the quality of the enlisted force than it does about the compatibility of status between those who wrote about the U.S. military and the officer corps as opposed to the enlisted force.

Compositional realities. How did the nineteenth-century peacetime enlisted forces differ from the nation's rank and file? The statistics support the image of the peacetime enlisted forces as disproportionately foreign born. In 1850 about 10 percent of the country's male population was foreign born; from 1860 to 1900, that figure went to about 15 percent.[15] From the 1820s to the 1880s, however, 25 to 70 percent of the army was foreign born, averaging at least 50 percent during the peacetime periods between 1840 and the mid-1870s. For example, of the five thousand recruits who entered the service in 1850–1851, 70 percent were born in Europe; about 60 percent of those came from Ireland, 20 percent from Germany, and 12 percent from England and Scotland.[16] Blacks, representing a declining percent of the population across the century (18 percent in 1820, 12 percent by 1990),[17] were substantially underrepresented in the military.[18]

Thus, during the nineteenth century military service attracted those trying to enter the mainstream more than those already in it. To judge the quality of those in the military, however, we need to compare their educational attainments with those of the larger society, their occupational skills with those of the civilian labor force, and their wages with the wages of the civilian labor force.

Let us look first at education. We can assume that members of the enlisted force were less educated than the average native-born white male. Then, as now, the military was a two-class system, but much more then than today, enlisted military jobs were primarily laborer and blue-collar jobs. Any reasonably efficient allocation of human capital would not staff the enlisted forces with the more-educated classes. Thus the educational levels of the nineteenth-century enlisted forces were probably somewhat below those of the rank-and-file, white, native-born population. The large percentage of foreign born suggests higher rates of illiteracy in English or in any language. Comparative data for 1850 indicate that Germany and the United States had about the same ratio of students to the total population. Other countries that supplied large numbers of recruits to the U.S. military, however, had lower rates, especially Ireland.[19] If foreign-born recruits spent their school years in their countries of birth, those from certain countries had fewer chances of attaining the educational levels of their counterparts in the United States.

If the nineteenth-century enlisted forces had limited education, then so did the nineteenth-century U.S. population. Although no reliable estimates exist of the population's educational attainment for specific dates before 1910,[20] in 1870 the U.S. Office of Education estimated that 2 percent of all seventeen-year-olds were high school graduates.[21] More recent data on educational attainment indicate that almost 30 percent of the cohort born no later than 1855 had four or fewer years of school and almost 10 percent were high school graduates with a median of 7.9 years of education.[22]

In sum, for much of the nineteenth century large percentages of the civilian population had little schooling. Although the immigrant contingent in the enlisted forces probably had less education than their white, native-born and blue-collar civilian counterparts, the educational differences between the two groups were probably not great.

Although nineteenth-century recruits were usually described as unskilled, the civilian labor force was not particularly skilled. Farmer and farm laborer occupations predominated in the civilian labor force for much of the century, representing 72 percent of the civilian male workers in 1820, 64 percent in 1850, 49 percent in 1880, and 38 percent in 1900.[23] As late as 1900 only 18 percent of the civilian labor force had white-collar occupations.[24]

The final indicator of quality is wages. Several nineteenth-century observers inferred on the basis of the military's low pay that anyone who enlisted at such rates must be of low quality—unemployable, dissolute, or worse (see the Poussin quote, above). I argue, however, that the pay issue—and what it implies for enlistee quality—must be interpreted in the context of the nineteenth-century economy. Specifically, after the Civil War,

- Military pay was no worse than civilian pay in some of the large blue-collar and farm laborer occupational categories.
- Military pay has to be interpreted relative to the availability and stability of civilian jobs that paid higher wages.

• The high immigrant make-up of the armed forces could have affected the relationship between wages and manpower quality.

There are no statistics that let us compare pre–Civil War military wages and allowances with the average annual earnings of different civilian occupations, although foreign observers commented on the discrepancy between an enlisted man's five dollars a month and a civilian laborer's one dollar a day.[25] These comments, however, neither consider military allowances nor compare the *annual* earnings of enlistees and civilian laborers. Civilian wage earners often did not have steady work, and their wage rates reflect the expected duration of their employment. Thus, from 1832 to 1860 civilian laborers employed by the day earned from 35 to 55 percent more per day than laborers employed on a monthly basis.[26]

The other wage data available for the nineteenth century—for 1865 and 1898—show that enlistees' annual pay was probably higher than that of farm laborers.[27] When we recall that in 1870 some 30 percent of the total male civilian labor force were farm laborers, military service may have been less unattractive economically than observers would have us believe. Comparing the 1898 annual wages for selected industries and occupations, including military service,[28] shows that enlistees received higher annual pay than manufacturing workers, bituminous coal miners, farm laborers, or public school teachers. (These first three occupations comprised 36 percent of the male civilian labor force in 1900.)[29] In sum, enlisted service was not a highly paid occupation; however, these fragmentary data suggest that enlistees were as well, if not better paid, than a substantial portion of the civilian labor force.

Military wages also have to be assessed relative to the availability and steadiness of civilian jobs, which nineteenth-century observers did not do when they talked about higher civilian wages. Unemployment levels were generally higher in the nineteenth century than in the twentieth as a result of labor market imperfections and seasonal and cyclical unemployment,[30] and a livelihood had to be patched together across the year.

The uneven geographic distribution of new immigrants, the lack of information about jobs in other places, and the high cost of transport combined to create serious unemployment in some areas, especially the Eastern coastal cities, and labor scarcities in others, especially the frontier states. Many workers could only work seven or eight months a year because agriculture, the major employer for much of the century, was notoriously affected by the weather. Before 1860 the second-largest employer of adult men after agriculture was the merchant marine. But because ocean trips varied in length—one or two months along the coast, five months from New England to the West Indies, and from six to eight months to Liverpool—between trips, sailors were often unemployed.

Nonfarm industry was also more subject to the weather in the nineteenth century than it is today, with outdoor workers losing four or five months a year. In the North and West grist and oil mills, the largest nineteenth-century manufacturing industry, hired only for the autumn or "so long as the mill can run before freezing up." Ironworks commonly shut down for several months during the winter. Weather also affected those occupations that depended on roads and internal waterways: the roads between towns were usually ruts that became impassable in winter, and the waterways closed an average of four months every winter. As it does today, outside construction ceased during the winter months in much of the country.

Finally, workers were subject to cyclical unemployment during the recessions and depressions of 1818–1820, 1837–early 1840s, 1857–1861, 1873–1879, 1885, and 1893–late 1890s. The effects of these economic downturns varied according to industry and location. The 1818–1820 crisis, for example, primarily and drastically affected manufacturing, but only about 5 percent of the labor force was employed in manufacturing at this time. Some of the crises, however, were severe and general. The depression of the 1890s was among the worst before the 1930s: unemployment reached 18.4 percent in 1894.[31]

High nineteenth-century military desertion rates are often interpreted as evidence of enlistees' inferior moral character.[32] However, these rates tell us more about problems in the civilian economy and men's use of military service to adjust to these problems than they do about the moral character of those in the military.

As I have already noted, the nineteenth-century economy had distributed supplies of labor unevenly—an excess in the East and a shortage on the frontier; seasonal unemployment was substantial; and there were periodic recessions and depressions. Minimum wage laws, collective bargaining, and unemployment insurance were nonexistent. The two major reasons men enlisted were economic—reasons that made them likely to desert. The first was to get free transportation from the eastern states to the western frontier where most army units were stationed and where there were shortages of civilian workers. The second was to patch together a year-round income. As General O. O. Howard observed in 1885,

Excellent young men every day solicit the privilege of enlisting, but they do it in a strait for work. A workman in Omaha has had from $1 to $1.50 wages, but in winter he is often discharged and not able to get work again until spring, so when a young man finds himself without means and without bread he enlists. Good offers in spring and summer tempt him to desert.[33]

A decade later an officer made a similar comment: "If desertion had varied in accordance with one standard, that standard has been the labor market."[34] The military's high desertion rates indicate high crossover between the civilian and military labor forces, which means that workers in each were similar.

Finally, what does the immigrant make-up of the armed forces imply about wages and quality? Nineteenth-century observers assumed that if military pay was low relative to civilian pay, enlistees must be low quality. They did not take into account, however, what economists call the reservation wage—the wage below which the individual declines to supply his or her labor—of the large percentage of immigrants in the army and navy. Nineteeth-century American wages for laborers were higher than European wages for the same occupation; for example, in 1850, wages of Dutch and German laborers were about fifty cents a week, whereas the average American wage was eighty-seven cents a day.[35] Thus, although military pay may have been lower than civilian pay, especially before the Civil War, it could nonetheless be attractive to recent European immigrants. Because of the many immigrants in the armed services, the possible difference between immigrant and native American wage expectations is not a trivial matter.

Wartime Enlisted Forces

If U.S. peacetime enlisted forces have been more select and less marginal than the public view suggests, U.S. drafted enlisted forces have been less representative than the public assumes.

The Civil War draft. The United States had federal conscription during the Civil War and World War I and during the years 1940–1947 and 1948–1973. The legendary inequities of the Civil War draft whereby a man could buy an exemption for three hundred dollars or a substitute for an agreed-upon amount, were partly responsible for the bloody draft riots of 1863.[36] The burden of the draft thus fell disproportionately on the working classes, causing both Confederate and Union soldiers to complain that they were caught in a "rich man's war and a poor man's fight."

The World War I draft. In an effort to avoid abuses of the Civil War draft, the 1917 Congress made decisions the responsibility of local selective service boards. A major National Academy of Sciences study, however, raises questions about the representativeness of the World War I draft.[37] Before September 1918, 21- to 31-year-old males were registered, and the study shows that more than seventh-tenths of all registrants were deferred. Of the 6,973,270 deferments and exemptions, 6.8 percent were occupational and industrial; 0.5 percent were religious; 51.1 percent were for various conditions of dependency; 8.9 percent, for current enlistment in the army or navy; 7.8 percent, for lack of physical, mental, or moral fitness to be a soldier; and 13.2 percent, for alien allegiance.

The academy concluded that those who received occupational deferments were "undoubtedly above the average of men in the same occupation"—and probably came disproportionately from the wealthier and better-educated classes. A slightly larger percentage of individuals were deferred or excluded because they did not meet physical, intellectual, or moral enlistment standards. (By definition, this group was below average and was probably concentrated among the poor and least well educated.) Dependency was the major source of deferments and, for this time period the relationships between dependency and representativeness criteria are not known.

The academy data suggest that foreign-born white male immigrants were somewhat overrepresented among white male draftees, that black registrants were apparently inducted at higher rates (34 percent) than white registrants (24 percent),[38] and that blacks were overrepresented relative to the total population. In 1920, black twenty- to twenty-nine-year-old males represented 10.1 percent of the twenty- to twenty-nine-year-old population, but provided 13 percent of all those drafted in World War I.

The academy data also indicate that World War I draftees had much higher illiteracy rates than the 1920 census shows for the general population. As the authors of the academy report observe, however, military literacy standards were usually higher than census standards. In general, World War I draftees had less education than their age cohorts. Relative to the twenty-five- to twenty-nine-year-old white population in 1920, the average native-born white draftee had less than five years of school and was much less likely to have had twelve or more years of school. Relative to the twenty-five- to twenty-nine-year-old nonwhite population in 1920, the total black draft had a slightly smaller percentage of those with less than five years of school, but only half the percentage of those with twelve or more years of school.

The World War II, Korean War, Korea-Vietnam interim, and Vietnam War drafts. Except for a fifteen-month hiatus in 1947–1948, the United

States had some form of military draft from 1940 to 1973. Data on the social makeup of the military for three episodes of war (World War II, the Korean War, and the Vietnam War) and one period of semipeace (the Korean-Vietnam interim)[39] for officer and enlisted veterans show:

- Before Vietnam, veterans' came from families with higher socioeconomic status than nonveterans. Veterans' families had higher annual incomes; their fathers, more prestigious occupations; they and their parents, more education.
- Average values on the above indicators for both veterans and nonveterans steadily increased from World War II to Vietnam, reflecting increasing constant-dollar family incomes, higher levels of education, and increasing proportions of the male labor force in prestigious occupations.
- The differences between veterans and nonveterans declined from World War II to Vietnam. By the Vietnam War, veterans and nonveterans were virtually indistinguishable from one another.
- Blacks were underrepresented among veterans for all military eras, but decreasingly so from World War II to Vietnam.
- Veterans were socioeconomically and educationally more homogeneous than nonveterans in all military eras, including the Vietnam War when the means for the two groups were virtually the same.
- From World War II up to the Vietnam War, those of the lowest socioeconomic levels were less likely to serve, whereas during the Vietnam War, those from both the lowest and the highest educational and socioeconomic categories were underrepresented in the military.

These data show that a draft does not reproduce the social and economic structure of the nation. More important for the goals of some national service proponents, even in World War I, but especially from World War II through the Vietnam War, the draft eliminated the most disadvantaged from the military. In other words, the draft did not serve to integrate this group into the social and economic mainstream.

THE POLITICS OF ENLISTMENT

If national service is to include military service, it will have to operate within the constraints and instabilities of the politics that frame military personnel policy. We like to think that military personnel policies, the resources devoted to them, and their consequences for the composition of the military reflect the objective requirements of national defense. In fact, of course, they represent the results of normal political processes— trades among multiple stakeholders that have different objectives for the enlisted force and therefore different compositional preferences.

This idea is hardly new. Eliot Cohen argues that "Clausewitz's dictim that war is a continuation of politics by other means means much more than that war is a tool of statecraft. It means that politics pervades war and preparation for it; that . . . military institutions are political institutions."[40] Samuel Huntington goes on to argue that

> the most distinctive, the most fascinating, and the most troublesome aspect of military policy is its Janus-like quality. Indeed, military policy not only faces in two directions, it exists in two worlds. One is international politics, the world of the balance of power, wars and alliances, the subtle and the brutal uses of force and diplomacy to influence the behavior of other states. The principal currency of this world is actual or potential military strength: battalions, weapons, and warships. The other world is domestic politics, the world of interest groups, political parties, social classes, with their conflicting interests and goals. The currency here is the resources of society: men, money, material. Any major decision in military policy influences and is influenced by both worlds.[41]

Discrepancies Between Compositional Images and Realities: Why?

Discrepancies between compositional images and realities are easily explained. Military personnel policies intervene between a given enlistment mechanism and actual enlistment. Under these policies, a volunteer mechanism never produces free flow entry and drafts never produce random selection.

A volunteer mechanism means that the military is subject to the same process of labor allocation that operates in the general economy. Because enlisted jobs consist primarily of blue-collar and low-level white-collar jobs, we can expect military applicants to come from the lower and middle parts of the nation's talent and socioeconomic distributions. Fluctuations in the civilian economy shift the distribution of applicant talent and socioeconomic characteristics up and down, but within a fairly narrow range. Military enlistment standards, such as medical and basic skill screens, however, shift the talent and socioeconomic composition of enlistees above that expected under free flow volunteer conditions.

Quality standards, by eliminating the less educated and physically fit and thereby limiting enlistment to those whose socioeconomic status is above the lowest rank, have the same effect under a draft as in an entirely volunteer military. As we saw from World War I on, however, occupational, educational, and dependency deferments limit the draft to those of lesser talent and lower socioeconomic status. Thus the combined effect of quality standards and deferments creates a draft more representative of the lower-middle and middle classes than would be expected under a truly random draft.

In sum, military personnel policies create continuity in the composition of the U.S. military, regardless of whether there is a draft. The discrepancies between our image of the composition of the military and the reality arise because different parties judge enlisted force composition relative to their own objectives. These objectives seem fairly consistent across time, probably because of continuities in the nation's social and political values and in the functional imperatives of war. The visibility of different values in the political process, however, varies according to stakeholders' power, domestic political priorities, and external or internal security threats. The values briefly discussed below relate to compositional preferences, not to the mechanisms (a draft or voluntary enlistment) by which that composition is obtained.[42]

Loyalty to civilian values. This objective can be traced back at least to the Roman army. A stress on loyalty flowered in Western Europe with the gradual transfer of power from kings to democratic governments. It reflects a fear that centralized military power will subvert democratic liberties through a military coup or a coalition of military and civilian leaders. This concern manifests itself in preferences for militaries as citizen institutions; for militias under state, not federal, control; and for citizen armies manned not by professional soldiers, but by civilians who turn soldier for the duration, who "are fresh from their civilian lives and look forward to their swift return to those lives."[43] This objective implies a small standing army, limited-time drafts, and a socially representative enlisted force.

Loyalty to the policies of the civilian leadership. Even in a society where everyone is created equal, some are more equal than others. As Machiavelli advised the prince, to stay in power, one must control the military. This objective implies enlisting soliders whose values are consistent with those of their military and civilian leaders. The army of the Roman Republic consisted of those who met certain property ownership qualifications on the theory that all who served should feel the desired "emotions of loyalty."[44] This goal implies an enlisted force comfortable with the status quo, such as middle- or upper-middle-class whites from less-recent immigrant waves.

Deterrent and combat effectiveness.   A standing army's purpose is to prevent wars and win those that must be fought. The image of effectiveness is crucial for deterrence; actual effectiveness, for winning wars. Whether image or reality, effectiveness requires reliability and competence. Stakeholders differ on the characteristics they associate with reliability, but concur in the characteristics associated with competence. Current weapons systems are examples of technical wizardry, and stakeholders assume that these weapons systems require commensurate skills. This assumption implies an enlisted force drawn from the better educated and higher-status groups in society, such as white males from middle- and upper-middle-class families.

Efficiency.   A given force composition is more efficient if it provides high-quality personnel for the same cost or the same quality for a lower cost. This objective, of primary concern to those with managerial responsibilities for the enlisted force, has become more important as economic analysis has increasingly affected the allocation of public resources in this country. For example, the services' educational standards for enlistment reflect a recognized relationship between graduation from high school and retention of enlistees. No optimal composition, however, has been identified for a fuller set of costs and benefits, such as recruiting, training, and job performance.

Equality of sacrifice.   This objective is rooted in the democratization of society. Social equality is exchanged for equal sacrifice in time of war. Tocqueville discussed why democracies find conscription at once necessary and desirable: "The government may do whatever it pleases, provided it appeals to the whole community at once; it is the unequal distribution of the weight, not the weight itself, that commonly occasions resistance."[45] That perceived "unequal weight" generated several American draft riots, such as the New York City riots during the Civil War. During the Vietnam War, the most recent winter of our discontent, the issue arose again because some believed that the war was being fought disproportionately by blacks and the poor. This issue also lies behind some ideas of national service: those becoming full citizens (the young) should earn the right of citizenship through military or nonmilitary service to the nation. This objective for our enlisted forces implies a socially representative military.

Access to military benefits and entitlements.   Today's military offers benefits such as food, shelter, clothing, medical care, income, and pensions as well as status transformations. Just as citizenship is said to carry the obligation of military service, so military service is said to carry the right to full participation in the society. A democratic society is under constant pressure to extend first the vote and then full citizenship to all its members. Past efforts of the socially less integrated to gain access to the military represent one instance of this pressure. In parts of this nation, blacks battled for a century just to exercise their right to vote. Black leaders based their calls to arms—such as during World War I—on the belief that combat service would prove the key to full and equal citizenship. Women's efforts to be allowed to enter combat are best understood in the same context. This objective implies a composition biased toward those less integrated into the mainstream.

When we review the implications of these different objectives, we see conflicting compositional objectives, with no single composition that satisfies all objectives. We also see the sources of the bobs and weaves that we observe in military personnel policy. External events perturb the basis for previous compromises by altering the relative saliency of the objectives that bear on compositional policy. Given the basic function of the military, military effectiveness is always important in defining compositional policy, which limits the extent to which military personnel policy can respond to objectives whose compositional implications may conflict with effectiveness.

CONCLUSIONS

Military service can meet some objectives of a national service program, but only under certain conditions, in limited ways, and in ways subject to shifts in military personnel policy. If we want national service to enhance the political, social, and adult status of youth, military service can help us achieve this end, for of all national institutions, it is unique in offering status transformations in exchange for contributions to a higher good. National service can achieve this end, however, only if those whose status could be enhanced get into the military. Military recruiting practices limit the extent to which national service can use military service to integrate the most socially marginal youth into mainstream society. The military—more selective under voluntary enlistment and less representative under a draft than is usually assumed—consistently draws from the upper-lower and lower middle classes.

Finally, if national service is to include military service, it will have to operate within the constraints of the politics that frame military personnel policy. Given the basic function of the military, the extent to which military personnel policy can respond to objectives whose compositional implications conflict with effectiveness will be limited. Thus, technological trends in the military promise to increasingly reduce the chances that national service can use military service to integrate the least educated and most disadvantaged into the mainstream.

At the same time, values other than effectiveness affect military manpower policy, with their visibility and impact varying according to changes in stakeholders' power, domestic political priorities, and external or internal security threats. Thus, the unstable elements that affect the military will likewise affect any national service program that has a military component.

NOTES

1. William Arkin and Lynne R. Dobrofsky, "Military Socialization and Masculinity," *Journal of Social Issues* 34, no. 1 (1978): 151–68.

2. Nuria Sales de Bohigos, "Some Opinions on Exemption from Military Service in Nineteenth-Century Europe," *Comparative Studies in History and Society* 10 (1967–1968): 261–89. This contract is neither unique to the United States nor emerged here. As Feld (1975) notes, the European nation-state and mass army invariably and not accidentally appeared together. The *levée en masse* (universal military service) followed the French Revolution, the Italians celebrated unification by instituting universal military service, and Prussia created a mass army in the process of creating the German state. Feld points out that "the very term *levée en masse* associated the general populace with the idea of active participation in the state. Conscription was as much a matter of social as of military policy. Military service and political rights were closely equated. According to the new political outlook the ballot was the minimal political right and military service the basic civic obligation. The former was widely considered to be justified by the latter. That is, military service represented a claim to full citizenship and was a conventional means whereby the disenfranchised gained civic rights." (p. 195.)

3. James B. Jacobs and Leslie Anne Hayes, "Aliens in the U.S. Armed Forces: A Historical-Legal Analysis," *Armed Forces and Society* 7, no. 2 (Winter 1981): 187–208.

4. Mark M. Eitelberg, *Military Representation* (Alexandria, Va: Human Resources Research Organization, 1979).

5. Michael Novak, *The Rise of the Unmeltable Ethnics* (New York: The Macmillan Company, 1972).

6. Bernard Beck, "The Military as a Welfare Institution," in Charles C. Moskos, Jr., ed., *Public Opinion and the Military Establishment* (Beverly Hills, Calif.: Sage Publications, 1971), pp. 137–48.

7. John Sibley Butler, "Symposium: Race and the United States," *Armed Forces and Society* 6, no. 4 (Summer 1980): 594–600.

8. Forms of the ASVAB in use from January 1976 through September 1980 especially inflated test scores in the lower categories of the Armed Forces Qualifying Test (AFQT). This test, which represents a combination of scores on selected subtests of the ASVAB, measures verbal and quantitative abilities. For example, the percentage of Fiscal year 1979 Department of Defense enlistees in the lowest AFQT category allowed to enlist, category IV, was 5 percent under the miscalibrated test and 30 percent under the properly calibrated test. (Data supplied by the Office of the Assistant Secretary of Defense for Manpower, Reserve Affairs, and Logistics.)

9. Individuals can be enrolled in school *and* working. I treated schooling as the primary activity for those working either part-time or full-time and enrolled in school.

10. I used four indicators of family socioeconomic status: father's education, mother's education, the Duncan socioeconomic score of father's occupation, and an index of reading in the home. (The survey lacked a measure of family income for all respondents.) The Duncan Socio-Economic Index (SEI) reflects the relative status of occupations such as receptionists, metal molders, electric power line workers and cable workers, with a weighted combination of the education and income of the average incumbent of the occupation determining each occupation's Duncan SEI score. The scores vary from 1 to 100: a judge, for example, has a Duncan SEI score of 93; an auctioneer, a score of 40; and a paperhanger, a score of 14.

11. For whites, the five activity groups have the same parental socioeconomic status order as for all males.

12. Francis Paul Prucha, *Broadax and Bayonet: The Role of the United States Army in the Development of the Northwest, 1815–1860* (State Historical Society of Wisconsin, 1953).

13. Donald Rickey, Jr., *Forty Miles a Day on Beans and Hay* (Norman: University of Oklahoma Press, 1977).

14. Ibid., p. 27.

15. U.S. Bureau of the Census, *Historical Statistics of the United States, Colonial Times to 1970*, Bicentennial Edition, Parts 1 and 2 (Washington, D.C.: U.S. Government Printing Office, 1975) pp. 15–18.

16. Prucha, *Broadax and Bayonet*.

17. *Historical Statistics of the United States, Colonial Times to 1970*, Part 1, 1975, Series A6–8 and A119–134, p. 8 and pp. 15–18.

18. At any point in the century black representation reflected a compromise among (1) black attempts to gain freedom and full enfranchisement through military service; (2) white attempts to frustrate the achievement of these objectives or to control the rate at which they were achieved; and (3) military personnel requirements. In general, blacks were more underrepresented under

peacetime volunteer conditions than during wartime. In wartime whites relaxed constraints on black enlistments to meet personnel requirements. (Jack D. Foner, *Blacks and the Military in American History* [New York: Praeger Publishers, 1974]).

19. Lawrence A. Cremin, *American Education: The National Experience, 1783–1876* (New York: Harper and Row, 1980).

20. John K. Folger and Charles B. Nam, *Education of the American Population, U.S. Department of Commerce, Bureau of the Census* (Washington, D.C.: Government Printing Office, 1967).

21. *Historical Statistics of the United States, Colonial Times to 1970,* Part 1, 1975, Series H598–601, p. 379.

22. Folger and Nam, *Education of the American Population,* p. 136. These data almost certainly overestimate the educational attainment of these survivors' cohorts, for social class is positively related to longevity and to educational attainment.

23. *Historical Statistics of the United States, Colonial Times to 1970,* Part 1, 1975, Series D75–84.

24. *Historical Statistics of the United States, Colonial Times to 1970,* Part 1, 1975, Series D182–232.

25. Prucha, *Broadax and Bayonet,* and Francis Prucha, *The Sword of the Republic* (Bloomington: Indiana University Press, 1977).

26. Stanley Lebergott, *Manpower in Economic Growth: The American Record Since 1800* (New York: McGraw Hill Book Co., 1964), p. 244.

27. *Historical Statistics of the United States, Colonial Times to 1970,* Parts 1 and 2, 1975, Series Y856–903, D705–714, and D735–738.

28. *Historical Statistics of the United States, Colonial Times to 1970,* Parts 1 and 2, 1975, Series Y856–903, D779–793.

29. Alba M. Edwards, *Comparative Occupation Statistics for the United States, 1870 to 1940, Sixteenth Census of the United States: 1940 Population* (U.S. Government Printing Office, Washington, D.C., 1943).

30. Lebergott, *Manpower in Economic Growth.*

31. *Historical Statistics of the United States, Colonial Times to 1970,* Part 1, 1975, Series D85–86, p. 135.

32. In 1823, 25 percent of the enlistments deserted; in 1826, 50 percent; in 1830, 25 percent (Prucha, *Broadax and Bayonet*); in 1866, 26 percent, and in 1871, almost 33 percent (Jack D. Foner, *The United States Soldier Between Two Wars—Army Life and Reforms, 1865–1898* [New York: Humanities Press, 1970]).

33. Foner, *United States Soldier Between Two Wars,* p. 9.

34. Ibid.

35. Lebergott, *Manpower in Economic Growth.*

36. Ulysses Lee, "The Draft and the Negro," *Current History* 55 (1968): 28–33, 47–48.

37. Robert M. Yerkes, ed. *Psychological Examining in the U.S. Army, Memoirs of the National Academy of Sciences,* vol. 15 (Washington, D.C.: U.S. Government Printing Office, 1921).

38. Foner, *Blacks and the Military in American History.*

39. The data come from two linked surveys, both conducted by the U.S. Bureau of the Census: the March 1973 Current Population Survey (CPS) and the August–November 1973 Occupational Changes in a Generation Survey (OCG). The World War I data pertain to enlisted draftees. The CPS and OCG data, describing populations from World War II to Vietnam, pertain to veterans, including officers. The officer content of the active duty military increased from 10 percent in World War II to 12 percent in the Korean War to 14 percent at the end of the Vietnam War (*Historical Statistics of the United States, Colonial Times to 1970,* Part 2, 1975, Series Y904–916, p. 1141; Table 614, *Statistical Abstracts of the United States: 1980,* 1980, p. 376). Because officers have more education and come from families with higher socioeconomic status than enlistees, these data represent upwardly biased estimates of the characteristics of our enlisted forces from World War II to 1973.

40. Eliot A. Cohen, *Citizens and Soldiers* (Ithaca, N.Y.: Cornell University Press, 1985), pp. 21–22.

41. Samuel P. Huntington, *The Common Defense* (New York: Columbia University Press, 1961), p. 1.

42. Stakeholders clearly differ in their preferences on this issue. Some prefer a draft, others prefer voluntary enlistment. Those with a more individualistic and free-market perspective prefer voluntary enlistment, and those with a more communitarian view, a draft. There is a loose, but imperfect, relationship between compositional and induction preferences. For example, those who want a composition that exposes Americans equally to the dangers of war tend to prefer a draft.

43. Cohen, *Citizens and Soldiers,* p. 124.

44. Eitelberg, *Military Representation,* p. 74.

45. Alexis de Tocqueville, *Democracy in America,* vol. 2, trans. Henry Reeve (New York: Vintage Press, 1945), p. 286.

Comment

Paul N. McCloskey, Jr.

Dr. Berryman's paper is an important contribution to military history. Military historians will take note of it. It confirms most of what I have observed in my lifetime about the makeup of the U.S. military in World War II, the Korean War, and the Vietnam War. My comments fall into two distinct categories: military service and civilian service.

The national service now is the military. Military service is the highest form of service and the most arduous form of service. The privilege we have of sitting here in this room at peace depends at the present time on two million young people who are prepared to fight.

The key ingredient in a military service, particularly in a time of peace, is that this service be combat-ready. Whatever the makeup of the military service is, no reasonable young men will volunteer to be combat-ready in the infantry—and certainly not the 400,000 that are needed each year—if they are given a forewarning of what combat-readiness requires: that in the summer you train in the desert or in the jungle; in the winter you train in the Arctic.

I am going to give you two anecdotal experiences. In 1950 we were not prepared to go to war. Suddenly Truman ordered in U.S. air and naval support in Korea, and the United Nations Security Council, in the absence of the Soviets, voted to commit a U.S. military force. We threw in four infantry divisions in the first three months of that war—the Twenty-fourth, the Twenty-fifth, the Seventh, and the First Cavalry divisions.

They were not ready; they had been eating ice cream in Japan. No troop commander wanted to lower troop morale by saying you will do a twenty-mile march every day, you are going to do 50 push-ups twice a day, you are going to do the things necessary to be combat-ready. Those American kids—eighteen and nineteen years old—were thrown into the breach and were massacred. Light Horse Harry Lee, a cavalry officer under General Washington during the Revolution, once said, "A government is the murderer of its citizens which sends them to the field uninformed and untaught, where they are to meet men of the same age and strengths mechanized by education and discipline for battle." The massacre of men in those first four infantry divisions thrown into Korea was a disgrace to American preparedness.

My branch of the service, the Marine Corps, was lucky. It called up all 138 of its reserve units in July. The first marine division with those reserves landed at Inchon, broke the back of the North Koreans, and then went up to the Chosin Reservoir. It turned out the marines were not prepared for combat either. Marines had been trained to fight in Haiti, Nicaragua, and the islands of the Caribbean. Nobody knew anything about fighting in the Siberian winds coming off Manchuria. The first marine division had about fifteen thousand fighting men who suffered 4,500 casualties from frostbite because they were not prepared to fight in Arctic conditions. American military power requires combat readiness. How do you get combat readiness unless you take people against their will?

We then came to the Vietnam experience. The draft was still in effect. The draft led to the disparity Dr. Berryman has referred to. If you look at the Vietnam-era figures, the makeup of the services was not that unrepresentative. But if you look at the combat units, it was. The country was 11 percent black people and 8 percent Mexican-American, for a total of 19 percent. But 43 percent of the men killed and wounded in Vietnam were black or Mexican-American. They bore a differential burden in defense of the freedom of this country.

Why did that occur? It is simple. In World War II, the draft law protected those who could get through college. We had a far lower percentage of people going to college so we had a deferment for those people. By the time of Vietnam, anybody who could get into college could avoid the draft. The other ways were to enlist in a reserve unit, the National Guard, or some unit that was not going to be called up. The disparity that Dr. Berryman refers to existed because bright young people understood the merits of the combat infantry relative to the air force, the navy, or some place less hazardous like going to school or getting married and having a child or some other means of deferment.

Young men took those options, which led to that disparity in the combat units.

It was not all bad. The second point she made, that service in the military is a means of upward mobility in society, is true. We honor our soldiers. We honor our veterans. We honor the experience. We hope it gives one judgment and a broadening of one's mentality. Growing up in the all-white suburb of San Marino, a place that was different from the world, I never saw a black person until I enlisted in the navy. Boot camp was an interesting experience.

Suppose the Congress and the president decide that the military needs 400,000 young men, 200,000, or whatever the number is. The country is better off if those people are a cross-section. I was in the Marine Corps on active duty when the Vietnam War started. I was in Congress when it concluded. I do not recall a single son of a congressman or senator being killed in Vietnam. The only person that I recall who served in the Vietnam War voluntarily was Chuck Robb. He married President Johnson's daughter and chose to serve. The Marine Corps tried to keep him out; the Marine Corps did not want famous people getting killed in combat. He insisted and went into combat.

The older you get, the more you get filled with fear. Those who are afraid in combat are more likely to be killed. It is so in an assault. [Oliver Wendell] Holmes [Jr.] said: "It is not well for soldiers to think much about wounds. Sooner or later we shall fall; but meantime it is for us to fix our eyes upon the point to be stormed, and to get there if we can." ["A Soldier's Faith," in Max Lerner, ed., *The Mind and Faith of Justice Holmes* (Boston: Little, Brown, 1943), p. 20.] That kind of attitude is easier for eighteen and nineteen-year-olds to have. I found in my own combat experience, the longer I was in combat, the more fearful I got. If I had been there much longer, I would have caved in, as I saw others do.

Another aspect of combat is that as young eighteen-year-olds joined us as recruit replacements, the first casualties were these replacements. They were not in good physical condition; they were not experienced. They had not had the rigorous, tough training that gave them a reasonable chance of surviving combat.

Because we are talking about national service, I want to make a flat statement that stems from a poll I took twice in my last two years in the Congress. I was asked to address the National Defense University which sent two hundred colonels and majors—selected for ultimate generalship because of their success in commanding battalions or regiments— over to the House to sit in a private session.

Because they had come right out of the field to attend this university,

I would ask them, "Gentlemen, are your troops combat-ready?" To a man they would say, "No, sir." I would say, "Would you mind if I went down to the White House and so advised the President?" They would remind me that this was an off-the-record conference. If the commander in chief says the troops are ready, so does every general, colonel, major, and the rest of the chain of command. There would be no word in public of what their opinions really were; you just do not undercut your commander in chief. If you do, you are cashiered or court-martialed.

Worse than that, in the late 1970s when the survey was done that Dr. Berryman relies on, the number of category fours going into the military was so high that many were failing the tests that were run in the combat commands.

Those running the tests found that American privates first class who were trying to fire the 90-mm tank cannons in Germany could not compete with Soviet gunners with proper training. They did not have the intelligence. They could be foot soldiers, but could they fire the cannons in sophisticated tanks? They could not.

The terrible truth is that our ability to fight a war—to land three divisions in Iran or fight on the European continent—depends on an immediate influx of reserves into sixteen or eighteen divisions. There are no reserves in this country today that we could send into combat as replacements without being murderers. If you have ever visited a National Guard unit, you will look in vain for a young man who can run three miles in twenty minutes. The whole purpose of the military is to have a combat-ready, confident reserve. This purpose is not being met by the all-volunteer forces.

On civilian service, I am going to draw on personal experience. I have practiced law in this community now for some 21 years. This community, built around Stanford in Palo Alto, runs on volunteer service.

To suggest a national program of civilian service from the top down is an outrage. First of all, it is unconstitutional. This government cannot impose involuntary servitude. The Thirteenth Amendment of the Constitution says so. Civilian service can only be mandated to support the morale of the armed forces, as I said when I referred to the Holmes case earlier. But for the national government to support the opportunity for every kid in America to perform some form of volunteer service is entirely appropriate.

I will give you two examples. In 1946, two Jewish ladies in this community who had escaped the Holocaust formed an organization to help the Japanese who were coming back from the internment camps. Those two ladies got together a group of kids who went out and collected washing machines and every accoutrement that people might need who were coming back to this community without assets. The leadership of the two elderly ladies and the work of the kids were cost-effective. Congress has now, 30 years later, voted $25 million to help the Japanese interned during the war. I can guarantee that what those volunteers did in this community was 100 times better than any governmental program for the same purpose could ever be.

Second example: In the late 1960s fifteen-year-olds were starting to steal cars. These fifteen-years-olds never listened to anyone over 30; they would not listen to their parents; they would not listen to the cops and ministers. There was only one class of people they listened to and that was seventeen- or eighteen-year-olds. So several lawyers conceived of a program called the Stanford Area Youth Plan. Stanford pioneered it; it is now in 70 universities. We put an eighteen-year-old Stanford football player with a fifteen-year-old voted by his principal most likely to steal a car next year. In seven years the program worked like a charm. We only had one problem: three Stanford kids were locked up for burglary or other incidents over the years. The program worked on local fund-raising. A group called the Stanford Buck Club that wanted to get big fullbacks and tackles to Stanford paid those athletes two bucks per hour—$30 per month—to spend time working with the kids.

I cannot conceive of a better way to try to stop people from using drugs than to get fifteen- to seventeen-year-olds to talk to 12-year-olds who are starting to use them. Now that is a volunteer program. Somebody will conceive it somewhere. Here in Palo Alto there is also a group of kids from Palo Alto High who tutor kids in East Palo Alto. This is a bona fide volunteer program.

I see the Bush administration, every time a program works around the country, honoring the person who conceived that program. Chances are that program cannot be duplicated. The two ladies who helped the Japanese probably could not be found in Dubuque, Iowa.

Now I want to outline my 1979 national service program for you. I almost had that political coalition that you spoke about as impossible. I had [Congressman G. V.] Sonny Montgomery [D-Miss.], who wanted better quality in the military, and [Congresswoman] Pat Schroeder [D-Colo.]. Whenever you can get Sonny Montgomery and Pat Schroeder on the same side, you have something going politically, and we did. It was called H.R. 2206. A majority in the House supported it. It would have passed except for the fact that Mr. Reagan was elected in 1980.

The bill was simple. We wanted to get people to volunteer for the military. We did not want a draft. We said, volunteer for two years in the military and we will give you four years of college benefit. Volunteer for six months of active duty in the reserve and after five and a half years of push-ups and running every day—so we know you are combat-ready—we will give you one year of college benefit. Or, if you do not like that, volunteer for the candy stripers, the Boy Scouts, or whatever in your local community. In order for your one year of volunteer work to qualify as civilian service, some leading citizen who is running a volunteer program will have to certify to your draft board—not a new federal bureaucracy, but three volunteer citizens who sit in every congressional district—that you have done your year. Once you have done that, then you have served your nation. You do not get any college benefits, but we recognize it. If you do not want to do any of those three things, then you go into the draft pool and you take your chances. If there are two million young men and two million young women and the military is only taking 400,000 and gets 300,000 volunteers, your chances of getting drafted are slim. The wisenheimers would soon realize that if you volunteer for nothing, your chances of getting drafted were not much. But with this plan, how could they complain that they were forced into involuntary service? They had their chance.

Mr. Friedman: Hadn't the draft ended by then?

Mr. McCloskey: The draft ended in 1973. In my judgment, it ended because Nixon saw that when he ended the draft, he would end all protest on the campus. The roar on the campuses became a squeak and it gave the president the time for that "decent interval" in South Vietnam before the government fell.

DISCUSSION

Mr. Moskos: You [Ms. Berryman] say in your paper that the data show incontestably that enlistees between the ages of seventeen and twenty-two are not drawn from marginal groups. This is probably the most provocative finding you come up with, but this may leave the impression that everything was hunky-dory in the all volunteer force in the late 1970s.

Ms. Berryman: It was not.

Mr. Moskos: There was concern in this period that especially the army and to some degree the Marine Corps were suffering recruitment problems. Bob Phillips did a study that breaks the data out by service. [Choongsoo Kim, Gilbert Nestel, Robert L. Phillips, and Michael E. Borus, "The All-Volunteer Force: An Analysis of Youth Participation, Attrition, and Reenlistment," Center for Human Resource Research, Ohio State University, May 1980.] If you look at those data, you will see that the army recruits were much lower in quality than the others, especially the navy and the air force recruits. By some measures on certain tests—knowledge of the world of work, the Rotter scale—the army recruits were comparable to the unemployed. The army was recruiting from marginal groups.

Ms. Berryman: What I was pointing out was the general pattern in the military. The AFQT [Armed Forces Qualifying Test] was misnormed, and the military did not realize it. The sergeants kept saying, we're getting kids we cannot train. When they renormed the test, they found that instead of 9 percent category fours, which is the highest percentage of this category legally allowed in the military, you had 42 percent at that point in the army. I do not know what they would have done if they had had properly normed tests.

Mr. Moskos: Had shortfalls.

Ms. Berryman: This came at a time when the army had recruiting problems. Nineteen seventy-nine was the nadir of that period. It is difficult to know what they would have done.

Mr. Bandow: It is one thing to acknowledge that the military faces problems and challenges. But the solution is a separate issue. It is clear that having a draft does not equal preparedness. You [Mr. McCloskey] gave the example of lack of preparedness in 1950 when there was a draft. When there are budget problems, the military has an unfortunate tendency to cut readiness spending instead of procurement and other things.

There are also many issues that are not related to national service or readiness. As long as you allow volunteers in the military and as long as you allow blacks to re-enlist, there will be a problem of equal representation—whether you have a draft or national service—because currently blacks enlist in larger numbers than whites. National service or military conscription will bring in a relatively small number of people and will not affect the composition much. Thus, as long as you allow volunteers in the military, you will not have equal representation. The same thing applies to overrepresentation of minorities in combat arms. We have seen from earlier wars that the college kid becomes the administrator or does the typing. The mix in the military will not be affected much by the method of getting people in.

The reserves are another issue. You cannot volunteer for the Individual Ready Reserve now. The Selective Reserves is still a problem. But from 1980 until now there has been dramatic improvement. There are still shortfalls in numbers, training, and quality, but because there has been a greater emphasis on improvement, things are getting better.

Mr. McCloskey: It is a bona fide value in the community to have a sense of duty. You have the privilege of being an American so you should serve in the armed services. There should be a sense that you have the duty to serve your country for a year or two in your youth. This is a praiseworthy thing. When the people come out of their period of service, they have a sense of higher dedication to the country and to community values. Most of the people I have seen in the armed services and in the Peace Corps have gone on serving. Most of the Stanford volunteers who go back to be interns in Washington go on to some kind of public service.

Mr. Barber: I listened with great interest to Pete McCloskey's comments about military preparedness and how it is murder to send in unprepared combat troops. I appreciate what he said about duty, but I am confused by the hostility he shows to service. The word *duty* to me suggests an obligation—something we have to do. A government that requires us to do something endemic to democratic citizenship is engaged not in an act of coercion but in an act of training for citizenship. I feel as strongly about democracy as you do about war. I do not want to see Americans go in unready for citizenship. Our democracy cannot survive unless Americans are citizens. Most Americans—adults and young people—are inadequate citizens who do not even bother to use the ballot, let alone do much else. The nation as a whole and our schools in particular have a responsibility to find ways to make people citizen-ready for the great enterprise of democracy.

That is not something that will happen simply as a consequence of market forces. It requires national planning. Whether it requires national coercion is an issue to debate. I am open to that debate. Citizenship requires a notion of duty and obligation, much like the one you suggested the nation has to ensure that its young people who go into battle are combat ready. Our citizens have to be ready for the democracy in which they will live, or they are going to lose it. I do not see any alternative to some governmental presence—not necessarily coercive, not necessarily required—in these things. I would have thought that Mr. McCloskey, so sensitive to issues of military preparedness and military responsibilities, might have felt a like concern for civic preparedness and democratic responsibility. That is what education-based community service is really about.

Mr. McCloskey: I have no problem with each student who graduates in political science going out and serving in a political campaign that year or in some capacity. My concern is that when the government hands down what the service shall be, it will be a make-work situation. It has to be meaningful service. The young person who does it has to believe he is helping his community. You can do that by going over to East Palo Alto [a predominantly black city on the San Francisco peninsula]. You can cut trails on the Skyline [the ridge of the Santa Cruz mountains on the San Francisco peninsula]. You can fight fires. You can help the local police in a neighborhood watch program. You can do a million things. I just have never seen a government program that was not ultimately a make-work program.

Mr. Barber: You are not ruling out a government requirement for service. You are just saying that you do not want service in a government program?

Mr. McCloskey: You have my program. My program would let you out of government service if you did your civilian service in some volunteer capacity. I just have never seen an effective, bureaucratically run service program. These kids at Stanford will come up with some way to serve this community. You tell a Stanford kid that he has to go into the Civilian Conservation Corps. He goes up to Auburn [a California city in the Sierra Nevada mountains] and sits in a camp. They do not do anything for ten days. He comes out of it with a bad experience.

Mr. Oi: On the make-up of the armed forces, the variations in the quality and other minor variations, throughout that whole period beginning around 1975 or 1976, the pay of the military, relative to civilians, was dropping steadily. That is when the army was running shortfalls and the proportion of the high-quality recruits went down. By the same token, Jim Miller [Chairman, Federal Trade Commission, 1981–85; Director, Office of Management and the Budget, 1985–88] and others are saying now that unless we do something about federal salaries, the quality of people at the deputy assistant secretary rank will go to hell in a basket. You cannot divorce these two. We are in a competitive market. You get what you pay for.

Mr. Anderson: You [Mr. McCloskey] raise an important subject. But it is a fallacy to argue that because people feel patriotic and because they feel that they have a duty to their country, that gives you the right to force everyone to fulfill that. That is the worst thing that you can do to encourage patriotism and a sense of obligation. The way to do it is through persuasion and example, not by saying the government has a right to coerce everyone.

Mr. Barber: The question is what coercion means. For two days, to the extent that we have been talking about rhetoric and ideology, not service, we have been talking about these two paradigms: the voluntary free market and the coercive state. But neither of them captures the reality of a so-called market that in many ways creates involuntary situations. The paradox of the so-called voluntary free market is that of the wolf in the henhouse saying, "We don't need a policeman here. Let's not encroach on the freedom of the hens." There are all sorts of wolves in the marketplace. There are wolves in the government. The government, however, belongs to us, unlike corporations, unlike the market. We vote for it explicitly, and we vote for it with a ballot: each of us—man or woman—has one. That is not the case in the market.

Mr. Szanton: I want to make several comments:

First, I have found this conference helpful in that I am now thinking about the problem in a different way than when I came, which is the definition of a helpful meeting. Second, there is more implicit agreement around the table than we have recognized. We have not recognized it because you can distribute this group along a spectrum at both ends of which there are a few highly vocal and highly articulate people. The people at one end feel strongly that the imperatives of citizenship or morality or social integration are sufficiently powerful to justify some form of mandatory or semimandatory mixing of youth at some stage in their lives. The people at the other end of the spectrum feel, in an equally principled way, that such actions imposed by government are illegitimate and have no moral, legal, or constitutional foundation. That leaves, however, many people somewhere between those positions, including (a) a portion of this panel and (b) a much larger proportion of the citizens.

The folks in the middle find themselves unhappy, uncertain, and confused for three reasons. First, they do not operate in the terms of a doctrine that quickly formulates the issue and gives them an answer. Second, the nomenclature we are forced to use in this debate is miserable. We cannot agree on what service means and whether national service means service to the nation, funded by the nation, or controlled by the nation. Third, they are confused because we are thinking at different times of different constituencies. In particular, the debate and our sentiments are twisted by the problems of the underclass. Having said that, I want to offer four propositions that would collect a fair degree of agreement even on this panel.

Proposition 1. Service involves sacrifice. Therefore no plan that offers material compensation and that asks no net sacrifice of those involved in the program should be regarded as service. Under these terms, the Nunn-McCurdy bill is not service.

Proposition 2. In the absence of an overriding national emergency, the government has no right to impose a service requirement on the population.

Proposition 3. Government might reasonably seek to encourage and stimulate genuinely voluntary service but should go no further.

Proposition 4. One partial exception to this rule is founded on the fact that there is one subpopulation of this society that is in unprecedentedly deep trouble. It is not only that its prospects are bleak, but that its family structure has also broken down in a way not found in any other society; its process of value formulation appear to be working poorly or perhaps perversely. We would clarify our discussion of national service if we segregated out that subpopulation—its problems, its needs, and what we want to do for it—from the rest of the population.

The last ten years have shown that young persons from that subpopulation can be profoundly reoriented through experiences of the sort the California Conservation Corps provides. Its program maintains a mythology of service, which is to say that it maintains the mythology that the participants are contributing more to society than society is contributing to them. In such programs the public investment in the participants may well exceed the monetary value of the work they do. It is nonetheless crucial to such a program's psychological impact that the participants feel that they are contributing to society, that people are depending on them, and that they are not dependents. They see themselves as doing constructive work, enduring a discipline, and gaining skills, and thereby they acquire self-respect.

The strongest argument for a mandatory universal service is that one wants to achieve not only those purposes but also social integration. That argument is insufficiently strong in that it calls "service" a program that is government supported and in which participants receive more than they sacrifice.

8

NATIONAL SERVICE AND ITS ENEMIES

Charles C. Moskos

National service proposals have traditionally failed to attract sustained policy attention for two seemingly contradictory reasons. Many proposals come across as vague and incomplete, omitting any serious discussion of such crucial matters as administration and costs. Other proposals are too formal and detailed, tending to ignore the social and historical experiences of actual service programs. All this changed, however, in the late 1980s with an outpouring of legislative proposals on Capitol Hill and editorial commentary across the country.

The catalyst for these developments was the Citizenship and National Service Act of 1989 introduced by Senator Sam Nunn (D-Ga.), Congressman Dave McCurdy (D-Okla.), and other congressional Democrats. Shaped by the Democratic Leadership Council, this legislation was both concrete in form and philosophical in content.[1] Although the bill did not move forward, its rationale and proposals coupled with the stature of its sponsors made it the focal point of much contemporary debate on national service.

This essay hypothesizes that this debate can be illuminated by looking at the opposition to the national service act. The opposition's distinguishing feature is that it comes from two directions: libertarian conservatives and conventional liberals. Another source of opposition is the human resources establishment within the Office of the Secretary of Defense. Although that office's opposition to national service parallels the support of the marketplace military favored by the libertarian conservatives, the specific focus of the military requires separate treatment. I will address the main arguments raised by opponents and offer rejoinders. My intention is not to defend all types of national service, but rather to keep the argument focused on the program envisioned by the Democratic Leadership Council and specified in the Citizenship and National Service Act.

The Nunn-McCurdy bill presented a nonmandatory program of comprehensive national service, embracing both civilian service and a citizen-soldiery. The bill would thus create a Citizens Corps of young people to perform such service for one or two years. The military side would include a new lower-paid citizen-soldier track for short enlistments coexisting with a professional soldier track, basically the present system. The civilian side would consist of expanded versions of the Peace Corps, Volunteers in Service to America (VISTA), and conservation corps plus a new component of social services overseen by a corporation for national service and a local network of councils. Such social services would be administered through existing voluntary associations and state and local government agencies.

Both citizen-soldiers and civilian servers would receive subsistence pay during the time of service, followed by generous vouchers for federal student aid or job training on completion of service. Students who perform some form of national service would become the main, though not sole, recipients of federal student aid. (Exemptions are made for those over age 26, for hardship cases, and for persons for whom no service position can be found.) This moves away from the present program under which the government gives $9 billion each year in loan subsidies and grants to college students without asking anything in return—a GI Bill without the GI.

The Nunn-McCurdy bill is based on three core principles. The first is that civilian and military service in peacetime have equivalent value. The second is that national service starts with the value of the service performed, not with the presumed good it does for the server. The third is that citizenship entails duties as well as rights. Each of these principles has in some way offended the interests and convictions of the libertarian right and the conventional left.

The notion that civilian and military service are antinomies can be traced to William James, often described as the progenitor of national service. James's 1910 essay "The Moral Equivalent of War" set the tone of the discussion for decades to come when he called for the same heroic and noble qualities in civilian service that he associated with warfare.[2] But by opposing what he termed the *peace-party* with the *war-*

party, James set up a contradiction that handicaps national service to the present day. Contrary to James, the virtue of military service rests not in its martial values, but in its character as one of the deepest forms of citizenship obligation in a democratic society—a quality true of civilian service as well. Military and civilian service, if not quite a seamless web, are, to the degree they contain civic content, cut out of the same cloth.

There has been some confusion among national service supporters about who is supposed to benefit—the server or the society—from the work performed. We have a military to meet a pressing national need, not to mature young people or improve their character. The same standard must be applied to civilian service. Focusing on the service invokes civic sentiments; focusing on the server invites negative stereotypes of the qualities of the server. Indeed, only when national service is cast in terms of meeting a genuine need can its positive, but necessarily derivative benefits for the server be achieved.[3]

In modern times both libertarian conservatives and conventional liberals de-emphasize the role of the citizen duties in favor of a highly individualistic rights-based ethic.[4] Whether political theorists favor an activist state handing out benefits, as liberals do, or a state that needs to be curbed, as conservatives do, the view of citizenship remains the same: individuals exist apart from one another bound by no meaningful obligations.[5] The Nunn-McCurdy bill points to a more balanced and nuanced formulation of citizenship duties and rights. To the degree practical, recipients of taxpayers' money should earn that money, especially when it is being used to increase the lifetime earnings of its recipients. The linchpin of the Nunn-McCurdy bill is to extend the principle of the GI Bill—an education or job training benefit for military service—to civilian service.

THE CONSERVATIVE CRITIQUE

The conservative critique of the national service act centers on three core issues and one facade argument. The facade argument is that any program along the lines of the Nunn-McCurdy bill is somehow un-American, akin to the Hitler *Jugend* or the Russian *Komsomol*. Any reading of U.S. history, however, that ignores the recurring connection between citizen duties and rights is intellectually dishonest. How can one dismiss the militia system of the colonial and early republican era, the common defense and general welfare provisions of the Constitution, the mandatory public schools of the Northwest ordinances, the partial conscription of the Civil War, the mandatory officer-training requirements of the early land grant colleges, the twentieth-century drafts in both peace and war, the Civilian Conservation Corps of the New Deal, the alternative service provisions for conscientious objectors, or the Peace Corps and VISTA? The history of the United States shows that notions of civic obligation periodically expand and contract. At certain times national service is held out as a civic ideal; at other times it is dismissed as misguided or utopian. Let us now turn to the more salient conservative criticisms of national service.

A Compulsory Scheme That Could Reinstate the Draft

This is a warranted fear. The system being proposed offers to national servers strong inducements—postservice educational and job-training benefits—that are much less available to those youth who do not serve. But the transition from the comprehensive (but nonmandatory) system proposed here to a compulsory program would be a momentous step that could not come about without widespread support. Such support would exist only if the comprehensive program were widely viewed as a great success. It seems perverse, then, to argue against a voluntary national scheme on the grounds that it might prove too successful.

More to the point is the objection that a comprehensive national service program could serve as a cover for reinstating a military draft. Indeed it might. But it is virtually unimaginable that a compulsory civilian program would be legislated (even presuming constitutional obstacles could somehow be overcome) before enactment of military conscription. If the draft were to come back, however, the prior existence of a voluntary national service program would surely create strong pressures to make that program compulsory for men, certainly, for women, probably. But why argue that any form of national service should be avoided because it might make a draft more palatable? Surely a palatable draft is better than a nonpalatable one. Again, the success of a program ought not be used as an argument against it.

Exorbitant Costs and a Massive Bureaucracy

A mandatory program involving millions of young people could certainly become a bureaucratic and financial nightmare. But the Nunn-McCurdy bill envisions a highly streamlined administration building on historical precedents and sucessful programs. Citizen-soldiers—approximately 100,000 annually, or one-fourth of the total annual military intake—would be absorbed into the existing armed forces with a minimum of organizational adjustment. Most of the envisioned 600,000 or

so civilian servers would also be assigned to existing institutions—
nonprofit organizations, schools, and hospitals. Of the remainder,
nearly all would serve in conservation corps, for which there is already
extensive organizational experience at state and federal levels. Any
scheme that seeks to impose a uniform system on a country as large and
diverse as the United States would collapse of its own weight.

Nonetheless, it must be acknowledged that comprehensive national
service will not come cheap. Every 100,000 civilian servers would cost
about $1 billion in public funds—and this does not take into account the
portion of the present federal student budget that would be redirected
toward civilian servers. About one-quarter of the outlay would come
from matching funds from state and local governments and sponsoring
agencies. Still, the federal expenditures would be substantial.

Yet there are some weighty items on the other side of the ledger.
The introduction of a citizen-soldier track to the all-volunteer military
would produce substantial savings in military personnel costs while
strengthening our reserve forces. Anything that gets people out of the
American underclass will lead to long-term reductions in costs associated
with welfare, unemployment, and crime—though admittedly there is no
sure way to quantify those savings. But the ways in which military service
and the GI Bill salvaged otherwise dead-end youth offer some guidelines. National service also means savings in the impending costs of
meeting the needs of an increasingly older and infirm population, costs
that otherwise would decimate family savings and stagger the federal
budget.

Market More Efficient than National Service

This view grows out of the conviction that even the most well-
intentioned intervention in the marketplace produces negative results.
This is not a frivolous argument, but it ignores the purpose of national
service, which is to perform work that the market does not deliver, that
is too expensive to be done by standard government bureaucracies, and
that can be done by nonspecialized workers. Indeed, to the degree that
many human services—care for the infirm, aged, and mentally ill comes
to mind—require menial labor combined with compassion, short-term
servers are best suited for these tasks, too often not performed at all.

During World War II, U.S. conscientious objectors performed alternative service in mental asylums, bringing an unprecedented humane-
ness to the handling of the mentally ill in this country. Today in the
Federal Republic of Germany some 70,000 conscientous objectors are
assigned to civilian service in lieu of military service. These young men

are assigned to social services in hospitals and sanitoriums, day-care facilities for the mentally and physically incapacitated, the ambulance corps, and, especially, nursing homes for the aged. They operate with a minimum of extra overhead because they are supervised by existing welfare and church agencies. Persons across the political spectrum recognize the usefulness of such *Zivildienst* (civilian service)—none of which displaces regular workers. In the United States a program of proportionate magnitude would involve close to 300,000 civilian positions in social services.

Any defense of national service must answer two questions. Are the means employed more likely to achieve the purpose than other means? Are the means more likely to achieve the purpose at lower cost than other means? If the answer is no to either one, then the activity is not suitable for national service. If it is yes to both, then national service is the practical means to meet societal needs that would otherwise go unmet.[6]

THE LIBERAL ASSAULT

The conservative opposition to the Nunn-McCurdy bill was predictable because of the right's general apathy toward citizen obligation and its outright hostility toward inteference in the market. More surprising was the vociferous opposition of the higher-education establishment and its liberal allies on Capitol Hill. Underlying the education establishment's attack was a visceral antipathy to a service-based criterion for federal student aid eligibility. Indeed, when the GI Bill lapsed after the Vietnam War and was reintroduced in 1985, the education establishment did not visibly lament its end or support its resurrection.

The nature of the higher-education establishment's opposition to the Nunn-McCurdy bill is revealing. For instance, that the proposal affected only able-bodied, unencumbered young students was lost in a welter of stacked congressional hearings and outlandish cost estimates.[7] At a time when students are protesting tuition increases in public universities and when the student default rate on federal loans is a scandalous $1.8 billion annually, the American Education Association and the College Board nevertheless stubbornly defended the present so-called needs-based system. Even more telling is that the higher-education establishment ignored the millions of middle-class families who need aid.

Opponents of the Nunn-McCurdy bill argued that linkage of federal aid to service would force only poor students to enter national service.

The proponents of the status quo, however, disingenuously overlook the regressive nature of the present system. In point of fact, the Nunn-McCurdy bill is infinitely fairer than the status quo. Here is why.

Negative Trends in Student Aid and Enrollment Will Be Reversed

The percentage of students receiving federal grants dropped from 31 percent in 1980 to 15 percent in 1984. Of that number, the proportion of black students receiving aid declined from 25 to 17 percent over the same period. This parallels a sharp decline in the percentage of poor, predominantly male, black and Hispanic high school graduates entering college over the same time and is accounted for mainly by the shift from student grants to loans during the 1980s. By putting a GI Bill–type grant in place of student loan programs, youth service widens access to higher education.

New Avenues for Underclass Youth

All student aid is regressive by definition inasmuch as it bypasses the bottom half of the youth population that does not attend college. Experience with existing local and state youth corps shows overwhelming enrollment—because of the steady stipend feature—by poor and minority youth. By expanding such youth corps, national service offers large numbers of youth, otherwise trapped in poverty, opportunities for college or vocational training. A civilian youth corps, like the original GI Bill, would become a way up for many poor young men and women.

Another important consideration is that infusing a middle-class element into civilian youth corps would preclude the debilitating and self-reinforcing stigma of programs targeted only on poor youth. A comprehensive program of national service would call on all our country's races and classes to take part in a common civic enterprise. If this possibility is ignored and time is allowed to slide by, the richest country in the world will enter the twenty-first century crippled by an unemployed, unassimilated, and embittered underclass.

More Student Benefits

The proposed ten-thousand-dollar educational voucher for each year of civilian service far exceeds the average federal grant (fourteen hundred dollars annually). Most important, linking national service to student aid would strengthen the constituency for student aid across the board. Moreover, the only public opinion survey on the issue shows better than three-to-one support for the proposition that students who receive financial aid for college should be "required to repay that support through some type of public service."[8] Consider this: in 1949 our country gladly spent 1 percent of its gross national product on the GI Bill—more than $45 billion in today's dollars.

Youths Act for Themselves

Determining eligibility for federal student aid under the present system is not only complex, but unfair because such aid does not necessarily go to the most needy, even among the college-attending population. Families that have not saved money have an advantage over same-income families that have. By basing eligibility on actions taken by the youth themselves, national service gives young people control over their educational future.

Gross Societal Inequities Addressed

The bill is designed to ensure that most servers would work in local agencies and voluntary associations. Thus national service would strengthen precisely those institutions in deprived communities where the need is greatest. The special energies of the organizations that achieved prominence in the struggle for civil rights could now confront the difficulties of the black underclass.[9] The preferential treatment on the basis of income of day care for children, of primary and secondary education, and in the handling of the aged and sick is one of the shames of our society. Youth participation in national service would reduce such inequities more than any other feasible program.

One other point must be made on service-based student aid. An amendment to the Defense Authorization Act of 1983, sponsored by Congressman Gerald Solomon (R-N.Y.), denies federal student aid to men between the ages of 18 and 26 who fail to register for the draft. The passage of this bill marked a signpost in the effort to restore civic obligations to those receiving student aid. Opposition to the Solomon Amendment, as the new law was called, was immediate. Opponents included pacifists, university presidents, and civil libertarians. The Supreme Court upheld the Solomon Amendment among other reasons because no student is required to seek student aid. The Solomon Amendment was a reaction, if not a full turn of the tide, against the notion that student entitlements were unconnected with civic duty.[10]

Latent union opposition   Although organized labor has not yet taken an official position on national service, the issue of job displacement is a serious one. The only acceptable answer is that national service must be restricted to work that otherwise would not be performed. The whole rationale for national service is that it meets needs not being filled by either the marketplace or the government. An extensive Ford Foundation study calculated that 3.5 million useful jobs could be performed by nonspecialized one-year servers without displacement.[11] Even if this figure is high, surely a program involving 600,000 civilian slots could be managed so as to have minimal effect on the regular work force.

At bottom, the labor substitution issue is more a political problem than anything else; thus it is essential that organized labor be represented on administrative boards at all levels, much as Franklin D. Roosevelt defused labor opposition to the Civilian Conservation Corps by appointing a union leader to head it. Labor must be allotted a policy-making role in a national service program. In an important sense, a national service system could even help labor, for reducing unemployment would tighten the labor market, thereby enhancing union bargaining power in the long term.[12]

Volunteerism One other source of opposition to the Nunn-McCurdy bill originates from proponents of volunteerism. These groups and proposals—represented by such diverse initiatives as Campus Outreach Opportunity League, Campus Compact, Senator Edward Kennedy's Serve-America bill, and, most significantly, President George Bush's proposal for Youth Engaged in Service (YES)—differ from genuine national service. The hallmark of volunteerism is to favor part-time service and uncompensated work over full-time and compensated service. I find singularly unpersuasive the view that only those who serve without reward are worthy of being called national servers. Only the extraordinarily idealistic (or perhaps neurotic) would serve without any recompense whatsoever. Volunteerism proponents also eschew any connection of civilian service with military service; the citizen-soldier concept especially runs contrary to the values of most supporters of volunteer service. Yet another distinction between national service and volunteerism is that the former typically stresses the importance of the service delivered whereas the latter emphasizes the good done to the server. Finally, volunteerists oppose linking service to student aid as such linkage makes use of an element of coercion. That the Nunn-McCurdy bill unabashedly rewards those who serve their country or community more than those who do not places the volunteerism establishment in opposition to the bill.

In congressional testimony in 1989, Energy Secretary James Watkins, a former chief of naval operations, supported both President

Bush's YES program and Senator Kennedy's bill. Opposing Nunn-McCurdy, Watkins states, "We believe service should not be financially compensated by the federal government. We feel that it is inimical to the very objectives we're trying to instill in young people."[13] Apparently Watkins did not see any contradiction between his testimony and his support of the all-volunteer force (AVF), the highest-paid military in our country's history.

DEFENSE DEPARTMENT CONFUSION

Ever since the inception of the AVF, the Office of the Secretary of Defense (OSD) has been hostile to any concept of a citizen-soldier. During the difficult recruiting times of the 1970s, OSD gamely insisted that high-quality recruits were entering the military—long after everyone else knew otherwise. OSD then shifted to claiming that no solid measures linking recruit quality and soldierly performance existed.[14] In the 1980s, OSD opposed two of the most successful recruiting initiatives in the turnaround of the AVF—the Montgomery GI Bill and the two-year army enlistment program. It was no surprise, then, that OSD has also come out strongly against the Nunn-McCurdy bill and its citizen-soldier option. The main OSD arguments and rebuttals follow.

GI Bill–Type Benefits for Civilian Servers Will Make Military Recruiting Difficult

It is foolish to argue that requiring service from college youth who now receive educational benefits with no service requirement will handicap military recruiting. A survey of youth who were offered the options proposed in the Nunn-McCurdy bill indicated that half of all male youth would choose a military option; one in ten, a civilian option; and the remainder choosing not to serve in any capacity. For women, about a quarter chose the military option; the same number, the civilian option, and about half elected not to serve.[15] In brief, the Nunn-McCurdy bill would create a new reservoir of potential military recruits. Indeed, the relevant OSD report contradicts itself by stating that military could not effectively handle larger numbers of recruits.[16] OSD to the contrary, nothing in Nunn-McCurdy can be construed as affecting the military's control over entering numbers and standards.

Citizen-Soldiers Would Create Large Training Costs

The citizen-soldiers would be a new stream of soldiers set by the army's need for two-year enlistments. When reserve components are included in the analyses (something OSD studies on national service have failed to do), savings occur in training costs.[17] In point of fact, reserve recruitment is best met by soldiers with prior service in the active force. In 1989 Army chief of staff Carl E. Vuono supported an enlistment option of two years in the active force, two years in the ready reserve, and four years in the standby reserve.[18] That military personnel trends, for both budgetary and personnel reasons, are moving toward great reliance on reserve components makes the case for the Nunn-McCurdy bill all the more persuasive.

Introducing a Lower-Paid Soldier into the Army Would Cause Discontent in the Enlisted Force

Invidious comparisons, some claim, would be made between those receiving less pay and those performing the same work and holding the same rank for more pay. Yet if the lower-paid citizen-soldier does feel put out, he can join the professional corps. Almost every army in the North Atlantic Treaty Organization except the United States has a two-track system much like the one described here. Our peacetime draft experience shows that many young men accepted short tours in combat arms over the technical-training advantages of a long enlistment and even accepted short tours as enlisted men over the compensation and privileges of longer-term officers.

Why Lose Soldiers Once They Have Been Trained?

This article of faith for OSD human resources analysts does not stand up to scrutiny. Long-term enlistees are less likely to complete their enlistments than short-term servers. Even during the best AVF years about three in ten of those who entered the army failed to complete a three-year enlistment. Certainly the military is more technical than it was a generation ago, but it is hard to argue that military readiness would suffer by having somewhat fewer career soldiers whose work could be done by an equivalent proportion of citizen-soldiers. In a citizen-soldier system, those leaving active duty would automatically enter reserve duty, thus building on the Total Force concept. Resultant personnel cost savings could then be directed toward the career force, precisely where technicians must be retained.

Underlying the whole OSD approach and its contract apparatus has been the myth that the AVF is less expensive than conscription. A look at some dollar figures (in constant 1986 values) gives us a sense of the changes in military compensation since the peacetime draft years (see the appendix for a detailed breakdown). In 1964 the average personnel costs for each active soldier were approximately $17,300, compared with $28,700 in 1986. The contrast in overall personnel costs is enormous. In 1964 the total bill was $79 billion (excluding retirement outlays); in 1986 the total was $100 billion. In other words, we are spending some $20 billion more for half a million fewer soldiers on active duty! Whatever the arguments against the draft, cost savings is not one. Indeed, it will be economics more than sociology that will bring the AVF into question.

The philosophy that underpinned the shift to an AVF tended to define military service in occupational terms rather than in institutional terms.[19] Such a redefinition of the military is based on a set of core assumptions. First, there is no analytic distinction between military systems and other systems, especially no difference between cost-effectiveness analyses of civilian enterprises and military services. Second, military compensation should be in cash (rather than in kind or deferred) and be linked to skill differences rather than to seniority. Finally, if end-strength targets are met in the AVF, concepts of citizenship are incidental concerns. If we are going to have armed forces based on cost-effective grounds—ignoring moral sentiments and civic dimensions—then we should hire Third World nationals and be done with it.

EMERGING PUBLIC PHILOSOPHY AND NATIONAL SERVICE

The national service act seems to have incurred the opposition of just about every interest group in the country.[20] Yet, even though the obstacles are considerable, I see three scenarios, not exclusive of one another, by which national service could be established. One is through the return of a military draft—a development that would surely create pressure for some form of alternative civilian service. A second scenario is for an energetic president to come forward and make the cause of national service his own. Just as the Civilian Conservation Corps was inaugurated by Franklin D. Roosevelt and the Peace Corps by John F. Kennedy, so national service awaits a president who is convinced that such a program is both good politics and good for the country.

The third scenario is the most problematic, but also the most desirable because it would foster public sensibilities to meet societal needs in national service terms. The public—already accustomed to thinking in such terms when it comes to military manpower, as is clear from the resilience of the citizen-soldier concept—is becoming more inclined toward such an approach with regard to civilian service, especially the conservation corps. The debate over the delivery of human services that pits those who favor a market approach against those who support the expansion of government agencies to deliver such services is becoming increasing sterile. National service means thinking of how national needs might be met in a different way and apart from either market arrangements or conventional government delivery of services.

To break out of this conservative versus liberal mind-set means no less than a paradigmatic shift in American thinking about policy. Yet such a shift is essential if we are to meet the challenges that currently confront our society.

For example, national service could help families cope with Alzheimer's disease, which afflicts about 5 percent of Americans over 65 and 20 percent of those over 80 and whose direct costs are estimated at $20 billion annually. The indirect costs are greater: the need for constant care places severe emotional burdens on relatives. Just to give family members a temporary break from caring for an Alzheimer's victim—either through home visits or adult day-care centers—would be a major help.

In recent years U.S. cities have been inundated with the deinstitutionalized mentally ill. Many of these would be better off back in institutions, but staff costs makes this financially infeasible. National service, which would provide low-level personnel for work in mental hospitals, offers a way out. The alternative is to allow cities to become increasingly crowded with people incapable of taking care of themselves and to make Americans increasingly callous toward the plight of the mentally ill on their doorstep.

Efforts to make standard public transportation available to the handicapped not only will lead to huge costs for the public at large, but also will leave untouched the many areas where public transportation is not readily available. With the introduction of national service, a paratransit system based on successful local models could become a nationwide reality. A cheap, alternative transportation system would not only be much less costly than where we are heading, but also offer a much more convenient mode of travel to those who need it the most.

Thanks to acidic paper, every year some 70,000 books in the Library of Congress crumble between their covers and at least 40 percent of the books in major research collections will soon be too fragile to handle. All films made before 1950 are in danger of turning to dust. Preserving these collections is tedious and extremely labor-intensive. Unless a national service program comes to the rescue, we are destined to lose a large portion of our cultural heritage.

The list goes on almost indefinitely, but the point is that we, the citizenry, must think about how national needs might be met through youths' serving their country and community. Political theorists as well as ordinary citizens are showing a growing appreciation of citizens' obligations and the importance of shared values. The new interest in the duties of citizens results from both the inadequacies of Marxism, with its materialist analysis and collectivist prescriptions, and the inadequacies of libertarianism, which offers a similar materialist analysis but with an insistent stress on the individual. Advocacy of national service is the political center reasserting itself against the right and the left.

APPENDIX. ───

COMPARISON OF DEFENSE PERSONNEL COSTS, 1964 VERSUS 1986
(IN 1986 CONSTANT DOLLARS)

	1964	1986
Direct Active Duty Personnel	$43.1 billion	$47.8 billion
Family Housing	1.8	2.8
Support*	6.0	11.8
Reserve Components	2.5	6.4
Retired Military Pay	4.2	17.3
Civilian Pay	26.3	31.3
Total	$83.9	$117.4
Number of Personnel		
Active Duty Military	2,687,000	2,169,000
Reserve Units	953,000	1,130,000
Civilian	1,175,000	1,112,000
Total	4,815,000	4,411,000

*Medical, recruitment, schools

NOTE: Inflation factor: 1964 = 1.0; 1986 = 3.5

SOURCE: Department of Defense, *Manpower Requirements Report FY1988* (February 1987), pp. (VIII 3–4.)

NOTES

1. In its broad contours the Citizenship and National Service Act of 1989 followed the line of reasoning given in Charles C. Moskos, *A Call to Civic Service* (New York: The Free Press, 1988). The main difference between what I proposed and the Nunn-McCurdy bill was my inclusion of high school dropouts in the purview of youth corps. In the text pertaining to the national service proposal, I have held to my original formulation.

I wish to acknowledge Will Marshall, a member the Democratic Leadership Council (DLC) and president of the Progressive Policy Institute, for his ongoing generosity with ideas and practicalities concerning national service. Marshall was the primary author of the DLC's *Citizenship and National Service* (Washington, D.C.: DLC, May 1988), which foreshadowed the Nunn-McCurdy bill. I am also grateful to Joel Berg of the Progressive Policy Institute for bringing new thought to an old subject. Although he does not always agree with everything I advocate, my debt is deep to Donald J. Eberly, who has been my longtime mentor in the area of national service. See Donald J. Eberly, *National Service: A Promise to Keep* (Rochester N.Y.: John Alden Books, 1988).

2. William James, "The Moral Equivalent of War," in *Essays on Faith and Morals* (New York: Longman, Greens, 1942), pp. 311–28. Originally published in 1910.

3. The insight that rehabilitation can best be served when the agency involved is not defined as rehabilitative was originally developed with regard to the latent functions of the armed forces. See Bernard Beck, "The Military as a Welfare Institution," in Charles C. Moskos, ed., *Public Opinion and the Military Establishment* (Beverly Hills, Calif.: Sage Publications, 1971), pp. 137–48.

4. On the connection between citizenship and national service, see especially Morris Janowitz, *The Reconstruction of Patriotism* (Chicago: University of Chicago Press, 1983) and Benjamin R. Barber, *Strong Democracy* (Berkeley: University of California Press, 1984).

5. A paradigm-making book that melds the economics of moral commitments with the prevailing utilitarian model of modern economics is Amitai Etzioni, *The Moral Dimension: Toward a New Economics* (New York: The Free Press, 1988).

6. I agree with conservative critics who find unpersuasive studies that compare the value of work performed by youth servers with what that work would have cost if done on the market. The question must always be, is the work important enough to warrant national service in the first place?

7. Perhaps the most irresponsible statement was the assertion of the research staff of the American Council of Education (ACE) that the Nunn-McCurdy bill would cost the federal government more than $50 billion a year to serve the same number of people now receiving federal student aid. See William D. Ford, "Bill in Congress on Public Service for Young People Shows Confusion

About Student Aid and Patriotism," *Chronicle of Higher Education,* March 15, 1989, p. A40. Although the ACE has backed away from this assertion in private correspondence, it has not publicly withdrawn its earlier statement.

The libertarian right faces a conundrum with service-based student aid. Opposed to federal student aid in principle, it nevertheless dislikes the "something for nothing" feature of the present system. Conservative elder stateman William Buckley has long proposed that the country's top colleges require students to spend a year in national service before they enroll.

8. 1983 Gordon Black poll. This New York state survey was conducted to test public sentiment toward a program like the Reserve Officer Training Corps for noncareer police officers.

9. A 1989 Urban League conference "lamented the shortage of black men in youth programs." "Urban League Parley Focuses on Help for Young Black Men," *New York Times,* May 4, 1989, p. 11. The connection between such a need and national service, however, has yet to be made by leading black organizations. Caring for the infirm elderly is a task that falls almost entirely on women, yet feminist organizations have never rallied behind national service.

10. By 1987 four states—Massachusetts, Mississippi, Illinois, and Virginia— had enacted laws linking state college aid to draft registration. A Tennessee law went so far as to prohibit enrollment of nonregistrants in state colleges and universities.

11. Richard Danzig and Peter Szanton, *National Service: What Would it Mean?* (Lexington, Mass.: Lexington Books, 1986).

12. No serious proposal exists to make national service an element of rebuilding the national infrastructure. Yet the Federal Highway Administration figures that bringing roads up to minimum engineering standards would cost $565 to $655 billion over the next twenty years. *Wall Street Journal,* August 30, 1989, p. 1.

13. "Bush Official Rejects Linking Aid, Volunteer Work," *Chicago Tribune,* April 22, 1989, p. 4.

14. A valuable summary of the literature dealing with quality/performance in the military is Juri Toomepuu, *Soldier Capability–Army Combat Effectiveness— SCACE* (Fort Benjamin Harrison, Ind.: U.S. Army Soldier Support Center, 1981). An insightful account of soldiers in the all-volunteer army of the 1980s is George C. Wilson, *Mud Soldiers* (New York: Charles Scribner's Sons, 1989); for the navy, see Wilson, *Super Carrier* (New York: MacMillan, 1986). An impressive treatment of military recruitment in historical perspective is Sue E. Berryman, *Who Serves? The Persistent Myth of the Underclass Army* (Boulder, Colo.: Westview Press, 1988).

15. These and other pertinent data on the positive effects of the Nunn-McCurdy bill on recruitment are given in Juri Toomepuu, *Effects of a National Service Program on Army Recruiting* (Fort Sheridan, Ill.: Research and Studies Division, U.S. Army Recruiting Command, February 1989). Because the Toomepuu analysis ran afoul of official policy, his report was initially suppressed. Even more troubling, high-level studies emanating from the Pentagon do not acknowledge, much less refute, Toomepuu's research findings.

16. See report attached to letter to Sam Nunn, chairman, Committee on Armed Services, U.S. Senate, dated July 11, 1989, signed by L. Niederlehner, deputy general counsel, Department of Defense. The report itself is unsigned with no letterhead.

17. Toomepuu, *Effects of a National Service Program on Army Recruiting.*

18. The so-called two plus two plus four enlistment has elements of the citizen-soldier track contained in the original Nunn-McCurdy bill. This enlistment was introduced on a trial basis in late 1989. Early reports indicated that the program was hugely successful in attracting young people into the army who would not have considered enlisting in the army for longer terms.

The concept of a lower-paid citizen-soldier track coexisting with a professional soldier track has also been proposed by the Heritage Foundation. See Stuart M. Butler, Michael Sanera, and W. Bruce Weinrod, eds., *Mandate for Leadership II* (Washington, D.C.: Heritage Foundation, 1984), p. 253, and Charles L. Heatherly and Burton Yale Pines, eds., *Mandate for Leadership II* (Washington, D.C.: 1989), p. 738.

19. A comprehensive treatment of the tendency to view armed forces in occupational rather than institutional terms is presented in Charles C. Moskos and Frank R. Wood, eds., *The Military—More Than Just a Job?* (Elmsford, N.Y.: Pergamon-Brassey's, 1988). In addition to the United States, eight Western nations are comparatively examined.

20. In the strange bedfellows department, conscientious objector groups have joined with the Pentagon in opposing the Nunn-McCurdy bill. See the newsletters of the National Interreligious Service Board for Conscientious Objectors and the Central Committee for Conscientious Objection.

Reaction to the Nunn-McCurdy bill has not been one of unrelieved opposition, however. The concept received editorial support in the *New York Times* and strong endorsement from columnists Mark Shields and David Broder in the *Washington Post,* as well as in much of the regional press.

Another philosophical strain that resonates with national service as a concept, if not in all the particulars given here, is neoconservatism. The first major publication of the ideas embodied in the Nunn-McCurdy bill appeared in Charles C. Moskos, "How to Save the All-Volunteer Force," *Public Interest* (Fall 1981): 74–89. At the Hoover-Rochester Conference on the All-Volunteer Force held at the Hoover Institution on War, Revolution and Peace in December 1979, Sidney Hook came to this writer to express his strong endorsement of the concept of national service. For neoconservative support of conscription, see Eliot A. Cohen, *Citizens and Soldiers* (Ithaca, N.Y.: Cornell University Press, 1985) and Philip Gold, *Evasions: The American Way of Military Service* (New York: Paragon House, 1985).

COMMENT

David R. Henderson

First of all, let me agree with you, Charlie [Moskos], about one argument. There is nothing un-American about national service. If Americans are advocating it, it is American.

It is also true that Charlie [Moskos] and everyone else who spoke here in favor of national service did not come out for a draft. I am pleased about that.

But I should add that Charlie admits that the fear that national service will lead to the draft is warranted. I want to expand on that by talking about some of the people who put together the Democratic Leadership Council [DLC] proposal. One of the people was Roger Landrum, who in 1979 favorably cited Chairman Mao's removal of youth from the city to the countryside as an example that "fire[s] some American imaginations." [Committee for the Study of National Service, *Youth and the Needs of the Nation* (Washington, D.C.: Potomac Institute, 1979), p. 28.] Charlie [Moskos] himself has said that if he could wave a wand, he would have national service be a compulsory program. [Jacob V. Lamar, Jr., "Enlisting with Uncle Sam: Is America Ready for a National-Service Program?," *Time*, February 23, 1987, p. 30.] Thank you for not having a magic wand.

Moreover what is striking are the four reasons the DLC itself gave for not wanting a compulsory program: the all-volunteer force is working, not enough women are in the military to justify drafting them (I do not know what that means), a draft would give no role to older citizens, and a draft would not address the nation's nonmilitary needs. [*Citizenship and National Service* (Washington, D.C.: Democratic Leadership Council, May 1988), pp. 13–14.] Absent from that list is any mention of the idea that there is something wrong with threatening innocent eighteen-year-olds with prison sentences.

Similarly, in a recent *Washington Post* article, Landrum gives three reasons for objecting to compulsory universal service: the cost is "out of sight," debates over compulsion are "an endless distraction," and administrative requirements are "a nightmare" [Roger Landrum, "The Citizen Corps is Already Under Way," *Washington Post*, June 2, 1988]. In other words, Landrum's only objection to compulsion, aside from cost, is debate and red tape, not prison sentences for eighteen-year-olds.

Charlie [Moskos] argues that only a successful national service program can pave the way for compulsion. He says, why worry? If it is successful, who cares? Well, if it is successful, opponents of compulsion still care. It is a different program. A successful voluntary program is different from the next step, which will be the draft.

Moreover, you can make an equally strong case that if national service fails, that will be how we get a draft. Consider the following scenario: National service is tried. The civilian service option hurts military recruitment by drawing from its target population. Both options fail to get the upper-middle-class kids that some advocates would like to see in the military and in civilian service. Those are both plausible.

The advocates then say we cannot get the broad representation we want without compulsion. Instead of calling for an end to the national service program that caused the problem for military recruitment, instead of advocating higher pay for the military, they say we have to go to compulsion.

If you think that is implausible, take a look at the bill Senator John McCain introduced a few months ago. At the time I was writing my *Barron's* article [David R. Henderson, "Who Needs a Citizens Corps?" *Barron's*, April 24, 1989, p. 9], they were putting it together. I interviewed a spokesman, Scott Celley. He said that McCain's goal with his voluntary proposal was to "start plugging people into positions and setting up networks with state and local officials." After two years, McCain would switch to a mandatory system of universal service with "disincentives" for those who do not participate. "Could one disincentive be a prison sentence?" I asked. Said Celley, "Under consideration would be a full range of possible penalties to ensure mandatory participation."

Charlie [Moskos] argues that national service would make the draft more palatable. [Moskos, *A Call to Civic Service: National Service for Country and Community* (New York: Free Press, 1988), p. 177.] Isn't a palatable draft better than an unpalatable draft? Yes, it is. That is not the issue. If it is more palatable it is also more likely. An unpalatable, nonexistent draft is better than a palatable one that exists.

The issue of cost has been much talked about here. I thought I would walk you through it. Here is a table that I put together.

COSTS AND BENEFITS
OF CIVILIAN COMPONENT
OF NATIONAL SERVICE
UNDER NUNN-MCCURDY BILL

Additional Budget Cost		*Additional Benefit*
Pay, health & life insurance, supervision	$5.7 billion	a. Nunn-McCurdy-Moskos scenario (i.e., no labor displacement): 600,000 × 2,000 hours per year × $5/hr. = $6 billion
Vouchers 600,000 × $9091	5.5 billion	
Total	11.2 billion	
		or
Offsets: Pell grants	− $2.5 billion	b. Walter Oi (some labor displacement):
Student loans 40% × $3.1 billion	− 1.2 billion	400,000 × 2,000 hrs. × $5 plus
Net additional budget costs	7.5 billion	200,000 × 2,000 hrs. × $7.50 = $7 billion
Including efficiency cost of taxes $7.5 billion × 1.4 =	$10.5 billion	

If Nunn, McCurdy, and Moskos are right, costs exceed benefits by $4.5 billion.

If Walter Oi is right, costs exceed benefits by $3.5 billion.

I put this together with the help of Will Marshall, who is the author of the DLC proposal. I asked him, what do you think this number or that will look like? If you look at the left-hand side that gives the additional budget cost, the $5.7 billion cost the DLC acknowledges. It is the DLC's number.

Panelist: How many participants would there be?

Mr. Henderson: There would be vouchers for 600,000 civilians. On the vouchers, I multiplied 600,000 by $9,091, because that is the discounted value of $10,000 one year from now. I add the $5.5 billion result to $5.7 million and get $11.2 billion. The offset—and this is where Will Marshall helped me—is $2.5 billion in Pell grants and $1.2 billion in student loans. Thus, there is a net additional budget cost of $7.5 billion. But when you raise $1 in taxes, it costs the economy more than $1. There are efficiency losses from taxes and administrative costs in collecting them. It costs about 40 cents on the dollar to collect taxes. If you multiply everything by 1.4 you get $10.5 billion as the net additional costs to the economy.

Of course, Charlie [Moskos] points out that there are benefits, and there are. Let us look at those. There are two scenarios here. In the Nunn-McCurdy-Moskos scenario, the program succeeds in avoiding labor displacement, which means that those workers will not be used in as high valued jobs as they would be if labor displacement is not avoided. They are not taking any existing jobs. This means when you consider that there are many jobs out there that are paying minimum wage or only slightly above, a generous estimate is that they will be working at jobs where their productivity is worth $5 per hour. A more plausible case could be made for $3.35 per hour, but I am being generous. If you take $5 per hour, the benefit is $6 billion. If you take Walter Oi's view that there will be some labor displacement (about 200,000 people displacing laborers whose time is worth $7.50 an hour), you get $7 billion as the benefit. If Nunn, McCurdy, and Moskos are right, the costs will exceed benefits by $4.5 billion. Ironically, if Walter Oi is right, the costs will exceed benefits by only $3.5 billion. So you do want labor displacement.

I am not critical of everything you [Mr. Moskos] said. I want to congratulate you on your critique of the liberal critique. You are on target. But both Charlie [Moskos] and Milton Friedman neglected the key point. They said that student aid money is taken from all taxpayers and is given to the lucky few who happen to be from middle and upper-middle class families. That is true.

But the key point is that all students—even kids from lower-income families who get the aid—who finish college are wealthy. An oil man in Texas who has not yet begun drilling is nonetheless wealthy. As Armen Alchian once said, if we subsidize people to exploit their brains in order to produce future income, that is like subsidizing a Texas oil man who hasn't earned the income from his oil yet. [Armen A. Alchian, "The Economic and Social Impact of Free Tuition," *New Individualist Review*, vol. 5, no. 1 (Winter 1968), pp. 43–44.] That is what is wrong with providing student aid without requiring anything in return. I agree with you totally. The DLC report pointed out that kids who complete college earn over their lifetimes $640,000 more than kids who do not go to college. [*Citizenship and National Service*, p. 11.] Government aid to higher education is a subsidy from the relatively poor to the relatively rich.

Of course, we disagree about what we ought to do about that. I think that we ought to get rid of the subsidy or at least have a loan system that makes the borrowers pay back the loans and has a higher interest rate that reflects the real risk.

Charlie [Moskos] talked about the fact that many people who advocate volunteerism have wrongly been opponents of his proposal. There I do not agree with Charlie. These opponents are right.

In Charlie's book he leads off by talking about a program where people are doing volunteer work on the Rio Grande in Mexico, and he says it has been going on for three centuries. [Moskos, *Call to Civic Service*, p. 1.] The government was not requiring this program three centuries ago, and the government is not requiring it now. The irony is that throughout his book many of the best examples Charlie gives of service programs that are working have nothing to do with government. He talks about the Guardian Angels [a nationwide volunteer anti-crime group that began in 1979 by patrolling the New York City subways to prevent crime] and says what a good program that is. He even says that they refuse to accept government money because doing so would undercut their control and undercut the value of the experience. [Moskos, *Call to Civic Service*, p. 80.] Are you listening to your own words, Charlie?

On the issue of national service's effect on the military, Charlie cites the study by Juri Toomepuu. The whole study is based on survey data. The survey asks, *What would you do if?* Those are the worst kinds of survey questions to ask. You are putting people in hypothetical positions and giving them only a few minutes to answer. They do not really know. They have not had time to think it through. Think of how you think through your decisions when you are going to spend $10,000 or $50,000. The present value of many of these commitments is $50,000. You are talking about eighteen-year-olds making these commitments. If you are asking for quick decisions, you will get many unthought-out decisions.

Charlie has pointed out in his paper that some military people objected to a two-tiered system in the military, with some soldiers paid differently from others, saying it would cause discontent. I agree with him that this is a poor argument. But I also want to point out that it is an argument that Charlie [Moskos] himself has made. Charlie has been a strong opponent of paying people different amounts when they are at the same grade and length of service. [Charles C. Moskos and John H. Faris, "Beyond the Marketplace: National Service and the AVF," in

Andrew J. Goodpaster, Lloyd H. Elliott, and J. Allan Hovey Jr., eds., *Toward a Consensus on Military Service: Report of the Atlantic Council's Working Group on Military Service* (New York: Pergamon Press, 1982), pp. 132–33.] I am glad to see that you are willing to pay people different amounts. Perhaps sometime I can talk you into bonuses, which are an effective way of paying people.

Charlie [Moskos] points out that three out of ten people who enlist for three years fail to complete their term and that short-termers tend to complete their enlistment more often than long-termers. He uses this statistic to argue, "who cares whether we get many short-termers in there?" But that is not the relevant statistic. The relevant statistic—when you have someone enlist for two years, a short-termer—is, how long does he stay on an average? When you have someone enlist for more than two years, a long-termer, how long does he stay on average? Those are the relevant statistics. The answer is that the one who enlists for a longer time stays for a longer time. The data that show that come from Juri Toomepuu. [Toomepuu, "Effects of a National Service Program on Army Recruiting," U.S. Army Recruiting Command, Fort Sheridan, Ill., 1989, p. 34.] Someone who enlists for two years of service tends to stay 3.74 years. That sounds strange, but some re-enlist. Someone who enlists for four years of service tends to stay for 5.27 years, staying over 50 percent longer. This really does matter. Why care that people do not stay a long time? Because it is expensive to train them and wastes money.

On whether the all volunteer force costs less than conscription, there are two sorts of costs at issue. One is the budget cost, and one is the social cost. Look at Charlie's table. The major reason for the increase in the budget cost is military retirement pay. You have to be in there twenty years to get it; it has nothing to do with volunteer forces versus the draft. Personnel support, another big item that went up, includes medical costs, which have been increasing. Syllogistics found that under a wide range of assumptions, we would spend more to get a military of equal effectiveness if we went to a draft. [*The Differential Budget Costs of Conscription-Based Alternatives to the All-Volunteer Force* (Springfield, Va.: Syllogistics, Inc., July 23, 1986).]

Finally, I want to say something about Charlie's use of the term *citizen-soldier*. (I am not only criticizing Charlie; he quotes in his book someone who used the term in a similar way two hundred years ago.) [Moskos, *Call to Civic Service*, p. 14.] Charlie uses the term *citizen-soldier* to talk about people who join for two years and then leave. That is a kick in the teeth to the two million people currently in the military. What are they, Charlie? Chopped liver?

Discussion

Mr. Moskos: Toomepuu based his study on survey data as opposed to those who *say* that everyone is now rushing to these civilian tasks. There is no survey data to show that. At least Toomepuu had some evidence that led him to a conclusion rather than the typical approach of the OSD [Office of the Secretary of Defense] and its contract apparatus ("Here is the conclusion we want") a la Syllogistics. Syllogistics never addresses the Nunn-McCurdy bill. Its report is moot. [*The Effects of National Service on Military Personnel Programs* (Springfield, Va.: Syllogistics, Inc., September 1988).]

Mr. Henderson: I did not use that Syllogistics report.

Mr. Moskos: All manner of studies by the U.S. Army Recruiting Command show there is a dual market, a concept that I was partly responsible for alerting people to. One is the economically motivated individual, and the other is the hiatus kid who wants a short break, does not know quite what to do, wants the GI Bill–type benefit, something between school and eventual adult employment.

The Guardian Angels do not want to have public funds, but they would accept scholarships, which is all I am asking for. [Curtis] Sliwa [founder and leader of the Guardian Angels] would be happy if they were given scholarships.

I actually want to pay the career force more. I do not call them "chopped liver"; I call them professional soldiers. They get a decent wage from the beginning, $17,000 equivalent for a private first class. On the other hand, we have citizen-soldiers who come in different models in different eras. They are militia persons in one period in our country's history; draftees, in another. In the late twentieth and early twenty-first century, we can have a new citizen-soldier under the national service rubric.

I want to add a few more remarks about the budget costs. I did not put retirement costs in my paper. But retirement costs will grow with an all volunteer force, as compared with a force that has more short-termers. If you have a large career force, you will have higher retirement costs down the road. My plan will save big bucks over the long haul. By the way, medical costs are higher not because medical procedures cost more but because there are more junior married people in the enlisted force. Just take the direct pay. You can save half a million career soldiers worth $5 billion a year. This is real money.

David [Henderson] and Doug [Bandow], you still have not talked about reserves. Remember, these men are not getting out of the army; they are going from their short-term active-duty tour into the reserves. You have to stick that into any calculation you make. This is something the opponents of national service never do.

Mr. Henderson: *Citizen-soldiers:* my point is simply that most soldiers are citizens.

Mr. Moskos: That is not the way it has historically been used.

Mr. Henderson: I know, and I would have objected 200 years ago.

My second point is that I used the Syllogistics study of the all volunteer force versus the draft. I was referring to that study. I agree that it did not cost out the Nunn-McCurdy bill, and I did not use it in that context.

The other point about reserves: A reserve year—as Mr. McCloskey reminded us and even people like Doug [Bandow] and me who think that our reserves are in rather good shape, agree—is not the same as an active-duty year. Not that reserve duty does not matter. But a year of reserve duty from a short-termer is not equal to a year of active duty from an active-duty person.

Ms. Postrel: I have a question and an unrelated statement.

On the one hand, one of the major ideas behind national service is creating a common experience analogous to service in the armed forces. Someone said yesterday that approximately 25 percent of the people in national service would be in conservation activities in places like Yellowstone. On the other hand, some people have stressed the community-oriented nature of the program. When I picture community, I picture local community. Congressman McCurdy in private conversation was emphatic that the local community would decide what it needed. Is there a tension here between creating a common national program that has the same effect on a broad cohort and creating localized programs that draw people into meeting the specific needs of their communities? Perhaps different people have different visions of national service.

I would also like to make a general point. In the arguments of the proponents of national service, I see two elements: an element of concerns over personnel and an element of moralism.

I think values are important. I am myself a moralistic person. But I would like to challenge the moralism I have heard here. So far no one has, except Milton Friedman implicitly. The proponents of national service suggest that something is deeply wrong with young people because they are not attracted to particular types of service. These moralistic proponents of national service look at people who were in college in the late 1970s and early 1980s and say, what is wrong with these people? They are only concerned about money. They are not concerned, poll data show us, about trying to change the world.

But if you think about what happened in the 1970s in this country, you will see that it was an understandable and justified response to the economic, social, and political turmoil of the time. I am in part speaking for my generation. We were less utopian than the preceding generation. We were right and are still right to believe that taking care of one's own private, familial, and community (narrowly conceived) needs is primary.

These national service plans have an underlying appeal to those who want to indoctrinate young people ideologically. No one in this room has been talking about having people study the works of Deng Xiaoping. But proponents of national service would like the purpose of national service to include ideological indoctrination in their moralistic attitude. Critics have ignored this problem with national service or waved it aside.

That said, the situation is changing. The proponents' problem is about to go away. The people who are in college now are much more interested in saving the world. Poll data show it. The Times-Mirror poll shows a new group it calls the Upbeats who are—I think wrongly—convinced that there are social causes that are both worth pursuing and likely to be successful. [Norman J. Ornstein, Andrew Kohut, and Larry McCarthy, *The People, the Press, and Politics* (Reading, Mass.: Addison-

Wesley, 1988.] The proponents are trying to solve a problem that is disappearing with the change in generations.

Mr. Eberly: We did not create the army to have a common experience, but one of the outcomes of basic training and other parts of the army is that you get a common experience. Much of what veterans of World War II were talking about as the best years of their lives were those common experiences. One outcome of national service will be such common experiences, which will be remembered well by the participants.

Ms. Postrel: I understand that model. But Congressman McCurdy is emphatic that the program would be localized and particular to the needs of the community. It would therefore—it seems to me—be fragmented. Different people want to design national service programs along different lines.

Mr. Burkhardt: We ought to ask the question, why do we have service in the first place? No one has addressed that issue. Bruce [Chapman] and I have some profound disagreements on other issues. But in his remarks he came the closest for me to answering this question. Ultimately the purpose of service is justice, whether it comes from the words of Jesus, whether it comes from what Mother Teresa has done, or Gandhi, or Martin Luther King, or others. If national service is established, the thing that will engage the imagination of young people is not greed, but the sense that they are contributing to equity and justice in this country. We can argue whether that is good or bad. But I am here to tell you that it is wonderful to see young people rise up because of their sense of justice.

Mr. Bandow: As one of the enemies of national service, I want to respond to a few of the points in Charlie [Moskos]'s presentation. For example, the GI Bill: I view the GI Bill as retroactive pay for people who were drafted and put into combat. I do not have any objections to a GI Bill used in that way; they deserved it.

On the issue of comparing military and civilian service today: the primary duty of the federal government is the defense of this nation. It has no higher duty. Solving social problems—many of which are located at state levels as opposed to the federal level—is simply a different order of duty. For the national government, the military has a much higher priority.

On the question of citizens' obligations: Charlie [Moskos] said that his libertarian opponents believe that citizens have no obligations to one another. That is not my view. There is a matrix of obligations—individually, within families, within communities, within organizations—that individuals have with one another. The important question is, what obligations should be enforced by the state or promoted by government programs? We have to be careful when we start picking out obligations and deciding those that should be enforced or promoted by law as opposed to obligations that are important and should be promoted by grass-roots organizations, by families, and in other spheres.

On the question of sacrifice, paying people, and what is a volunteer: one should not expect volunteers to serve without any reward, but before you call something service—according to the sense of service that I get from your [Mr. Moskos's] book, from the DLC's book, and from other books—it should, as Peter Szanton suggested, require some sacrifice. [Charles C. Moskos, *A Call to Civic Service: National Service for Country and Community* (New York: Free Press, 1988); *Citizenship and National Service: A Blueprint for Civic Enterprise* (Washington, D.C.: Democratic Leadership Council, May 1988).] The payments provided by your [Mr. Moskos's] proposal and the DLC proposal are far above that. They do not require sacrifice. In the military, seventeen thousand dollars is a fair wage, considering some of the jobs that people in the military do. There is a sacrifice. You put in long hours. It is not a nine to five job. You are on an aircraft carrier helping bring in multimillion dollar planes. You are engaged in tasks in which you are called on to risk your life. The military should be run on the basis of a call for duty and with the idea of sacrifice, and I agree with some of your criticisms.

David [Henderson] and I were on a panel [Association for Public Policy Analysis and Management meeting, Seattle, 1988] with [sociologist] John Faris [vice president, Cole and Weber, Inc., Seattle advertising firm]. I agreed with much of what John said about occupational and service models. He made many good suggestions about how the military should attract people and what values it should emphasize in its recruiting program. There should be a call for sacrifice. The problem with these [national service] programs is that they are paying way above that. They will provide no sense of sacrifice.

Finally, there is the question of the expense of the all volunteer armed force versus the draft. I am skeptical about aggregate numbers. You have to look at the cost of the first two years of people who would be drafted. The total pay for people in the first two years of service is about $6 billion. Even if you cut pay in half for draftees, you are not going to save much money. You will get higher turnover. You will have higher training costs. You will have to have higher pay to keep a consistent career force and to bring people in because retention will be lower. You have to look at a much more disaggregated figure as opposed to the total sum you put in your paper.

Mr. Moskos: Let me address the thrust of the remarks here about intermediate organizations. The Nunn-McCurdy bill is designed to take advantage of these groups. Groups like Bob Burkhardt's and the college work programs—these are intermediary groups. There are thousands more examples. All of them say they could use an infusion of more federal funds. This is where debate would have the most value and help clarify things the most.

By the way, Doug [Bandow], the GI Bill is not just for combat soldiers, it is for women, who do not bear combat arms.

Mr. Bandow: Now you are referring to today. But you talked about the 1949 figure. That expense came because of war veterans.

Mr. Moskos: The great majority of GI Bill users in 1949 were not combat soldiers. Do not think of it as a reward for combat. That is a misstatement of what the GI Bill is, and the current one is not that either.

On the savings: I disagree with you on the budget figures. Let us look at personnel costs in 1986, the last year for which we have official data available, and in 1964. Look at the numbers. Do not get complicated; just divide the denominator by a numerator and see what the costs are. It is much more expensive under the AVF [All Volunteer Force]. There are a thousand arguments against the draft. But please do not say that the AVF is cheaper than the draft.

One other thing: you [Mr. Bandow] too did not bring in the reserves.

Mr. Bandow: David [Henderson] handled it.

Mr. Moskos: Training costs do not increase if they go into reserves. Every reservist, if he has no prior service, must be trained just like an active-duty soldier. General [Carl E.] Vuono, the chief of staff of the U.S. Army, has said that he would prefer no nonprior service entry. I do not want to get too technical, but the idea is that every reservist comes out of the active-duty force or the citizen-soldier track.

Mr. Henderson: On the budget costs, Doug [Bandow] is right that you need to disaggregate the data. If you are talking about a draft, unless Charlie [Moskos] is advocating a tsarist-style draft where you draft people for 25 years, you do not look at the whole career force. You look at first-termers because that is the length of time that people would be drafted for. That was Doug [Bandow]'s point. Perhaps the Department of Defense quit publishing this aggregate data because you [Mr. Moskos] kept misusing it. [laughter]

Mr. Oi: From 1964 to 1972, real wages were climbing at about 2 percent a year. That will raise the costs. From 1984 on, real wages have been rising again.

Furthermore, the budget cost is an irrelevant cost. The social cost of the effort is the all-important one. That is the relevant cost. By any calculation, it has to be lower on a volunteer basis, especially when you include the avoidance costs. Under the draft, we had people fathering children, running off to Sweden, and doing other similar things. It was expensive.

People are in error about the common experience. Under the Nunn-McCurdy bill's plan, the local national service councils will cut contracts with local service agencies. If you cut a contract with [the] rape crisis [center], you go with rape crisis. If you cut one with the Al Sigl sheltered workshop, you work in the Al Sigl sheltered workshop. Is this what we think will constitute a useful training experience? No. It is a waste. It is providing labor resources to service agencies that have connections with national service councils.

That is not the spirit of national service as I heard it talked about in the 1960s.

Mr. Chapman: We have this problem before us: The Nunn-McCurdy bill is dead in the water. We have a piece of legislation before us [the National and Community Service Act (S.1430)] that includes a demonstration program. What will the demonstration project test? What will this demonstration program tell us about needs that we do not know already? There is an infinity of needs out there. Won't we find out that if we offer people jobs, they will sign up to do them, and that there are many things that need doing?

Mr. Moskos: If there are many things in society that need doing, then let us do them. What is the problem? We will find out if this is a better way of doing them than not doing them.

Let me give you an example. Here is a case where national service makes sense. In everything I have ever written or said, I have two criteria: (1) Is this the best way to do it? (2) Is this the cheapest way to do it? Only then do you use national service. Otherwise, forget the idea. Court decisions now mandate that all buses have lifts for handicapped people. Congress will spend billions of dollars on them. They usually are broken. They get everybody else angry when they are waiting for the bus. Only about 1 percent of those who could use them, use them.

The paratransit systems do not work either. They take too long to come, and you have to make reservations a long time in advance. Here is a market failure. Yet this is also something that is too expensive for the government to hire regular civil servants to do. The Germans use conscientious objectors to do such paratransit work. In the United States, the Vera Institute [of Justice] in New York uses felons to do this work.

This is a vital service. The use of national service people would save the taxpayers zillions of dollars. Everybody will be better off.

Mr. Henderson: Deregulate taxis.

Mr. Moskos: Paratransit is a good example of how national service could be used.

9

A SUPPORTING ROLE FOR THE FEDERAL GOVERNMENT IN NATIONAL SERVICE

Donald J. Eberly

William James chose Stanford University as the setting for his most famous speech, "The Moral Equivalent of War," which he gave at an assembly of the full university on February 25, 1906. In it James called for

> a conscription of the whole youthful population to form for a certain number of years a part of the army enlisted against Nature. . . . To road-building and tunnel-making, to foundries and stoke-holes, and to the frames of skyscrapers, would our gilded youth be drafted off, according to their choice, to get the childishness knocked out of them and to come back into society with healthier sympathies and soberer ideas.[1]

His speech was hardly a prescription: Would all youth be drafted or just the gilded ones? Would they have a choice of being drafted or a choice of assignments once drafted? Still, his speech has been a source of inspiration to many of its readers and influenced programs such as the Civilian Conservation Corps and the Peace Corps.

Whatever James's intentions, and I believe his purpose was more to inspire than to prescribe, the only U.S. draft for civilian purposes has been an alternative service program for conscientious objectors during times of a mandatory military draft.

A youthful mobilization resembling James's moral equivalent of war is needed for human and environmental services among old folks and children, the poor and the homeless, the illiterate and the ill-housed, those imprisoned and in mental institutions and for our polluted air, our acid rain, and our scarred earth.

Young people need work experience, a chance to explore careers, a higher sense of self-confidence and civic pride, a chance to develop a service ethic, and opportunities to work with different kinds of people in common endeavors. The weakened social fabric of the United States needs good citizens and future leaders with firsthand experience in tackling important social and environmental problems.

Any one of these reasons is enough to justify at least a modest moral equivalent of war; put together, they make a compelling case for what I have been referring to for nearly forty years as national service. The name is not crucial. What is critical is the way national service is designed and operated. Because these features are vital and because so many different national service plans are being floated nowadays, I shall first briefly outline what I mean by national service.

DESIGN AND OPERATION

Until 1966, I had given little thought to the detailed operation of national service, thinking it a job for the experts, but in May of that year, I convened a conference on national service. A few weeks later Burke Marshall asked me to prepare a plan for national service for consideration by the National Advisory Commission on Selective Service. The plan that I submitted to the commission—and that I have continually updated on the basis of evaluation, experience, and current conditions—has the following framework: A national service foundation would set guidelines for national program operation, stipulating that those in service must meet human or environmental needs and that they may not displace regular employees or volunteers.[2] It would make grants to state and local organizations that direct the program and would provide a GI Bill for the further education and training of those who complete their service agreements. Five percent of its budget would be set aside to experiment with variations on the basic national service model.

At the local level, young people would register at seventeen and receive information about the service opportunities open to them when they turn eighteen. The local grantee would determine which public and nonprofit agencies qualify to sponsor national service participants and invite them to list openings. The list of openings would be made available to labor unions and others who might challenge them as falling outside the guidelines. The youthful applicants would then examine acceptable positions and interview for those that interest them. When sponsor and applicant agree on an assignment, they then fill out an agreement form specifying the responsibilities of each. That agreement is then presented to the grantee, who approves it if all is in order. That agreement also becomes the major point of reference for settling disputes between the sponsor and the server.

The server would receive a $6,200 annual stipend, 10 percent of which would be paid in cash by the sponsor, who also assumes responsibility for the supervision and training of the servers it engages. The sponsor receives no money from the grantee. The $620 annual payment, as well as supervisory, training, and other costs, comes from the sponsor's budget.

National service, then, would be characterized by low entry standards and high performance standards. Admission would be open to everyone willing to serve; continued enrollment in national service would be contingent on living up to the service agreement reached between the young person and the sponsoring agency.

Existing federal programs such as the Peace Corps, Job Corps, and Pell grants that might be affected by national service would remain in place for several years. Should a peacetime draft be reinstituted, persons completing two years of national service would have the same draft status as those completing two years of military service.

These principles, I am confident, can launch national service today, can see it grow to enroll several hundred thousand young people in a few years, and can provide the above-mentioned benefits to those in need, to those who serve, and to the United States.

I shall attempt to shed some light on where we are with national service and where we should be going with it by first responding to its major critics. Second, I shall outline two test projects designed to inform the national service debate. Third, I shall make a few observations on the current national service scene.

As expected, the pervasive issue in these three areas concerns the role of the federal government. Those of us who look at national service and see the promise of service, youth development, and citizenship would like to unleash governmental resources to accomplish the promise. Those who look at national service and see the threat of bureaucracy, boondoggle, and slavery want to keep the government out of it.

In deciding what government should and should not do, I take as my guide Adlai Stevenson's comment on Woodrow Wilson: "He taught us to distinguish between governmental action that takes over functions formerly discharged by individuals, and governmental action that restores opportunity for individual action."[3] National service as described above can restore the opportunity for individual action. To distinguish between it and other national service proposals, I shall refer to it as Cadets in Service to America (Cadista) and to those in service as Cadets.

Issues and Answers

It will take a Pentagon-sized bureaucracy to run national service. Not at all. Cadista will be about as decentralized as the Defense Department is centralized and appropriately so because the problems are national, but the solutions are local. Sponsoring organizations' providing the necessary supervision and training to those who serve and making a cash contribution to the endeavor help ensure that Cadets contribute and have a fruitful experience. Costs to the government are reduced by the sponsor's contribution and by the savings resulting from the high ratio of Cadets to program monitors.

It will be a boondoggle because the jobs will be useless. Doug Bandow refers derisively to national service as "building playgrounds, handling police paperwork, and installing smoke detectors in senior citizens homes."[4] However, Dan Evans, the former Washington governor and senator, says these little things add up. Referring to the chore services and shopping that volunteers in a national service test project performed for elderly residents in the Seattle area in 1973–1974, Evans says it helped them "remain independent and in their own home as an alternative to continuous care in a nursing home or similar facility. . . . If you can help an elderly person remain independent for three months longer, it more than pays for a whole year of the volunteer."[5] Also, the Cadista requirement of a significant contribution by the sponsors will keep to nearly zero the number of useless placements.

We can't afford it. Yes we can. Studies show that the value of services rendered will equal or exceed the cost of the program to the federal government.[6] The other outcomes—work experience, career exploration, better citizens, increased awareness of the needs of others—are bonuses.

National service would be unconstitutional and a return to slavery. This refers to a form of service that would put anyone in prison who refused to serve. It may or may not be constitutional, but as an idea with few supporters and of little interest to congressional advocates of national service, mandatory service is irrelevant to today's national service debate.

There is not that much work to do. There is much work to do. Surveys over the past 25 years show a need for the work that could be done by three to five million young people in national service.[7] Cadista's system for matching people with jobs, however, as with any such system in a democracy, is imperfect. I am satisfied that public agencies and non-profit organizations can usefully engage up to one million participants in full-time service. Beyond that, test projects (see my discussion of research and development below) are needed to determine the upper limits.

Why do we need national service when millions of young people are already volunteering? Certainly that volunteer work deserves applause. But it amounts to only about four hours per week, with half of that devoted to sectarian religious work and other activities ineligible for government support. Also, there are many activities—from day-care centers to conservation corps—where full-time service is required. Yet the number of 18–24-year-olds in full-time, year-around service at the end of 1988 in such programs as the Peace Corps, Volunteers in Service to America (VISTA), the California Conservation Corps, and the New York City Volunteer Corps was only 8,500.[8]

Some say that few young people would show up for national service. A few proposals for national service—in particular those that would pay participants little or nothing for full-time service—would have a hard time recruiting people. In looking at survey and other available data, I concluded that a steady-state Cadista would have enrolled about one million people in 1980 and, given the changes in the population and economy since then, I would expect a similar program in 1990 to enroll about half a million young people.

National service is a stalking-horse for a military draft. This seems unlikely under present conditions. Although the military services are struggling to meet their enlistment quotas (evidently because of a drop in the youth population and in the rate of unemployment), there are signs that the United States will soon reduce the size of its active duty military forces. Pressures have been building for some years to reduce U.S. troop strength in Europe and the Far East. Now, with Gorbachev's many initiatives and with Soviet generals testifying before the Congress, the pressures are increasing. A significant U.S. troop reduction would almost certainly relieve the military's recruitment difficulties until the youth population starts to rise.

Joseph S. Murphy contends that those who volunteer for two years of national service will lose that time to those who go directly to college.[9] In Cadista, the reverse is more apt to be the case. In the Seattle project, for example, participants reported on a standardized career progress test that their service experience advanced them two rungs up on a ten-rung career ladder and that their long-range expectations were two rungs higher than they would have been without the service experience. Both results were significantly above the norm.[10] Former Peace Corps and VISTA volunteers report that they learned more than they contributed while in service.[11] That Cadista gives Cadets a major voice in their service assignments will help ensure that Cadets consider the service experience worthwhile.

Leave college student aid programs the way they are. Other than adding a GI Bill for national service, Cadista would not change them. But there are other forces at work. With a student loan default rate now at $1.9 billion per year, something has to give. Let us be open to new ways of providing aid so changes come gradually. It is not necessary to force the issue by taking the Nunn-McCurdy-Moskos approach, but I would not be surprised to see the gradual and partial replacement of existing student aid programs with the GI Bill. This will result in (1) more students because Cadets who were not college bound will have their educational appetites whetted by the service experience, (2) better students because they will have better ideas of what they want to study and what careers they want to pursue, and (3) more total money for student aid because the earned benefits under the GI Bill will be more popular with Congress than current programs.

Bandow says that "dumping money on private groups would corrupt them, changing their focus from helping people to collecting government funds";[12] a volunteer coordinator had a similar refrain: "You'll have to pay us to take these kids off your hands." Private groups, however, would not receive a penny from Cadista. In fact, sponsors would have to rearrange their budgets or raise new money to provide for the necessary supervision, training, and dollar contributions. Such money would come from sources that support particular activities. Thus, a day-care center might receive money from the local United Way, a baby food company, and the Department of Health and Human Services.

National service will impose high opportunity costs. Although controlled tests have yet to be performed that will enable us to predict opportunity costs, indications are that they will be small. The largest single group of Cadets almost certainly will be unemployed and looking for constructive work; the next largest will probably be in college with little sense of purpose and would welcome the opportunity to do something useful, to find themselves, or to test their careers. Even those young people for whom opportunity costs are the greatest—those who enter Cadista from paying jobs—will enter at least in part because they believe it will improve their lives.

National servers will displace regular workers and volunteers. Legal prohibitions and opportunities to challenge openings before they are filled will keep this number close to zero. What will be interesting is the extent to which Cadista will create new jobs and promote adaptation to new needs. Some jobs will be created by sponsors as they hire supervisors and trainers, and some positions filled by Cadets will be transformed into jobs filled by regular workers.

I don't want the federal government deciding what national servers will do in Peoria. It will not. Decisions in Cadista are made locally at three levels: by the grantee when it decides what organizations qualify to receive Cadets, by the sponsoring organizations when they submit applications for service to be performed, and by the youthful participants when they decide where they would like to serve.

RESEARCH AND DEVELOPMENT

The National and Community Service Act (S.1430) offers the best hope in years for significant testing of national service. Just how much the demonstration programs provided for under this bill would break new ground and how much they would reconfirm what is already known about national service is not yet clear.

The two test projects that will best inform the national service debate would measure the demand and supply parts of the national service equation. The demand side of the equation should be determined by guaranteeing Cadets to all the eligible organizations in a given area, say a midsized city including surrounding suburbs and a contiguous rural area. Most would volunteer from within the test area; others would be transported in. A similar area would be designated as a control. Such a test would take two or three years to reach its steady state and another three or four years to be properly tested.

The supply side of the equation should be determined by offering civilian and military opportunities to all young people in an area like the one described above. The test would run for eight years so fourteen-year-olds could plan in advance. Measurements would be made of the number who serve and their demographics and how their time in service affects future education and careers. At the end of these tests, we would have a realistic idea of the optimal size of national service in the United States.

On the basis of survey data and previous Cadista-type projects, my hypothesis is that the first test will show a demand for Cadets equal to 1 percent of the population of the test area; the second test will show 15 percent of the young people choosing military service, 25 percent choosing Cadista, and the remainder choosing neither.

The federal government's role in these test projects should be in their design, financing, evaluation, and coordination with Cadet recruitment and service projects in other areas. Administration and education should be local responsibilities.

RECOMMENDATIONS AND CONCLUSIONS

I conclude with a few observations about national service directed at those individuals and groups in positions to make major decisions about national service.

To those politicians and educators interested in the interaction between service and education I would say: *Exploit the potential of service learning but do it carefully.* Service learning is defined by its originators as integrating "the accomplishment of a needed task with educational growth."[13] This two-way street wherein the service informs the learning and the learning informs the service, when properly utilized, has enormous potential. Too often, however, what passes for service learning is little more than remedial education unrelated to the service activity.

We cannot dump service learning on the nation's schoolteachers and college professors because they are not equipped to handle it. For every hundred teachers at a typical school or college, no more than five or ten can properly deal with service learning.

But we can make headway. The government can, for five years, help finance the appointment of full-time service-learning coordinators in our schools and colleges. These people would organize service-learning programs to balance the service needs of community agencies, the educational goals of teachers, and the altruistic, exploratory, and experiential interests of students. Government funding would be phased out at the end of the five-year period.

Colleges and universities could introduce four-year baccalaureate degrees that would include a year of national service, set up learning contracts and seminars, and assess the learning that comes from the service experience. The government should encourage the academic recognition of service experiences, but should not compel or control such recognition.

To President Bush I would say: *Tell the American people what to expect from national service.* Thus if we spend $200 million to support a Cadista-type national service, Americans can expect at least $200 million worth of services performed, together with the several benefits acquired by virtually all of those who serve.

On the other hand, if we spend $50 million on a Youth Engaged in Service (YES) to America–type national service, they can expect mostly exhortation and advice. Mr. Bush's press release on the day of his YES to America announcement said, "The president's national service initiative focuses on the most critical domestic challenges facing the nation today."[14] Yet there was nothing in the announcement, or in the White House briefing for nonprofit agencies that I attended, to convince me that YES will have a measurable impact on our "most critical domestic challenges." The evidence suggests that $50 million for YES will have less impact on those critical challenges than $50 million for Cadista.

Lessons from other nations tend to fortify this conclusion. Although both Mexico and Indonesia urge university students to contribute to the health and education of peasants and farmers by serving several months in the countryside, these are mere shadows of those programs that were in place when there was enough financial support to meet the needs of the students for transportation, food, and shelter. By contrast, Nigeria and West Germany financially support the young people in their national service programs, which have been significant both for the nations and for those who serve.[15]

As much as I applaud the first president to establish an Office of National Service in the White House, it needs much more muscle to achieve the stated goals of YES to America.

To the Peace Corps I would say: *Shift from the present one-way street to programs that are bilateral and multilateral.* In terms of a benefit-cost ratio, the Peace Corps may be our best investment since the GI Bill. But to keep up with the times, it should sponsor exchanges of American volunteers with those in other countries and join with nations around the world in endeavors like a world conservation service or an emergency relief corps.

To those running youth service programs I would say: *Continually test service activities on the frontiers of human and environmental needs.* These frontiers must be tested for two reasons. First, today's service areas may fade away as they are taken over by robots or paid employees. Second, national service organizers may acquire a fatal lassitude if they fall into the trap of doing what is easiest and seek to replicate the experiences offered young people year after year instead of building next year's program on this year's experiences. I shall cite three examples of frontline service projects.

James B. Jacobs recommends the use of national service participants in prisons: "National service volunteers would not easily identify or sympathize with the staff subculture; they would become an institutionalized watchdog that the permanent cadre would not trust to maintain the secrecy and silence that deter public scrutiny. Brutality, excessive force, and racism might decrease."[16]

Hans R. Huessy writes that professionals who try to give mentally ill and mentally retarded patients the caring they need

> "burn out." They cannot sustain it. But for a time-limited period all of us can make a nearly total commitment. Volunteers who serve six to twenty-four months can give of themselves to meet the needs of these unfortunate members of society. . . . Professional consultation without the caring does not work. Caring without professional input also does not work. The professional input can be bought. The caring can come only through committed service.

He added that this superior caring system can be had for "one-tenth the cost of current professional programs."[17]

The dedication of which Huessy speaks and the testing of which I speak exist in youth service programs around the country. Two days before Christmas 1988 there was an oil spill at the mouth of Grays Harbor on the coastline of Washington State. A Department of Wildlife official recounted his experience with members of the Washington Conservation Corps.

> I will probably always remember a WCC crew loading dead, oiled birds into my pickup for transport to the Aberdeen hatchery late on Christmas Eve. When I asked where they would be staying that night, they cheerfully informed me that they would probably stay right there in the Ocean Shores public works shop.
>
> "We've got about 40 live oiled birds here," one of them told me. "Somebody's got to see that they're all right."
>
> The crew had already worked a ten- or twelve-hour day by then. I drove back to Aberdeen feeling a bit more humble about just how hard I had been working.[18]

That kind of performance and dedication renews my confidence that young people can tackle the tough jobs in society just as they have tackled the tough jobs on the front lines of armed combat over the years.

Today we are faced with many tough civilian jobs that need doing, and we know that many young people are willing to serve where needed. So let us join the need with the resources and launch an updated version of James's moral equivalent of war.

To get there, we do not need a Pentagon to run boot camps and direct service projects. What we need is a three-legged stool, a small, quasi-governmental office that will (1) bring the nation's leadership to bear on challenging young people to serve on the frontiers of human and environmental need, (2) provide the financial support to enable all young people who want to serve to do so, and (3) support continual testing and evaluation to keep national service up to date.

One leg of this stool is in place and the other two are underconstruction. President Bush and many other national leaders are challenging young people to serve. The legislation pending in the Senate—which proposes spending $330 million in the first year—will move us into a time of universal service opportunities and provide the necessary tests and evaluations. If we are to give national service the stability its various manifestations have not had over the years, we must hammer the other two legs into their sockets.

NOTES

1. William James, "The Moral Equivalent of War," in John J. McDermott, ed., *The Writings of William James* (New York: The Modern Library, 1968), p. 669.

2. National Service Secretariat, *A Plan for National Service* (New York: November 1966). Most of the plan has been published in Donald J. Eberly, *National Service: A Report of a Conference* (New York: Russell Sage Foundation, 1968).

3. Earl Latham, *The Philosophy and Policies of Woodrow Wilson* (Chicago: University of Chicago Press, 1958).

4. Doug Bandow, "The National Service Debate," *Christian Science Monitor*, June 21, 1989.

5. National Service Secretariat, "An Interview with Senator Daniel J. Evans," *National Service Newsletter*, no. 43 (December 1983): 3.

6. U.S. Congress. Senate. Committee on Labor and Human Resources, *Hearings: Presidential Commission on National Service and National Commission on Volunteerism*, 96th Cong., 2d sess., 1980, p. 141 (reports on the value of work done by members of the Young Adult Conservation Corps); Kappa Systems, Inc., *A Cost/Benefit Analysis of the Program for Local Service* (Arlington, Virginia: Kappa Systems, Inc., 1975) (reports on the benefit-cost ratio of a national service test project conducted by the ACTION agency); Donald J. Eberly, "Base-line for

a Future National Service," *Youth Policy* 10, no. 1 (January 1988): 21 (reports on the benefit-cost ratio of several current state and local youth service programs).

7. Greenleigh Associates, *A Public Employment Program for the Unemployed Poor* (November 1965): pp. 28, 29; "First Comprehensive Survey in 13 Years Finds Need for Several Million People at National Service Level," *National Service Newsletter*, no. 35 (January 1979): 2; Richard Danzig and Peter Szanton, *National Service: What Would It Mean?* (Lexington, Mass.: Lexington Books, 1986), pp. 17–45.

8. National Service Secretariat, *Results of the 1988 Youth Service Survey* (Washington, D.C., 1988).

9. "Service With A Smile," *New York Times*, August 6, 1989 education section.

10. Kappa Systems, Inc., *The Impact of Participation in the Program for Local Service on the Participant* (Arlington, Va: Kappa Systems, Inc., 1975), chap. 2.

11. Donald J. Eberly, *National Service: A Promise to Keep.* (Rochester, N.Y.: John Alden Books, 1988), p. 65.

12. Doug Bandow, "National Service Debate."

13. Atlanta Service-Learning Conference, *Atlanta Service-Learning Conference Report, 1970* (Atlanta: Southern Regional Education Board, 1970), p. 2.

14. Office of the Press Secretary, The White House, *Points of Light Initiative.* Washington, D.C., June 22, 1989, p. 6.

15. Donald J. Eberly and Michael W. Sherraden, *The Moral Equivalent of War? A Study of Non-Military Service in Nine Nations* (Westport, Conn.: Greenwood Press, 1990).

16. James B. Jacobs, "The Implications of National Service for Corrections," *New Perspectives on Prisons and Imprisonment* (Ithaca: Cornell University Press, 1983), p. 210.

17. Cited in Coalition for National Service, *National Service: An Action Agenda for the 1990s* (National Service Secretariat, Washington, D.C., 1988), p. 3.

18. Doug Zimmer, "Quick Response and Hard Work Earn Praises for WCC Crews, *Esprit: A Bulletin of the Washington Service & Conservation Crops* (Olympia, Washington: Washington Youth Employment Exchange, Summer 1989), p. 2.

Comment:
The Dirty Work Philosophy
of National Service

Martin Anderson

National service is a strange, rather shadowy public policy. From a distance it has a certain glittering allure, caressed by puffy clouds of benevolence and self-satisfaction, doing good works for others and feeling good about doing them. But almost always on closer inspection, when one penetrates the soft, slippery words that describe the proposed policies, one finds the sharp fangs of coercion and compulsion, a faint whiff of envy and hatred of the young, and an ideological yearning for elements of a totalitarian society.

Today an understanding of what national service is all about is obscured by an imprecise use of language. The term *national service* is often used indiscriminately to describe proposed public programs that differ vastly in their content and in what their effect would be. The two public service programs that are today described as *national service* differ radically: one kind of public service is *voluntary*, free of any coercion or compulsion, a form of public service in which citizens freely choose to give of their time and effort and money, a form of pure benevolence; the other kind of public service is *compulsory*, where good deeds are done out of fear—the fear of going to jail (straight compulsion) or the fear of devastating financial loss (economic coercion).

The idea of national service is a controversial, divisive issue because these two very different forms of public service keep getting mixed up. Properly understood, there is almost no controversy among the overwhelming majority of Americans today. Americans like the idea of *voluntary* public service; Americans also believe the idea of *compulsory* public service is morally repulsive.

So why does the controversy continue, as it has for most of this century? We have hundreds and hundreds of public service programs—in the towns and cities, in the states, and at the federal level. We have the Peace Corps and the Job Corps and VISTA. We have available opportunities for just about anyone who would like to spend time and energy serving others. In 1989, President Bush proposed an expansion of the federal effort, Youth in Service to America (YES), that promises to fill any existing gaps in the vast network of public and private opportunities to serve—no controversy here. There is also no real controversy about the kind of national service programs that call for the widespread conscription of America's youth. Emphatically rejected by all but a handful, politically speaking they are nonstarters with about as much appeal as concentration camps.

The national service controversy continues because the proposed programs are not exactly what their proponents claim. The programs that still stir controversy are those that claim to be voluntary but that contain core elements of coercion or compulsion or the intent to one day become compulsory and universal. The argument is not about whether we like voluntary or compulsory programs. That argument is settled and is likely to remain settled for at least our lifetimes. No, the argument today is whether a proposed national service program is voluntary or compulsory, one which young people freely choose or one into which they are coerced.

THE HIDDEN AGENDA OF COMPULSION

The issue of compulsion is central for all those who favor a large-scale, universal program of service to the state, especially if they believe, which they do, that *all* young people should somehow be made to participate. For they know that only official laws compelling the young to serve, backed by the threat of real punishment including jail, will ensure that everyone serves.

"Any effective national service program will necessarily require coercion to insure that all segments of the American class structure will serve," wrote Charles Moskos, one of the most persistent and effective advocates of large-scale national service, in 1971.[1]

"Only if it were mandatory and universal could national service impose a roughly equal burden on all citizens," concluded the report of the Democratic Leadership Council in 1988.[2]

Michael Walzer, the philosophical guru of modern national service, was even more explicit in 1983 when he wrote that an effective national service program "would require an extraordinary degree of state control over everyone's life, and it would interfere radically with other kinds of work."[3]

But despite the conclusions that these undeniably intelligent men are led to by analysis and reason, they do not openly propose universal compulsion of the young. Why? Simple political expediency. They know they cannot achieve what they want if they tell the truth. So they do the next best thing. They set aside their true goal and propose programs they hope will advance their goals without alarming the general public. For example, the 1988 report of the Democratic Leadership Council candidly admits they doubt "that the American people would accept such a coercive and intrusive—not to mention costly—program."[4]

Professor Moskos admitted in 1988 finding himself "in the awkward situation of rebutting my own former position" (the one he took in 1971),[5] but not awkward enough to renounce the delights of compulsion. When it came to the military draft, a part of any compulsory national service program, Moskos was one of those rare individuals who saw the draft as something good in and of itself, unlike most people who, even if they supported the draft, saw it as a necessary evil. In 1980, Moskos stated flatly, "I am one of those former draftees who look upon conscription as a moral good."[6]

Over the years Moskos's lust for compulsion never dimmed. "If I could have a magic wand, I would be for a compulsory system" Moskos told *Time* magazine when asked about national service in 1987.[7] Then he bragged to a columnist for the *Chicago Tribune* that his latest effort, the legislation introduced by Senator Sam Nunn of Georgia in 1989, was "just this side of compulsion, but we don't cross the line."[8]

Professor Moskos is only the latest of many who have tried to persuade Americans to adopt compulsory national service. The accepted grandfather of national service, quoted reverently by all believers who came after him, is William James, the philosopher who was the father of pragmatism. In a speech given in 1906, *The Moral Equivalent of War*, James stated unashamedly that everyone should be compelled to serve the state for a "certain number of years."

"If now—and this is my idea—there were, instead of military conscription a conscription of the whole youthful population . . . the injustices would tend to be evened out, and numerous other goods to the commonwealth would follow." James pointedly called this kind of national service a "blood-tax."[9]

James's blood-tax was but a pale copy of the plan fictionalized 22 years earlier by the famous novelist Edward Bellamy. Bellamy's book *Looking Backward* proposed to turn the United States into a military-industrial dictatorship, where government, military, and business merged into one giant fascist whole. Universal compulsory military service would be required of all the young men and women of the nation. All would be compelled to work for the state at whatever jobs they were assigned. Applying compulsion in some ways more rigorously than a modern communist state, Bellamy sketched out a blueprint of what might be called the ultimate totalitarian state. in the latter part of the nineteenth century, *Looking Backward,* arguably the most evil book ever written by an American, became a runaway best-seller and even today is referred to with some reverence by the proponents of compulsory national service. Moskos, for example, calls Bellamy's novel part of "socialist utopian thought," acknowledges that compulsory youth service "was the cornerstone of his new social order," and then gives Bellamy credit for first introducing the "concept of civilian service by youth" and presenting a "military analogy to describe the organization of civilian service, a trademark of much subsequent national-service thought."[10]

Another early proponent of compulsory national service in the United States was Randolph Bourne, a young radical opposed to World War I who, in a 1916 article for the *New Republic,* called specifically for an "army of youth." Bourne envisioned two years of compulsory state service for all young men and all young women. He tried to lull people's fears of compulsion by asserting that it would be compulsory only in the sense that it called everyone. "Between the ages of sixteen and twenty-one they *shall* spend two years in national service [emphasis added]."[11] The details of his 74-year-old plan are remarkably similar to today's proposals for national service.

Two more-recent advocates of compulsory national service are Margaret Mead and Terrence Cullinan. Margaret Mead—a world-renowned anthropologist until it was discovered after her death that her most famous work was fraudulent (she was either deceived on certain research findings or she made them up)—was influential in her day, and in 1967 her call for compulsory national service for both young men and young women was taken seriously.

Mead saw in national service far more than a few good works in society; she saw that universal national service had great potential for massive social engineering. For example, she urged that part of the "institution of universal national service would be the postponement of marriage until the service was completed," pointing out that such compulsory service "would replace for girls, even more than for boys, marriage as the route away from the parental home." Mead was sensitive to the prospect of compelling young men and women to live and work together at this age and proposed that the program be "varied to suit the different circumstances, allowing for groups of both boys and girls who wished for time to mature before being forced into the continuous company of the opposite sex."[12]

Terrence Cullinan is without question the most frank and direct advocate of compulsory national service. In 1968, Cullinan, a 1964 graduate of Stanford University, argued that without compulsory national service "the goals of true democracy simply will not be attainable." His logic ran like this:

> Failure to make national service compulsory would deny its values to those needing them most. The most disadvantaged, smothered in ghettos or in rural isolation, would simply not respond to a voluntary system. . . . The social inertia of these deprived individuals can only be overcome by positive compulsory action. Conversely, the affluent and unconcerned—those for whom a final explosion of social tensions would be most dangerous—are unlikely to grasp the full significance of those tensions unless forced into confrontation with them.[13]

To back up this rather breathtaking totalitarian view, Cullinan asserted that the "best proof of the value of compulsion to the advantaged is the established Ethiopian compulsory programs."[14]

Cullinan denies that compulsory national service will "spawn a Hitler Youth" or that it would mean "regimentation and lack of individuality" or that it would "destroy individual capability for life-planning." He summed up his case for compulsory national service with a succinct statement: "Should we not finally muster the courage to compel?"[15]

Most of the men and women who fought for compulsory national service over the years are now dead, their specific plans and arguments interred with them. But the echoes of what they longed for still resonate, as their dream is carried on by others. Today the most sophisticated and dogged advocate is Donald J. Eberly, who has devoted most of his life to the concept of national service.

Although Eberly supports and advocates large-scale national service programs, he has always been careful to downplay the issue of compulsion. He proposes voluntary national service programs, deftly sidestepping the question of whether they would inevitably lead to a compulsory program.

The last time Eberly addressed the issue of compulsion directly was in 1968.

First, he put forth his arguments for compulsion:

A compulsory program would guarantee the involvement of millions of youth each year attacking poverty, ignorance, and disease.

It would prevent it from becoming an elitist program like the Peace Corps or a poverty program like the Job Corps.

It would remove the inequities of a system in which some serve and others do not.[16]

Against that powerful array of procompulsion arguments, he then meekly alluded to the case for individual freedom—"the traditional case of the civil libertarian that any form of compulsion is an infringement on the freedom of an individual"—and promptly undercut even that weak statement of the case in his next sentence: "My problem with that argument is largely personal: I was compelled to enter the army but I came out with the feeling of greater freedom than when I entered."[17]

Eberly then argued that his "major problem" with compulsory service is that it "would tend to lessen the quality of service performed and the value of the service experience to the individual."

His final argument against proposing a compulsory program was that it would be "superfluous." He asserts that a properly run voluntary program will "attract millions of young men and women" and thus it will "not be necessary to create the elaborate machinery needed for a compulsory program."[18] Eberly's strategy seems crystal clear. He understood earlier and better than most that the necessary compulsion to make a large-scale national service program work was repulsive to the American people. He has thus artfully presented a one-sided argument for compulsion, giving only the weakest of arguments in defense of personal freedom and then slipping to the false conclusion that compulsion is not necessary anyway. This allows him to advocate a voluntary program to satisfy those who detest compulsion, yet leaves him a clear opening to move swiftly back to a compulsory program if it should become "necessary."

Eberly's goals are the same as those of Moskos and Cullinan and Mead and Bourne and Bellamy and James. If one has any doubts about Eberly's allegiance to William James's program, these can be easily resolved by reading the first paragraph of the dedication of his 1988 book, subtitled *A Promise to Keep*. The dedication, written to his grandchildren, is signed "Grandpa."

You may some day read these words in a history textbook: "Following a 1906 speech by William James in which he advocated a moral equivalent of war, the debate on national service waxed and waned for nearly a century before it was finally adopted by the United States."[19]

If Eberly and others who profess to favor voluntary national service are sincere, then let them denounce compulsion and flatly state that they will support no national service program that embraces it, for until then, prudent people will assume that compulsory national service is their secret, cherished goal.

All those like Mr. Eberly and Professor Moskos who favor large-scale national service programs confront a dilemma. If on the one hand, the program is truly voluntary and noncoercive, you will not get millions of young men and women to sign up. On the other hand, if you propose a compulsory program that would work in the sense of forced labor for millions of American youth, you will not get any program. You are damned if you do and damned if you don't. One won't work, and the other you can't get.

The hidden agenda of many national service programs is compulsion—concealed only because it is politically unacceptable and because it is necessary for large-scale national service to work. Some may think that questioning the motives and sincerity of the advocates of national service should not be done in polite intellectual discourse. But the importance of what is at stake and the necessity of understanding all aspects of the argument overrides that nicety.

One important detail that is left out of all discussions of compulsory national service, one item not dealt with by Bellamy, James, Walzer, Eberly, or Moskos, is what to do with the girls and boys who defy the call. What do you do to them if they refuse to serve? What punishment do you inflict on them? Do you arrest them, handcuff them, and haul them off to jail? Do you prosecute them, try them, and imprison them? How do you enforce compulsory national service?

The advocates of national service could easily erase our suspicions of their romance with compulsion by denouncing it for the evil that it is and by saying that they would never support any national service program that embraced the compulsion of the young. But they don't. They may say that they would accept a voluntary program, but it is clear from their writings, from whom they cite as experts, that they would dearly love a compulsory program if only they could figure out how to get the rest of us to go along.

We have hundreds of volunteer programs now. President Bush's proposal would extend and amplify these programs, probably beyond the limit of any demand for them. Logically, all the advocates of national service should be singing the praises of Bush's proposal, but they cannot without fatally compromising their carefully crafted position on compulsion. As President Bush stated, the first principle of his YES service program is that it is "voluntary—truly voluntary. You don't need to be bribed with incentives and threatened with penalties."[20]

This flat rejection of compulsion by President Bush is the key reason the program is unacceptable to many advocates of national service. Their proposals are stalking-horses of one variety or another for what they really long for—widespread compulsion of the youth of America. Not a single one of their programs contains a Shermanesque rejection of compulsion. They all leave the door wide open. And that is why—until that policy door is closed—we should view all such "volunteer" national service programs with skepticism.

THE DIRTY WORK PHILOSOPHY

The agenda of coercion and compulsion embedded deeply in nearly every national service program proposal leads to a puzzling question. Why do these people want to coerce and compel the young so badly? What, over the years, has powered this urge to control young men and women, to make them do things they do not want to do? What was so important to those Democratic political leaders who in 1988 wanted a national service program so badly that they were willing to call for phasing billions of dollars of federal aid to higher education in order to get an effective way to coerce young people? What on earth would make such intelligent, savvy men and women do such a stupid thing politically?

There is only one answer: They thought it was the right thing to do. They felt that what they would achieve justified the immorality of the coercion and compulsion intrinsic to their plans. But what was it they wanted to achieve? The clues lie in the ethical base of compulsory national service.

Like all great public policies, compulsory national service is driven by a moral engine, a set of specific moral beliefs that guide, with sureness and precision, those who believe them. To discover the moral beliefs that allow adults to push for the compulsion of the young with no compunction whatsoever, we must go to the writings and teachings of the philosophers of national service mentioned earlier. These three important philosophers have set down the moral foundations for the political activists who now push for universal national service programs.

The first is Edward Bellamy. A lawyer by trade, he drifted into journalism and wrote editorials for the *New York Evening Post,* but found his true calling as one of the most successful novelists in U.S. history.

His book *Looking Backward,* a hymn to a totalitarian state, sold more than a million copies in the latter part of the nineteenth century—and still sells to this day among the intelligentsia. Written when Bellamy was only 38 years old and sporting a black, bushy handlebar mustache, his novel contains the philosophical inspiration for the professional philosophers who followed.

The second, and by far the most influential, is William James, the brother of the novelist Henry James. William was the leader of the philosophical movement of pragmatism, a school of thought that was dominant in the United States during the first quarter of the twentieth century and then fell from favor. James suffered serious mental illness as a young man, but later recovered fully.

The third and last philosopher to have an impact on the national service movement is Michael Walzer, currently a fellow at the Institute for Advanced Study in Princeton, New Jersey. Walzer's 1983 book, *Spheres of Justice,* is cited by Moskos as best exemplifying the "contemporary shift toward a reemphasis of citizen duties."[21]

Proposals for national service policy are the final links in a chain that goes back to these philosophers. The current legislation introduced by politicians like Senator Nunn and Congressman McCurdy is heavily influenced by the writings of the prime advocates of large-scale national service programs such as Donald Eberly and Charles Moskos. In turn, the writings of Eberly and Moskos draw heavily for their philosophical foundations on the earlier writings and speeches of Edward Bellamy, William James, and Michael Walzer.

But why only these philosophers? Why do the advocates of national service refer again and again to the writings of these men? What did they say that distinguished them from other philosophers and writers? These three men wrote a great deal in their lifetimes, and it is difficult to conclude what exactly made them the philosophers of national service. But two major ideas separate them from many other philosophers who lived and wrote when they did.

The first idea that set them apart from their philosophical colleagues was a peculiar view on the morality of doing dirty, distasteful, and dangerous work in a society. The basic thrust of their philosophical view is that all the dirty, distasteful, and dangerous work of any society *should be shared equally* by all the people in the society. No exceptions—woman or man, rich or poor, skillful or not—every single soul must do his or her share of taking out the garbage, preparing the dead for burial, cleaning toilets, guarding violent prisoners, and taking care of those sick and dying from deadly, contagious diseases. For these philosophers, these tasks are a moral imperative.

Because they consider parceling out the dirty work of a society to all citizens equally to be a fundamental moral issue, something as ethically compelling as one of the Ten Commandments, they see no problem with using compulsion to secure that end. No more than others see anything wrong with using compulsion to apprehend people who kill and steal. To achieve justice, the philosophy of national service implies, it may be necessary at times to compel people to act against their personal will.

The second idea that makes these men the philosophers of choice for national service is their notion that the youth should do the work. There is not enough dirty, dangerous work to go around, so make people do it for a year or two or more while they are young. That way, everyone will be forced to experience things that are dirty, humiliating, or dangerous for a period of time in their lives. Using young men and women neatly solves the problem of not enough dirty work for everyone. It also has one other great, though morally questionable, advantage. Young people are optimally vulnerable—mature and physically strong enough to do dirty work—and almost defenseless against compulsion if the society inflicts it on them, for they have the wisdom and judgment and power of sixteen- and seventeen-year-olds. They cannot vote; they have no real political power.

So if you begin with the philosophical premise that all of society's tasks that are dirty, humiliating, or dangerous should be equally shared by all—if this is one of the building blocks of your notion of a moral, just society—then it does not take too long or too much intelligence to conclude that compulsion is necessary and justified and that adolescent boys and girls are the ideal compellees. You may argue that the philosophical principle of shared dirty work is intrinsically evil or bizarre, but if you accept that premise you cannot argue with compulsory national service as the public policy solution.

The principle of an equal distribution of dirty work, however, is such a peculiar, bizarre notion that it is difficult to believe that intelligent men and women seriously advocate it. The overwhelming majority of people would ask, shouldn't trained nurses and doctors take care of people with deadly, infectious diseases? Shouldn't professional trained guards, preferably large, strong ones, guard violent prisoners? Do we all really need to take turns hauling the city's garbage to the dump? Yes, this is exactly what the philosophers of dirty work mean.

"Is it not an appropriate goal for social policy, however, that all the *dirty work* [emphasis added] that needs to be done should be shared among all the citizens," wrote Walzer in *Spheres of Justice,* one of the clearest expositions of this view.[22] As he explained it,

The question, in a society of equals, who will do the dirty work? has a special force . . . the necessary answer is that, at least in some partial and symbolic sense, *we will all have to do it* . . . this is what Gandhi was getting at when he required his followers—himself, too—to clean the latrines . . . people should clean up their own dirt [emphasis added].[23]

Professor Walzer did not leave the national policy implications of this philosophical view open to speculation, for he argued that "work of this sort might be done as part of a national service program."

"Indeed," he continued, "war and waste seem the ideal subjects of national service: the first, because of the special risks involved; the second, because of the dishonor. Perhaps the work should be done by the young, not because they will enjoy it, but because it isn't without educational value."

That, in a nutshell, is the philosophical essence of compulsory national service. The dirty work of a society must be shared equally. It should be part of national service (and here Walzer adds a perverted twist) *because of the dishonor.* And the young should do the work.

Preceding Walzer by some 77 years was William James. In his now famous speech "The Moral Equivalent of War," delivered on the campus of Stanford University in 1906, Dr. James spelled out a plan to draft young men to do civilian work. (This was 1906, so young women were not considered or even mentioned.) As Donald Eberly approvingly describes James's plan in his book *National Service*, the so-called moral equivalent of war would come about by "conscripting young people to do the work of society that was risky, tough, and unpleasant."

Professor James left Harvard University in early January of 1906 and traveled westward, accepting five thousand dollars to spend six months at Stanford. At the end of his three-thousand-mile journey he was fatigued and soon came down with a painful bout of gout. When his wife joined him in the middle of February, the pain was so bad he was hobbling about on crutches. So he was probably in a somewhat cranky mood when he sat down and wrote what was to become his most memorable speech.[24]

In that famous speech he spelled out the moral underpinnings of his idea of a just society, his utopia. Curiously, that part of his speech that is critical to understanding why he proposed what he did is never quoted by his followers and admirers. Here is what Professor James told the students at Stanford on that balmy, damp day—February 25—in California:

There is nothing to make one indignant in the mere fact that life is hard, that men should toil and suffer pain. . . . But that so many men, by mere accidents of birth and opportunity, should have a life of *nothing else* but toil and pain and hardness and inferiority imposed upon them, should have *no* vacation, while others natively no more deserving never get any taste of this campaigning life at *all—this* is capable of arousing indignation in reflective minds. It may end by seeming shameful to all of us that some of us have nothing but campaigning, and others nothing but unmanly ease [emphasis added].[25]

In James's extreme egalitarian philosophy it is clearly implied there should be an equal sharing of "toil and pain and hardness," the "campaigning," as he called it, the dirty work of society.

James had a specific program for achieving his utopia. He proposed that a young man in his teens be forced to serve the state for a "certain number of years." These young conscript laborers would be sent

to coal and iron mines, to freight trains, to fishing fleets in December, to dish-washing, clothes-washing, and window-washing, to road-building and tunnel-making, to foundries and stoke-holes, and to the frames of skyscrapers, would our gilded youth be drafted off, according to their choice, *to get the childishness knocked out of them,* and to come back into society with healthier sympathies and soberer ideas. *They would have paid their blood-tax* [emphasis added].[26]

The transparent hostility of James toward young men, for whatever reason, is obvious. There is a streak of cruelty here (fishing fleets in December?), of a barely concealed, seething lust to control the young, to hurt them, to crush the innocent enthusiasm for which the old so often envy the young. James's program of conscripting the young is often referred to with respect and reverence by the advocates of national service, but the dark side of his plan—knocking the childishness out of children, a blood-tax for youth—is never criticized.

In Edward Bellamy's fictional totalitarian society, created more than one hundred years ago, the dirty work was also reserved for the young. Indicting all previous societies, especially free ones, Bellamy argued that in them the "reward of any service depended not upon its difficulty, danger, or hardship, for throughout the world it seems that the most perilous, severe, and repulsive labor was done by the worst paid classes."[27] In Bellamy's society, "all needs of this sort can be met by details from the class of unskilled or common laborers." That army of unskilled conscript labor was where "all new recruits belong for the first three years of service . . . three years of stringent discipline," a "severe school." The term of service in Bellamy's industrial army began when young people finished school, at age 21. For three years they served as common laborers doing whatever tasks the rulers decreed. Then they were "free" to apply for better work, serving as conscripts until the age of 45.

In both the fantasy of Bellamy and the real-life proposals of James and Walzer there is a common theme. Dirty work—that which is dangerous, degrading, or difficult—must be shared equally. All citizens must, for a period of time, when they are just on the threshold of adulthood, perform conscript labor. In effect, all adolescents become slaves for several years doing the dirty work of society.

The practical consequences of the shared dirty work philosophy can be seen in the specifics of some of the proposed national service programs. What kind of work will the boys and girls do? How does the abstract philosophy translate into specific jobs?

Most national service advocates have said relatively little about the kinds of work they would assign to their millions of young charges. In 1971, Margaret Mead acknowledged that national service in any form "arouses anxieties." She then clearly addressed the fears that all parents would have for their children:

> Young people not yet regarded as either mature or responsible will leave their homes, the supervision of their parents, the constraints imposed by their peers, and be plunged into situations which are variously seen as dangerous, frightening, filled with temptation and opportunities for mental and moral corruption. . . . In civilian service the images that are aroused are girls away from home, unchaperoned, mixing with all sorts of people whom it would be inappropriate for them to marry, likely to get attacked, raped, impregnated, exposed to every sort of moral, physical, and social danger. . . . The picture of girls at eighteen, lined up, stripped, weighed, examined, within the brutal disregard of human dignity characteristic of the boot camp, and subsequently sent to other parts of the country, to the wild West, or the urban slum, the race conscious South, or the backwardness of a rural community, hostile to all strangers, is bound to be frightening.[28]

And so it is. Unfortunately, Professor Mead did not specify what particular jobs she had in mind for the young that were so frightening.

But some have not been so reticent. Randolph Bourne, carrying on from where his mentor William James left off, wrote in 1916:

> I have a picture of a host of eager young missionaries swarming over the land, spreading the health knowledge, the knowledge of domestic science, of gardening, of tastefulness, that they have learned in school. . . . We might even come to the forcible rebuilding of the slovenly fences and outhouses which strew our landscape.[29]

Times have changed since Bourne put forth his vision; fortunately the outhouses are gone, somehow replaced with indoor plumbing without the help of his "eager young missionaries."

The national service advocate who has been most explicit and articulate in explaining exactly what the young people would do in a modern national service program is Charles Moskos. Arguing that national service provides cheap labor ("the practical argument for national service is that it can be a means of providing services that the government cannot afford"), Moskos spells out a number of specific ways this cheap labor might be employed. Some tasks are relatively benign, such as being a teacher's aide or working in a library making braille books for the blind. But those job assignments would be for the lucky ones. For many others these are the job prospects that Moskos candidly predicts:

State Prison Guards

Noting that eighteen-year-olds are eligible to serve in some states as state prison guards, Moskos states that "national servers could even act as guards." He acknowledges that being a prison guard is dirty work: "Stress is high. Prisons are dangerous, and inevitably some national servers would be injured." From this acute and perceptive observation Moskos then concludes that such service "should profoundly enrich the later education and personal development of the servers."[30]

Maybe I am missing something here. But surely taking innocent, untrained young boys and girls and putting them in direct daily contact with hardened criminals, men convicted of brutal crimes like rape and murder, is folly of a cosmic order. Do we seriously intend to assign untrained teenage girls to work directly with the dangerous psychopaths our prisons now contain?

Some have already done it. Alec Dickson, an ardent advocate of national service, felt that we were in "danger of becoming too protective of the young" and exulted that "the fun is to be opening doors to people who would never, never have dreamt they could be volunteers." Here, in a special case that occurred in England, is an example of what Dickson considered to be fun.

> We have even been placing girl volunteers in institutions for young male offenders. At this moment, in a school for delinquents, our volunteer is not only a girl but is totally and irrevocably blind. They could watch her walk into a wall or a door if they wished—but their reaction on seeing that she needs them is heart-warming.[31]

AIDS and Alzheimer's Disease

Moskos suggests a special program to match the "needs of those afflicted with a particular disease, Alzheimer's and AIDS being preeminent examples."[32] Young, untrained boys and girls taking care of people afflicted with the contagious, deadly disease of AIDS? Changing their bandages? Young, untrained boys and girls taking care of old people afflicted with a heartbreaking disease that robs them of their memory and their ability to think and reason? What are we thinking of? It would be an injustice to both the servees and the servers. Men and women striken with AIDS and Alzheimer's disease need the skilled care of trained professionals, not teenagers playing doctor and nurse, and untrained youths should not be needlessly exposed to the infectious dangers of any deadly disease. To force or coerce them into such a situation would be evil.

Day-Care Centers

Moskos proposes that national youth servers take care of the nation's children: babysit for children at home while the parents are gone and act as day-care workers at day-care centers where parents can leave their children. This is a dubious proposition. In recent years day-care centers run by adult professionals have had many serious cases of child abuse and neglect. Do we really want to staff day-care centers with teenage boys and girls from different backgrounds? Do we really want to let young strangers into our homes to care for our children? This is an idea that needs a little more work.

U.S. Border Patrol

Moskos suggests that national service youth should work with "the United States Border Patrol."[33] Work with? Does this mean they will be involved in tracking down and apprehending dangerous drug smugglers? Will they try to stop the flow of illegal aliens across our southern borders? Patrolling the national border is serious police work, work that should be done by trained, adult professionals.

Mental Institutions

Young people serving as aides in mental institutions seems to be a favorite of many national service advocates. Such work would certainly expose innocent young men and women to a dark side of life and force them to experience, up close, the tragedy and humiliation of mental illness. But it would be a profound disservice to the patients. What they need is more and better professional care, not some teenagers staring at them, wondering what to do.

Aid to the Homeless

One specific suggestion made by the Democratic Leadership Council is to have the young men and women involved in national service "aid the homeless."[34] But how? Most homeless people are single men who are either mentally ill, drug addicts, or alcoholics. These problems, tragic and primarily personal, desperately need professional help. What is a young girl of seventeen, untrained, relatively naive, going to do when confronted with a dirty, drunk alcoholic? How is she supposed to deal with a cocaine or heroin addict infected with AIDS? What is a young boy of 17 supposed to do with a 60-year-old woman who is mentally ill and insists on sleeping on the sidewalk? We will not help the homeless by forcing our young men and women to share their pain.

Of course, some favor national service not because it entails the sharing of society's dirty work, but because it may help them achieve other goals they desire—bringing back the military draft or helping the poor, aged, and disabled, for example. But those who favor compulsory, large-scale national service generally have a different goal. They have a moral imperative that is aimed at the server rather than the servee. The experience of the person who serves is of paramount importance for them, not the services provided. This peculiar moral dimension sets apart the prime movers of national service from the policy hitchhikers.

Professor Moskos makes this moral sentiment clear in one of his earlier articles urging a compulsory national service program: "If America's privileged youth would really like to demonstrate their *moral concern* for our country's underclasses, they must be willing to put up with an *extended period of indignity* on par with those very same underclasses [emphasis added]."[35]

This moral imperative—the idea that to be moral one has to suffer indignities and that in a moral society dirty work is required of all— inevitably leads those who so believe to embrace compulsion or coercion as the key means of achieving that kind of national service.

SUMMARY

The peculiar philosophy of sharing the dirty work of society with young men and women lies at the heart of all compulsory national service proposals. If you believe that it is morally just for everyone to be required to do a share of society's dirty work, then a universal national service program that coerces or forces young men and women to carry out that work will logically follow. The ultimate philosophical goal of that program is not to provide service for others; that is only a secondary result. The first and primary goal is the participation of all in the dirty work; that is the mark of morality, of justice, in that kind of society.

If, however, you believe that sharing the dirty work equally is a bizarre philosophy or, as I do, a morally repulsive one, then you will most likely come down on the side of a voluntary service program only large enough to accommodate the desires of those who wish to participate.

Those who are generally opposed to large-scale national service programs suspect that they are stalking-horses for universal, compulsory national service. For those who favor large-scale programs, but avow they should be voluntary, it would help allay the fears of the rest of us if you would assure us of two things: (1) you do not believe in sharing the dirty work of society equally, and (2) you oppose forcing or coercing people to serve.

Until then I for one shall remain suspicious.

Notes

1. Charles C. Moskos, *A Call to Civic Service: National Service for Country and Community* (New York: The Free Press, 1988), p. 179, and Moskos, "The Social Equivalent of Military Service," *Teachers College Record* 1 (September 1971): 10.

2. "Citizenship and National Service: A Blueprint for Civic Enterprise," Democratic Leadership Council (May 1988): 50.

3. Michael Walzer, *Spheres of Justice: A Defense of Pluralism and Equality* (New York: Basic Books, 1983), p. 175.

4. "Citizenship and National Service," p. 51.

5. Moskos, *Call to Civic Service*, p. 179.

6. Charles C. Moskos, "How to Save the All-Volunteer Force," *Public Interest* (Fall 1980): 84.

7. "Enlisting with Uncle Sam," *Time*, February 23, 1987, p. 30.

8. Richard Dennis, "National Service Offers an Idea Whose Time Has Gone," *Chicago Tribune*, August 9, 1989, p. 17.

9. William James, "The Moral Equivalent of War," Documents of the American Association for International Conciliation (New York 1910), p. 17.

10. Moskos, *Call to Service*, p. 30.

11. Randolph Bourne, "A Moral Equivalent for Universal Military Service," *New Republic*, July 1, 1916, reprinted in Martin Anderson, ed., *The Military Draft* (Stanford: Hoover Institution Press, 1982), p. 400.

12. Margaret Mead, "A National Service System as a Solution to a Variety of National Problems," in Anderson, *Military Draft*, p. 442.

13. Terrence Cullinan, "The Courage to Compel," in Anderson, *Military Draft*, p. 454.

14. Ibid.

15. Ibid., p. 455.

16. Donald J. Eberly, *National Service: A Promise to Keep* (Rochester, N.Y.: John Alden Books, 1988), p. 93.

17. Eberly, *National Service*, p. 16.

18. Ibid., p. 94.

19. Ibid., p. 1.

20. George Bush, in remarks delivered to Youth Engaged in Service, June 21, 1989.

21. Moskos, *Call to Civic Service*, p. 6.

22. Walzer, *Spheres of Justice*, p. 175.

23. Ibid., pp. 174–75.

24. Gay Wilson Allen, *William James: A Biography* (New York: Viking, 1967), pp. 450–51.

25. James, *Moral Equivalent*, pp. 16–17.

26. Ibid., p. 17.

27. Edward Bellamy, *Looking Backward: 2000–1887* (New York: Modern Library, 1951 edition, originally published in 1887), p. 71.

28. Margaret Mead, "Women in National Service," *Teacher College Record* 73 (September 1971): 59–62.

29. Bourne, "Moral Equivalent," in Anderson, *Military Draft*, p. 401.

30. Moskos, *Call to Civic Service*, p. 149.

31. Mora Dickson, ed., *A Chance to Serve* (London: Dobson Books Ltd., 1976), pp. 124–25.

32. Moskos, *Call to Civic Service*, p. 152.

33. Ibid.

34. Ibid., p. 37.

35. Moskos, "Social Equivalent," p. 12.

Discussion

Mr. Eberly: A brief comment in response to Martin. I was once upon a time an experimental physicist, and I still think of myself as experimentally oriented. If you would be willing to conduct a test of voluntary national service along the lines I have outlined, with no implications for a mandatory service program, we could agree on a set of criteria and measurements that should be made to find out if it is something that we should pursue. It would only take $40 to $50 million to find out. We spent a long time debating it up in the rarefied air in Estes Park, Colorado.

Mr. Anderson: Speaking as an experimentally oriented person who has a masters in engineering, that sounds like an interesting prospect. First, I would have to know what the goals of the experiment are. What are we trying to show? If you will say to me that you have renounced compulsion, that you do not like it, that you do not think it will work, that you do not think it is desirable, that the voluntary programs are the way to go, then we may get an Anderson-Eberly Bill.

Mr. Eberly: That comes pretty close to where I am. The goals, Martin [Anderson], would be to test my Cadista model—which is voluntary—to see the value of services rendered and the value of the service experience to the Cadets, and then to compare the values of these outcomes with the cost of the program.

When you have as much white hair as I have, you know that circumstances can change rapidly. As unlikely as it now is that America will need a draft in the foreseeable future, it could happen. And if we were to return to a peacetime draft, I probably would call for draftees to have a choice between military and civilian service, as I did in the 1950s. At that time, it looked as if the draft would be here for a long time to come. The question was how could you improve it? In other words, I was quite willing to work with the conscription system then in effect. My major point to the Burke Marshall Commission [National Advisory Commission on Selective Service, 1966–67] was, do not let national service get entangled with the Pentagon or the Selective Service System because you, Anderson, Friedman, and others were already talking about a volunteer armed force. I knew that if national service were integrally linked with the draft, that it would collapse with the end of the draft. I wanted to have it apart from the draft in what I called in those days the National Foundation for Volunteer Service. [Testimony reprinted in Donald J. Eberly, ed., *National Service: A Report of a Conference* (New York: Russell Sage Foundation, 1968), pp. 513–55.] Today I am neutral on the question of the draft and the all-volunteer force. I do not believe I have ever said that I favor one over the other. Other people decide those things.

Mr. Anderson: In the world of politics, neutrality does not count.

Mr. Wycliff: The issue on the table is proposed legislation that does not contain compulsion plus a piece of legislation that may contain something tantamount to compulsion that may be objectionable to some people. Why are we fighting tomorrow's war today?

Mr. Anderson: Because that is the way to win it.

Mr. Chapman: I would like to point out the Peace Corps is an atypical volunteer program although it is constantly cited by advocates of national service as an illustration of how fine that program would be.

The Peace Corps is an elite program. It is made up of top flight university graduates and some older people; it is not made up of seventeen-and eighteen-year-old unskilled young people who in many cases are living at home and who make wages in the program above what they could get on the open market. The Peace Corps people have higher skills, higher education, are more mature, and, furthermore, could be making more money in the outside world. They are making an economic sacrifice as part of their service. If we believe that sacrifice does constitute a part of service, then you would certainly have to hand that to the Peace Corps people.

But that is not what is being proposed in any other program under the rubric of national service. Therefore, when we start talking about what national service would be like, you cannot use the example of the Peace Corps. What you have to look at is CETA [Comprehensive Employment and Training Act] and some of the poverty programs of fifteen years ago, many of which fell on their faces and were dropped because of various problems.

Don [Wycliff], when you say we have a piece of legislation on the table, I must respond that although we have had the Nunn-McCurdy bill, I do not know anybody who believes that bill is alive today.

Mr. Wycliff: My point is that no piece of legislation that I know of has any element of compulsion.

Mr. Eberly: The only one is the one Senator McCain introduced, and in that he calls on the president to figure out how it will be compulsory.

Mr. Anderson: May I respond to that? I am a little baffled too. You [Mr. Wycliff] are right. The current legislation has no compulsory features, though there was economic coercion in the original Nunn-McCurdy bill. My question then is, why are people reluctant to renounce compulsion, to say not only is it a political loser, but it is not good, to say we do not want it, and it is not the kind of a program we could thrive on?

Mr. Wycliff: You [Mr. Anderson] spoke approvingly of Mr. Burkhardt's program in San Francisco, and I noticed some signs of assent elsewhere on the panel. Insofar as this program is supported by taxpayers' funds, it would incur the same criticism that Mr. Friedman made about any national service program: It takes the money of people who do not know or do not care about something to support it. What is it about a federal program that does precisely the same thing that is so objectionable?

Mr. Anderson: There are two distinct issues. One is the issue of compulsory or economic coercion. It is possible to have a local program (such as Mr. Burkhardt's) that is funded with federal money. It is true, as Milton [Friedman] says, that the people who contribute the money did not do so voluntarily. There is a great deal of difference between that type of program and [a compulsory] one that is controlled by the federal government or the state government. You can have a local government that is just as totalitarian as any federal government.

I would offer a caveat about taking federal money. The public service program at Stanford University does not take federal grants. Why? Because they are a pain in the neck. That is one reason Hoover Institution does not take federal money. You have to fill out all the forms, you have all the restrictions, and all the little strings are like a sticky web when you get your hands in the federal money box.

Mr. Wycliff: That is the Hoover Institution's choice. That is not a reason why the federal government should not make it available.

Mr. Henderson: I was one of those nodding my head, and I noticed you [Mr. Wycliff] saw me. I was nodding because when Marty [Anderson] was talking about the San Francisco program, I thought it was run with voluntarily contributed funds. I see your point. I see the principle you are driving at.

Given that Bob Burkhardt has the funds, he is doing a good job. But I do not approve of forcing taxpayers to give funds. I agree that there is no difference in principle between the federal, state, and local governments.

Mr. Wycliff: So it is not a constitutional objection?

Mr. Henderson: It is, based on the takings clause of the Fifth Amendment.

Mr. Eberly: Robert [Burkhardt], what is the breakout of your support from federal, state, and city governments and the private sector?

Mr. Burkhardt: Thirty-three percent, federal money; 33 percent from the State of California; the other third is a combination of corporate, foundation and local nonprofits, city agencies, and private support.

John Judge, former military counseling program director, Central Committee for Conscientious Objectors, Philadelphia: I have been doing draft, military, preenlistment, and veterans counseling since the mid-1960s. I have talked to thousands of young people over those years who have made these decisions or were involved in these decisions. I feel that the discussion here is a rarefied, mostly philosophical debate.

I do not think national service would be an issue right now if it were not for the reality of what I call the poverty draft or economic conscription, which has been used since the end of the paper draft to force people into the military. I do not disagree with Ms. Berryman's analysis of the composition. But I do not agree that therefore the military is not an employer of last resort. It may be the individual's last resort and not the military's last resort. Economic conscription extends up into the lower middle classes and forces people in, and the military can pick and choose what level of person it wants. So I would still argue that we are operating under a draft.

I became involved with this issue in the late 1960s when the [Lt. Gen. Lewis B.] Hershey memorandum on channeling revealed what the draft did. [See U.S. Selective Service System, "Channeling" Memorandum (1965), in John Whiteclay Chambers II, ed., *Draftees or Volunteers: A Documentary History of the Debate Over Military Conscription in the United States, 1787–1973* (New York: Garland, 1975), pp. 493–500. Hershey was the director of the Selective Service System.] He said that the draft accomplishes in American society what foreign dictatorships do to their youth. He said it was like an "uncomfortably warm" room with a number of preselected doors.

Similarly, what is happening in the current period is based on the shrinkage of the baby pool that Mr. Eberly mentioned. But what is going on is much less benign than he suggests.

The military knows that. My mother was a manpower analyst for the Department of Defense for 30 years. She had the national annual draft call down to a hundred people either way five years in advance. The military knows that in the 1990s it has to get one out of every two warm male bodies. In the late 1970s, the director of defense education at the Pentagon laid out the plan that is coming into effect now: All post-secondary education in society will be tied more closely to the military. [Thomas W. Carr, "Education in the Military: A Look into the Future," in Franklin D. Margiotta, ed., *The Changing World of the American Military* (Boulder, Colo.: Westview Press, 1978), pp. 413–20; Carr, "Education and the Military: The Future," *News Notes* [Central Committee for Conscientious Objectors, Philadelphia], vol. 30, no. 5 (Holiday 1978).] National service is only the liberal alternative to enforcement so that the liberals can pat themselves on the back for creating jobs and giving an alternative to conscientious objectors.

I have no reason to be anything but cynical about any program that has government involvement. Somebody here was even trying to suggest the Selective Service was not really the government. It is, if anything, worse than the rest of the government and always has been, in my experience.

You talk about these matters in the abstract, but when you take a grid and put it down over the real lives of young people, you are in a different ball game. If you cut Title IV educational funds at this point, all you are doing is closing off one more option for the people who have no other economic opportunity. In the same way, [Congressman Gerald] Solomon [R—N.Y.], by requiring draft registration, attempted to cut off all but a few choices. [The Solomon Amendment to the Defense Authorization Act of 1983 blocks federal college aid to all men between the ages of eighteen and twenty-six who do not register for the draft.]

Under the McCloskey bill [the National Youth Service Act of 1979, whose chief sponsor was Congressman Paul McCloskey, R-Calif.] or the more recent ones, the choice that will be made by young people between civilian and military service will be made in a high school setting with military recruiters telling young people what will be good for them and what looks better from the front end: the military option. That is what they will be forced to take. That is what this is about.

Regardless of the motives of other people who are proposing national service out of liberal ideals, the effect is the same. It is a matter of coercion even though there is nothing explicit written into the legislation saying so. It is economic conscription. The most venal social planners will want to become involved once they have the warm bodies to play with. A few may be philosophical idealists. In reality people will be forced into making the choices that are wanted of them.

It is time for us to take a look at what is behind this issue, namely, the size of the U.S. military. We need to begin a public debate about that. It should not be decided behind closed doors by the National Security Council and the Joint Chiefs of Staff. It is a public issue. I am not talking about a fifteen-year debate between Mahatma Gandhi and John Wayne as to whether we should have a military. If we are going to have a military, there is a legitimate public concern about what that military is, how big it is, what it costs, who goes into it and how, whether they are treated with respect when they are in, whether promises made on the way in are kept, whether you can get out as easily as you walked in, and what happens to the veterans. Those are the issues I have dealt with over the last twenty years. They will not be different if people are interacting with a conscript service that takes away social benefits and exchanges them for these vouchers.

We are going exactly where they want us to go. That director of defense education [Thomas Carr] I mentioned—he and others want the military to replace the church, the home, and the school—to be the major socializing institution for America's youth—that is still on the agenda, regardless of any side discussions. I do not have any reasons to be idealistic about national service or think that it will go in the direction of solving social problems. I have seen nothing but the opposite from such plans over the years. On the other hand, if there is a voluntary job worth doing, people will do it.

Mr. Bandow: The size of the military is an important issue. I have done considerable work on Korea and the question of the American military commitment to Korea. The size of the military force is something that we should address.

But I do have a problem with the term *economic conscription*. What happens now is that the military is offering an extra opportunity. In my view, many kids do not have adequate opportunities, but that is a separate problem. You should not close off military opportunities. You make everyone worse off if you close off the volunteer system.

Robert Knight, Media Fellow, Hoover Institution: This gentleman [Mr. Judge] was talking about what he considered misplaced idealism. Why do the proponents of national service have so much faith that this program will remain within bounds? Mr. Eberly referred to a small quasi-government office, at least initially. Mr. Wycliff said he hoped legislators would exercise restraint and suggested prayer as a means of effecting that. Where do you get your faith that this will not turn into a huge boondoggle, especially if it does not work as envisioned within a few years? Mr. Henderson had a good point—that if it does not draw sufficient numbers of middle-class kids in and if it draws away from the military—there would be tremendous pressure to make it compulsory. How would you answer that?

Mr. Eberly: You would have built-in controls by requiring the sponsor to provide $600 in cash and the necessary supervision and training, which today would be worth $1,500 or so per person per year. That is a little over $2,000 investment by the sponsor. If people are goofing off, the local office will hear about it quickly because they are losing money, losing their investment. On the reverse side of the coin, to take Charlie Moskos's example of providing paratransit services as is done in West Germany, Walter Oi said that cannot work under a voluntary program. He says he has seen places where they have tried it. It gets corrupted because the handicapped people, the disabled people, exploit that chauffeured service the way we see in Washington, D.C., with the spouses of the VIPs going shopping, to social affairs, and to various other activities.

In a Cadista, or voluntary national service program, a person may well sign up as a chauffeur because many young people enjoy working with automobiles or minibuses. When the inevitable happens—I am sure Walter Oi is right in that regard—their agreement says that the purpose of this transport is to take people to their medical care, welfare benefits, jobs, school, or university. When abuses occur, then the cadet or the participant will have a legitimate gripe and can take it up.

In the Seattle project [Program for Local Service, 1973–74] that I have alluded to several times, there was a ratio of staff to what we called volunteers of one to one hundred. That was at a time when the program managers of VISTA and the Seattle project were in the same office of ACTION [the federal agency to aid volunteer work] in Washington, D.C. VISTA had a ratio of one staff person to ten volunteers. We had a whole order of magnitude less supervisory staff. That is just one example.

Mr. Wycliff: We have no assurance that it will not get out of control. Life does not work that way. Legislation does not work that way. When you write legislation, you write in controls. You have a GAO and an FBI. You have a Congress or a city council. You have a press and eager beavers in academia. You keep on acting like a citizen. You keep on going to the city council meetings, reading the budget, and asking, what is going on here? The idea of national service is to cause people to appreciate their citizenship.

Mr. Oi: If you sign up on a contractual basis to be a driver for the Lighthouse For the Blind, how does that contribute to citizenship training or develop citizenship? How do you protect against the political influence? You are getting this driver for $620. We know how long it takes to train a driver. The question is, how do you prevent this from turning into a political football between the local national service council and the host agency?

Mr. Bandow: Don [Wycliff], I want to respond briefly to your question about the federal versus the state and local. I object for three reasons to federal government involvement in a program such as Mr. Burkhardt's or others'. One question is, who has the money? It is an illusion to act as though the federal government has it. There is a $161 billion deficit in 1990. This is not the case in many states. The state of California is in much better financial shape than the federal government. We have to stop looking at the federal government as if there is a federal cornucopia. You can get more money by running the printing press, but it is a bad economic policy. Instead you have to make choices at the federal level. We cannot act as if there is this endless stream of money.

Second, who has the responsibility? Under our constitutional scheme, some responsibilities are fundamentally national, for example, the defense of the nation. I do not see how you can have states or counties or localities defend the nation. Meeting social needs in the way the San Francisco Conservation Corps strikes me as being fundamentally a local or a state responsibility, not Washington's responsibility.

Mr. Wycliff: So the locality or the state may do these things?

Mr. Bandow: My more ideological self would have the same objection Milton Friedman has, but I live in the real world. The question is, what is my range of objections? I have a strong objection to the federal government having a program like that. If you want a program like that, it has to come from the local level, not from the top. That is an added reason to object.

The third reason is the belief that accountability and financing should be together. Programs run best if the people running the program have to pay for it. If you hand out free money, it gets misused. If your local organization or local city government can get the money from the federal government, it does not have nearly as much incentive to treat it correctly. They are not responsible for raising it. I remember a local bond initiative on a water project while I was at the Stanford Law School. People said, isn't this wonderful? We should vote for this project because 90 percent of the money comes from the federal government. The way they were looking at it, if it was providing us with one dollar more in benefits than their share of the funding—the 10 percent—they should be for it, irrespective of the overall benefits and costs. This was because they had free money floating in. So my argument is, if it is going to be run locally, it should be paid for locally. That is your own money. If you spend your money, you treat it much better than if someone hands you the cash.

INDEX

ABOUT THE EDITOR

Williamson M. Evers is a Visiting Scholar at the Hoover Institution whose work concentrates on political philosophy and public policy. He was chairman of the Hoover Institution Conference on National Service in September 1989. He has written on national service for the *New York Times*. He held a National Fellowship at the Hoover Institution in 1988–89 and was a visiting political science professor at Emory University in 1987–88. He was editor in chief of *Inquiry Magazine* from 1977 to 1980. He has published scholarly articles on the policy governing the press in socialist societies; the economic sociology of Plato and Rousseau; Peter Kropotkin's ethical theory; social contract doctrines; the law of contracts; and the rights of children. He received his Ph.D. in political science from Stanford University in 1987 and wrote his dissertation on liberty of the press in political theory.